through & fire water

through
& fire
water

An Overview of Mennonite History

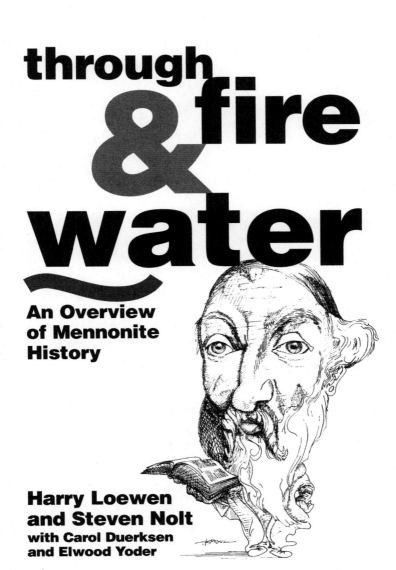

Harry Loewen
and Steven Nolt
with Carol Duerksen
and Elwood Yoder

HERALD PRESS
Scottdale, Pennsylvania
Waterloo, Ontario

Library of Congress Cataloging-in-Publication Data
Loewen, Harry.
    Through fire and water : an overview of Mennonite history / Harry
  Loewen and Steven Nolt, with Carol Duerksen and Elwood Yoder .
      p. cm.
  Includes bibliographical references and index.
  ISBN 0-8361-9015-7 (alk. paper)
    1. Mennonites — History. 2. Anabaptists — History. 3. Church
history. I. Nolt, Steven M., 1968 –   . II. Duerksen, Carol, 1954–   .
III. Yoder, Elwood, 1956 –   . IV. Title.
BX8115.L6484   1996
289.7'09 — dc20   96-12242
                                                              CIP

The paper in this publication is recycled and meets the requirements of
American National Standard for Information Sciences—Permanence of Paper
for Printed Library Materials, ANSI Z39.48-1984.

All cartoons are by Mike Burrell. All *Martyrs Mirror* etchings are from *The
Drama of the Martyrs;* used by permission of Lancaster Mennonite Historical
Society, 2215 Millstream Rd., Lancaster, PA 17602-1499. Elwood Yoder created
the maps. Photos are by Jan Gleysteen, unless otherwise credited where they
appear. Paraphrases of Scripture are provided by the authors, and quotations
from KJV are adapted. Except where noted, direct quotations are from the
New Revised Standard Version Bible, copyright 1989, by the Division of Christian
Education of the National Council of Churches of Christ in the USA, and are
used by permission.

THROUGH FIRE AND WATER
Copyright © 1996 by Herald Press, Scottdale, Pa. 15683.
All rights reserved.
  Published simultaneously in Canada by Herald Press,
  Waterloo, Ont. N2L 6H7.
Library of Congress Catalog Card Number: 96-12242
Canadiana Entry Number: C96-930338-6
International Standard Book Number: 0-8361-9015-7
Printed in the United States of America
Design by Gwen M. Stamm. Cover art by Mike Burrell (cartoon of
Menno Simons, for whom Mennonites are named)

05 04 03 02 01 00 99 98 97 96 10 9 8 7 6 5 4 3 2 1

Through Fire and Water

We preach, as much as is possible,
  both by day and by night,
    in houses and in fields,
      in forests and wastes,
        hither and yon,
          at home or abroad,
            in prisons and in dungeons,
          in water and in fire,
        on the scaffold and on the wheel,
      before lords and princes,
    through mouth and pen,
  with possessions and blood,
with life and death.

We have done this these many years,
  and we are not ashamed of the Gospel of the glory of Christ.
    For we feel His living fruit and patience and willing sacrifices
      of our faithful brethren and companions in Christ Jesus.
      We could wish that we might save all mankind
        from the jaws of hell,
      free them from the chains of their sins,
    and by the gracious help of God
  add them to Christ by the Gospel of His peace.
For this is the true nature of the love which is of God.

Menno Simons, Reply to Gellius Faber, *1544* (Writings, *633*)

For no one can lay any foundation other than the one that has been laid; that foundation is Jesus Christ.

1 Corinthians 3:11

This is the one who came by water and blood, Jesus Christ, not with the water only but with the water and the blood. And the Spirit is the one that testifies, for the Spirit is the truth. There are three that testify: the Spirit and the water and the blood, and these three agree.

1 John 5:6-8

Contents

Preface and acknowledgments

This book is designed as an introduction to church history and the Mennonite faith story. It was written with several audiences in mind: individuals who want to learn more about Anabaptists and Mennonites, congregations looking for a way to teach youth and adults about Mennonite origins and beliefs, and students in Mennonite high schools in Canada and the United States.

To encourage discussion, the book includes essays on five topics important to Anabaptists through the centuries: the church, following Jesus in daily life, nonviolence and peacemaking, the relationship between church and state, and outreach. These themes are also addressed in *Cloud of Witnesses*, a video series available from Mennonite Board of Missions, Harrisonburg, Virginia.

The book represents a cooperative effort by several Mennonite groups in North America. The development council established by the Mennonite Secondary Education Council included David Brubaker, Mary Friesen, David Graybill, Gerald Hughes, Harry Loewen, Levi Miller, Steve Ropp, Orville Yoder, and Elwood Yoder.

Harry Loewen wrote the Introduction and chapters 1-6 and 10-12. Steven Nolt wrote chapters 7-9 and 13-15 and the Epilogue. Carol Duerksen and Elwood Yoder worked closely with the writers in developing the general direction of the book and the section-ending focus essays, each headed by a question for today. Mike Burrell created the cartoons.

The manuscript has benefited from suggestions made by numerous readers. Special thanks go to Myron Dietz, John Friesen, James C. Juhnke, and Elmer S. Yoder for their advice. In addition, Richard Thomas and J. David Yoder deserve recognition for their support and encouragement.

The Canadian Association of Mennonite Schools and the Mennonite Secondary Education Council pray that this book will deepen the faith of all who read it and will renew their appreciation for the Anabaptist-Mennonite story.

Elwood E. Yoder, Project Coordinator
Harrisonburg, Virginia
Spring 1996

Introduction

Ghosts and echoes

Disturbing a church service

On Sunday, January 29, 1525, there was a great commotion in a church near Zurich, Switzerland. Just as the Reformed pastor was about to preach, a tall young man stood and asked him in a loud voice, "What have you come to do?"

"I am going to preach the Word of God," the pastor replied calmly.

"Not you but I have been called to preach!" the young man shouted back.

Ignoring the disturber, the pastor began to preach. But the young man interrupted and talked back to him rudely. Unable to continue, the pastor stepped down from the pulpit and headed for the door.

Angry voices came from the congregation, which clearly sided with the preacher. The pastor was asked to continue his sermon, and the young man was ordered to sit down and not disturb the service. As the pastor resumed, the young man struck the pew with a stick and shouted, "It is written, my house shall be a house of prayer, but you have made it a den of thieves."

The troublemaker had gone too far. The deputy magistrate, who was attending the service, approached the young man and told him to keep quiet or face arrest and imprisonment.

The young man was Georg Cajacob, nicknamed "Blaurock" (German for *blue coat*) because of the jacket he usually wore. He belonged to a group of radical believers called Anabaptists.

George "Blue Coat" seemed to be just a big troublemaker. For one thing, this grown man couldn't keep quiet during church.

Blaurock's zeal for reforming the church eventually led to his arrest, trial, and torture. On September 6, 1529, he was burned at the stake for what was called his "heretical faith."[1]

From nun to Anabaptist teacher

When she was a child, Elizabeth Dirks was taken to a convent near Leer in East Friesland, Germany, to become a nun. At the age of twelve, she heard about the burning of a heretic who did not believe in the sacraments of the church. Wishing to learn more about the mass and infant baptism—and why some people rejected them—Elizabeth began reading a Latin Bible. The more she read, the more she doubted the teachings of her church.

When Elizabeth became a young woman, she found it hard to keep her doubts to herself. She talked to the other sisters about the things that troubled her. Suspected of heresy, Elizabeth was imprisoned in the convent for a year. With the help of other nuns, Elizabeth escaped, disguised as a milkmaid.

Elizabeth found refuge and support with local Anabaptists. She attended their worship services, received baptism,

Between 1535 and 1592, at least 110 Anabaptists were tortured and executed in the Castle of the Counts of Flanders, Ghent, Belgium. Many were burned at the stake just outside the castle's main gate.

and became an active member of the church.

For a while, she lived quietly with a widow named Hade-wyck. But both women had a strong desire to share their faith with others. Putting caution aside, they began talking of their beliefs with all who would listen.

Elizabeth and other Anabaptists shared insights. There is evidence that she conferred with Menno Simons, an early Anabaptist leader whose name was used to label Menno-nites.

In 1549 Elizabeth was arrested. Her accusers called her a teacher of heresy and falsely said she was Menno's wife.

At her trial Elizabeth's answers were courageous and to the point.

Etching by Jan van Luyken in *Martyrs Mirror*

Joriaen Simons and Clement Dirks were burned in Haarlem, Holland, 1557. When the authorities tried to burn Joriaen's Christian books, the crowd grabbed them out of the fire and saved them. As a result, *Martyrs Mirror* **says, "The truth was spread the more."**

"Are you married?" she was asked.

"I have no husband," Elizabeth replied.

"We demand to know who your friends are."

"I will not tell you, . . . for that would mean their destruction."

Ivan Moon

Hans Denck, a South German Anabaptist leader during the 1520s, believed that one's faith needed to result in works of love. Denck said that no one could truly know Christ unless they followed him in life.

"Tell us who the persons are whom you have taught."

"O my lords, leave me in peace about my fellow believers, but ask me instead about my faith. I shall tell you gladly about it."

As the interrogation continued, Elizabeth was asked about the sacraments, infant baptism, the pope, and many other teachings of the church. To the end she remained strong and did not betray her faith or her fellow believers.

In the torture chamber, the executioner applied thumb-screws to Elizabeth's fingers until blood squirted out the nails. Then the authorities ordered that she be undressed in preparation for torture on the rack.

"O my lords," she pleaded, "do not put me to shame, for no man ever touched my bare body."

The executioner applied screws to her shins, one on each, stretching and dislocating her joints. Elizabeth cried out in pain and prayed, "Help me, O Lord, your poor handmaiden."

When her tormentors saw she would not recant, they condemned her to death by drowning. Elizabeth Dirks died on May 27, 1549.[2]

Facing armed killers

In the 1880s, a number of Russian Mennonites migrated to Central Asia to escape military service and find a place where they could live their faith freely. They found, however, that violence followed them.

The Mennonites did not know the customs of the Muslim groups who lived around them. One day, visitors from the Turkmen tribe came to Heinrich Abrahms' and offered to buy his wife, Elizabeth. Abrahms, of course, declined. The enraged men shot and stabbed him to death.

Elizabeth escaped to a neighbor and reported the murder. In the meantime the visitors robbed the Abrahms' household and left to divide the loot.

Mennonite young men organized a search party. Though they were unarmed, they discovered the group's hideout and confronted the killers. A Mennonite named Peter Unruh called them "thieves and murderers." The Muslims raised their guns and were about to shoot Unruh for having insulted them.

Johann Drake stepped forward, put his arms around Unruh, and said, "Brother, I will die for you." Facing the gunmen, Drake said, "Take me in place of this man. There is no one who will miss me or cry for me since my parents are both dead. I am willing to die for this man, for he has a wife and small children."

"This we cannot do," one of the killers said. "Our religion does not allow it. Get out of the way so we can kill the man who called us thieves and murderers."

Drake refused and kept his arms tightly around Unruh.

The gunmen consulted among themselves. Lowering their weapons, they said, "We grant both of you your freedom." They mounted their horses and rode away.

Later the government authorities captured several bandits and brought them to justice. Even after this incident, the Mennonite elders did not allow their members to carry guns. They did not want to violate the principle of nonresistance.[3]

Handcuffed and beaten

John J. Yoder's ancestors came to Pennsylvania seeking peace, freedom of conscience, and economic opportunity. But the American dream became a nightmare for John when the U.S. government drafted him in 1918 during the closing months of World War I.

The twenty-four-year-old from Geauga County, Ohio, boarded a train for Camp Greenleaf, Georgia. Of the four hundred men on board, he was the only conscientious objector.

At the camp, the officers demanded that John put on a uniform and help with noncombatant work. He refused. Across

Esther and Elmer S. Yoder

**John (1893-
1961) and Emma
(1900-1987)
Yoder near their
home in the
Amish Menno-
nite community
of Hartville,
Ohio, 1956.
During World
War I, John suf-
fered for his
conscientious
objector beliefs.**

the United States during World War I, some 2,300 conscientious objectors took similar stands—refusing to wear a uniform, work in the camps, or drill with the other soldiers.[4]

John's background had not prepared him for what lay
ahead. "You do not realize how a person's faith is tried
here," John wrote on March 13, 1918, just days after arriving
at the camp.[5]

But the ordeal had only begun. One day the officers called
John out from confinement and beat him with a heavy

broom handle. For a time, John thought he might die of his injuries. His spinal cord never fully healed, and he lived with pain the rest of his life.

In handcuffs and accompanied by an armed military officer, John was taken to Camp Meade, Maryland, in August. He and the officer engaged in friendly discussion aboard the train. John explained that his refusal to cooperate with the military was not a result of stupidity or ignorance, but because he took the teachings of Jesus seriously.

Even though the war was ending in Europe, the officers at Camp Meade were determined to break John's will. One day when the temperature was nearly one hundred degrees, they put him in a sweat box barely large enough for him to enter. They closed the door and said he might not get out alive. For five hours, John could not move and was barely able to breathe. Yet the experience did not take away his resolve.

In a change of policy, the U.S. War Department decided to let conscientious objectors work on farms until the war was over. John finished out the year on a farm in Lancaster County, Pennsylvania. Upon receiving his blue dishonorable discharge paper on January 17, 1919, he returned home to Ohio.

Many peace churches also were suspected of disloyalty to their country and severely criticized in the media. Writers in the *Kansas City Star* and the *Chicago Tribune*, for example, denounced conscientious objectors as slackers, cowards, parasites, and religious fanatics.

Theodore Roosevelt, suggested that COs be sent to the most dangerous areas of the war. He believed they were not fit to live in America.

What the voices tell us

The ghosts and echoes from the past tell us something important about Anabaptists. These followers of Jesus paid a high price to live by a faith that was unpopular. They were willing to suffer, even die, for the truth they had found.

These believers did not always show political wisdom or good manners in expressing their beliefs. Yet there is no doubt of their sincerity and commitment. They were genuine radicals because they looked back to the roots, the beginnings of the Christian faith in apostolic times. They had experienced new life and sought to follow Jesus and live by the faith he established.

What made them so certain about what they believed? Would we today be willing to suffer and die as they did? Has the fire that burned within the Anabaptists dimmed in their spiritual descendants, the Mennonites of modern Europe, North America, Asia, Africa, and South America? Or is such faith still evident among Mennonites today? This book will try to answer such questions.

How do we know what happened in the past?

History is a series of stories told from letters, diaries, government documents, other written materials, and artifacts. Mennonite history focuses on the events of the sixteenth-century Anabaptists and their spiritual descendants, covering a period of almost five hundred years.

The study of history, including Mennonite history, is not like the study of mathematics or science, where objectivity is easier to achieve. Historians need to choose among many documents, stories, events, and movements. When analyzing similar historical events, different historians will arrive at widely varying conclusions. Yet a credible historian will be fair, as objective as possible in weighing the evidence, and sympathetic toward the movement, events, and people described.

Historians have not always lived up to these standards in writing about the Anabaptists and Mennonites. For more than three hundred years, writers distorted the Anabaptist story. They pushed it to the margins of history and dis-

Africa Inter-Mennonite Mission

Bukungu Mishumbi, the highly respected treasurer of the Mennonite Church in Zaire, 1965-1981, giving money to a North American missionary. The steel drum served as the church's safe.

missed the radical Reformers as dangerous heretics or misguided fanatics.

Not until the nineteenth century did historians such as non-Mennonites C. A. Cornelius and Ludwig Keller portray the Anabaptists in a more balanced light. In the twentieth century, Mennonite and non-Mennonite historians such as Harold S. Bender, Roland H. Bainton, and George H. Williams have revised the Anabaptist story and tried to set the record straight.

The writers of this book want to tell the Mennonite story sympathetically, yet fairly. They seek to be critical in their approach—to include both the good and the bad. However, the writers identify with their story and the faith principles that have guided Mennonites through the centuries. They hope that the reader will discover many aspects of the Anabaptist story and come to respect and love the heritage that over one million Mennonites throughout the world have made their own.

Pentecost to the early 1500s

1

The apostles build the church

Drunk with wine?

The people in Jerusalem on the day of Pentecost looked and listened in amazement. Romans, Jews, Arabs, and visitors from other parts of the Mediterranean world watched as simple men and women addressed the crowd in many languages.

"Don't these people come from Galilee?" some of the onlookers said. "How can they speak to us in our native languages?"

Others sneered: "We don't have to listen to this babble. They are filled with new wine!"

Peter stepped forward and said, "Dear friends, the people you see and hear are not drunk. It's too early in the day to drink wine. You should know that."

There was a murmur in the crowd, then silence. People were ready to hear more.

"What you see," Peter continued, "is a fulfilled prophecy from the book of Joel: 'I will pour out my spirit on all flesh; your sons and your daughters shall prophesy, your old men shall dream dreams, and your young men shall see visions. I will pour out my spirit.'"

People listened with open mouths. In the heart of his message, Peter spoke of Jesus of Nazareth, who came to redeem his people from their sins, and was rejected and put to death. But God raised Jesus from the dead and elevated him to sit at the right hand of God. "Therefore," Peter said, "let all Israel know that God has made Jesus, whom you crucified, both Lord and Messiah (Christ, the anointed king)."

Most people in the crowd no longer mocked. Instead, they thought about what Peter had said.

"What shall we do?" they asked. "Repent," Peter replied, "and be baptized in the name of Jesus Christ. And you too will receive the gift of the Holy Spirit."

According to the book of Acts, about three thousand people accepted the invitation to become Jesus' followers that day.

Who was the man of Nazareth? What made Jesus so special, and why did he attract people from all age groups and social classes? Why did the Anabaptists seek to follow him and make him the center of their faith and life?

The Gospels portray Jesus

The books of Matthew, Mark, Luke, and John focus mainly on the last three years of Jesus' life—his teaching, suffering, death, and resurrection. We learn little about Jesus' looks, his childhood, or his teenage years.

The Gospels are not detailed biographies. Instead, they are statements of faith, written to tell readers that Jesus is the promised Messiah, who came to redeem people from their sins. Each Gospel writer tells the story of Jesus in his own way. Yet Matthew, Mark, Luke, and John agree on the major points.

According to the Gospels, Jesus preached repentance and invited people to enter the kingdom of God. Those who accepted his message became his followers. Eventually his enemies killed him. But Jesus was raised from the dead and later ascended to be with his Father in heaven.

In his teachings and life, Jesus emphasized love. He commanded his followers to love God, their neighbors, and even their enemies. This comes through most clearly in the Sermon on the Mount (Matthew 5—7), a passage central to the faith and life of the Anabaptists of the sixteenth century.

Jesus put the needs of people ahead of institutions, customs, and traditions. He violated Sabbath laws by healing people and allowing his disciples to pick grain. When religious teachers criticized him, he said the Sabbath was made for people, not the other way around.

Jesus told many stories about peoples' problems. He felt deeply about women and others oppressed in society. Children especially were close to the heart of Jesus. They were examples of how people ought to trust and have faith as citizens of his kingdom.

Jesus recognized the sinfulness of human beings and their tendency to do evil. But he also believed that people could answer God's call to justice and choose to follow him in day-to-day life. Jesus said God's power was available to anyone who would reach out in faith and claim it.

Jesus came to live and teach and heal

According to the Gospel writers, Jesus stood out among his contemporaries. He healed sick people, cast out evil spirits, and taught with great authority. He amazed people with his spiritual and emotional powers. They knew him as a teacher, and some thought of him as a prophet in the tradition of Old Testament leaders.

Yet Jesus was also an ordinary human being. He liked to be with people, enjoying social gatherings, good fellowship, and friendship. His relationship with Lazarus and his sisters, Martha and Mary, indicates that he had both male and female friends. When Lazarus died, Jesus wept and comforted the sisters. On occasion Jesus became angry, especially when people forgot what it means to worship God. For example, he drove the money changers out of the temple and overturned their tables.

Jesus had a sense of humor and a keen eye for the ridiculous. He laughed at his metaphor of the self-righteous man who had a huge log in his eye and yet tried to pluck a speck from his neighbor's eye. Jesus told of a strict person who worried so much about details and purity that he removed the smallest gnat from his food and drink, then swallowed an entire camel with hair, hooves, and bumps.

We never hear of Jesus being ill, but we do read about his human weaknesses. He became tired and needed to rest. He often withdrew from the crowds to renew his strength in prayer and contemplation. He suffered in body and spirit, but this pain was inflicted by others. He was a man "acquainted with grief," but this grief was for others who were to benefit from his suffering and death.

The people of his time viewed Jesus as a radical. He followed Jewish traditions and religious laws, but he went beyond what people were used to. For example, he agreed that the Old Testament allowed revenge, killing, and even war. Yet he often added, "But I say to you," and taught that hatred and violence were not acceptable among his followers (Matthew 5).

Jesus' relationships with women were especially radical for his time. His disciples were amazed at his conversation with a Samaritan woman about intimate details in her life. He protected a woman caught in adultery whom the religious leaders wanted to stone to death. At Jesus' crucifixion, the men disciples fled in fear, while women remained with him to the end. And when Jesus rose from the dead, women followers were the first witnesses of his resurrection.

Jesus was the Son of God

For the Gospel writers and their readers, it was much easier to identify with a human Jesus than with Jesus the Son of God. Yet they told his story so readers might believe that Jesus came to bring the redemption of humankind through his whole life, ministry, death, and resurrection.

Jerusalem, birthplace of Christianity.

The Gospels refer to Jesus as the Messiah, the Son of God. As a young person in the temple, Jesus spoke of needing to be about his Father's interests. Mary and Joseph pondered Jesus' words, knowing that he did not mean his earthly parents (Luke 2). In arguing with religious leaders, Jesus claimed that he existed even before their ancestor Abraham (John 8:58). When he was baptized by John, a voice from above called Jesus "my Son, the Beloved" (Luke 3:22).

The Son of Man is thus also the Son of God. Christian leaders have debated this mystery to establish correct teaching in the church. The Gospel writer John identified Jesus with God's revelation and communication to humanity, the Word (Logos) who was in the beginning with God and through whom all things were created. In Jesus, this Word became flesh. New Testament writers demonstrate that only through the human-divine Jesus Christ could humankind be reconciled to God. As the ascended and exalted Lord, Christ became the foundation and head of the church.

The apostles build the church

Just before his suffering and death, Jesus told his disciples that it was good for him to leave them, for then the Comforter, the Holy Spirit, would come to guide them. After his ascension the disciples and other followers of Jesus, about 120 persons, waited in Jerusalem for the Holy Spirit to come. Then, according to the book of Acts, the Holy Spirit was poured out upon the disciples at Pentecost. This event empowered them to become Jesus' witnesses throughout the world (Acts 1:8), as Jesus built his church on them (Matthew 16:18; Ephesians 2:20).

After the coming of the Holy Spirit, Jesus' followers found new power to speak about Jesus and what it means to acknowledge Christ as Savior and Lord. *Before* Pentecost, Jesus' followers felt discouraged, and some of them were ready to return to their old occupations as fishermen. *After* Pentecost, with their hope and faith renewed, they spoke boldly about their risen Lord and invited people to repent of their sins and to join the community of believers.

No persecution or suffering could stop them from proclaiming the gospel. They witnessed in Jerusalem, then continued in outlying regions, and eventually in many parts of the known world. These leaders were building the church on the foundation of Jesus Christ (1 Corinthians 3:10-15). According to the memory of the first Christians, most of the disciples and early followers of Jesus were martyred for their faith—but not before they had planted the seed of the worldwide church.

Paul travels and teaches

The greatest missionary to the non-Jewish world was the apostle Paul, a Jewish religious teacher and at first a persecutor of Christians. When Paul traveled to Damascus to round up followers of Christ, Jesus appeared to him in a vision.

That event changed Paul completely. He renounced his actions against Christians and became a servant of Christ. He considered himself an apostle, for like the other disciples of Jesus, he had seen the risen Lord and was proclaiming the good news.

As a missionary to the Gentiles, Paul went around in the Roman Empire, establishing congregations and strengthening Christians in their faith. Traveling by land and sea, Paul went to Asia Minor (present-day Turkey), into southern Europe, and perhaps as far as Spain. He and other apostles wrote letters to the churches, dealing with matters of Christian doctrine and teaching. Paul regularly spoke out against false teachings and un-Christian behavior.

Church tradition says that Roman soldiers martyred both Paul and the apostle Peter for their faith.

The church spreads rapidly

By the fourth century, the Christian church was establishing itself throughout the Roman Empire. What accounts for this rapid spread of Christianity and its victory over many old pagan religions?

Historians have suggested several reasons for the success of Christianity in the first five centuries. Edward Gibbon's

The Decline and Fall of the Roman Empire, published in England in 1776, provides one of the best analyses of Christianity's success.

First, according to Gibbon, the converts were zealous missionaries. They took seriously the great commission of Jesus to go into all the world. They proclaimed the gospel to all people, baptized them, and taught them the Christian life.

Second, Christians believed in life after death with the promise of future rewards. This appealed to many people whose pagan religions did not give them such a "blessed hope."

Third, the early church claimed miraculous powers, another drawing point for many people. The miracles reported in the Gospels, healings in following centuries, and especially the resurrection of Jesus, the greatest miracle of all—these led people to believe that Jesus was indeed the Lord of all.

Fourth, the early Christians not only believed the truth of the gospel, but they also acted and lived according to this belief. Greek and Roman society was deeply impressed by the ethical standards of the early Christians, their love for one another, and even for their persecutors and enemies.

Fifth, the organization and unity of the church convinced the Roman emperors that Christianity could contribute to the unity of the empire. They thus favored the Christian religion over other religions.

Other historians have proposed additional reasons for the success of the early church:

• Christianity satisfied the spiritual needs of society.

• Society was impressed with the heroic suffering and death of Christian martyrs.

• The church's teaching of monotheism (the belief in one God) and the doctrine of the incarnation of Jesus (God becoming human) appealed to people who were turning away from the gods and goddesses of the old religions.

• The support of later Roman emperors greatly boosted the expansion of early Christianity.

Along with this, the Greek and Latin languages were spoken in the Roman Empire, so Christians had little difficulty communicating their faith to others. The *pax romana* (peace of Rome) made it possible for Christians to travel safely by land and sea throughout the empire. Over Roman roads, built for the rapid transportation of armies, Christian missionaries carried the gospel to all corners of the empire and beyond.

Christians suffer persecution

Christians experienced at least ten periods of persecution during the first three centuries. One of the most cruel persecutions took place in Rome in A.D. 64 under Emperor Nero. According to some accounts, Nero set fire to the city, then blamed the Christians for the destruction.

Nero wrapped Christians in hides of wild animals and threw them to the dogs to be torn to pieces. He had others fastened on crosses and set on fire to illuminate a circus which Nero staged for the entertainment of the crowd in his own gardens. ·

The last persecution came under Emperor Diocletian in 303. Christian church buildings were destroyed and sacred books burned. Christians were removed from places of honor, tortured, and killed.

Christians were tormented because they refused to offer sacrifices to the old gods, acknowledge Caesar as their lord, and serve in the military.

In Asia Minor a Roman official burned a Christian town and its inhabitants. Romans stole Christians' property in Rome. In Egypt, Palestine, and Syria, Christians were mistreated and killed until well into the fourth century.

The early church leader Tertullian (160-220) wrote that the blood of the martyrs became the seed of the church. He

Maximilian of North Africa

Some Christians suffered persecution because they
refused to serve as soldiers. Consider Maximilian's
North African story of martyrdom in 295. Just over
twenty-one years old and fit for military service, Maximilian had to appear before Dion, the proconsul of
Africa. When they tried to put him in a soldier's uniform, Maximilian said repeatedly, "I cannot serve as a
soldier. I can't do evil because I'm a Christian." The
proconsul said, "There are other Christians who serve
as soldiers." Maximilian replied, "They know what
they can do, but I can't do evil." Officials asked his
father to change Maximilian's mind. The father, however, supported his son and said, "He is old enough.
He can make up his own mind."[1]

Maximilian was sentenced to die. His courageous
witness and death made a powerful impression on the
Christians of his time and on succeeding generations.
The medieval church made Maximilian a saint, and
Christians throughout the ages have tried to emulate
his courage and steadfast life.

■ ■ ■

meant that the suffering of Christians contributed to the
growth of the church.

There is much truth to this. It might be noted that the persecutions of Anabaptists in the sixteenth century were even
more severe than those of the early Christians. Roman emperors martyred less than two thousand Christians. In the
sixteenth century, however, under Christian rulers, some
four thousand Anabaptists and early Mennonites were
drowned, decapitated, and burned at the stake.

Persecution nearly destroyed the Anabaptist movement. It
is almost a miracle that Anabaptist Christianity survived
and today flourishes throughout the world.

The massive, round prison tower of the Rheinhessen Castle once held many Anabaptist prisoners. Those who gave up their faith had only their fingers cut off and crosses burned into their foreheads with a red-hot iron. Those who remained steadfast were beheaded, drowned, or burned at the stake. The Hutterian *Chronicle* places the number of Anabaptists executed in this castle, near the Rhine River in Alzey, Germany, at 350.

Christians disagree about war

Until 174 there is no reliable evidence that Christians served in the military. With the possible exception of Cornelius and the soldiers who came to John the Baptist, the New Testament has little to say directly about whether a Christian can be a soldier. Until well into the second century, Christians assumed that military life contradicted the teachings and example of Jesus.

What did Christians object to? Historians point out that a soldier's occupation in Roman times was the opposite of what Christians believed and practiced. A soldier's duty included shedding of blood on the battlefield, torture in the law courts, execution of criminals, swearing an unconditional military oath of absolute obedience to his commander, worship of the emperor, and sacrifices to idols of pagan religions. Even in peacetime, the behavior of soldiers was such that no self-respecting Roman, not to speak of Christians, would voluntarily join the army.[2]

In 313 Emperor Constantine made Christianity legal and respectable in his empire. Soon Christians in increasing numbers joined the military voluntarily or remained in the army after they accepted the Christian faith.

One hundred years earlier, church leaders such as Tertullian and Origen had written against Christians going to war, arguing that nonviolence was central to Jesus' teaching and life. But after Constantine, church leaders such as Ambrose and Augustine taught that Christians had a duty to defend their country, especially when the war was considered just.

By the 400s, an extraordinary thing happened: non-Christians were excluded from the Roman army, and only Christians could serve as soldiers! Ever since, there have been Christians who serve their country militarily and Christians who refuse for the sake of conscience.

Constantine becomes a Christian

How did this new phase in the development of Christianity come about? In 312, Constantine was in a military struggle with his rival for the throne. Preparing for battle against Maxentius, he had a dream. He reported later that he saw a cross of light in the heavens bearing the inscription "Conquer by this sign!" He made a banner showing a spear and a cross as a monogram using the first two Greek letters of the word *Christ*. Led by this symbol, Constantine won the battle and took possession of Rome.

By Constantine's time, Christians had become numerous and influential in the Roman Empire. The emperor knew the church could become a powerful partner in his attempts to unite and govern his realm. In 313, he elevated Christianity to be one of the important religions of the empire.

In time, Christianity became the official religion of state. Constantine granted many privileges to the church, made Sunday an official day of rest, had his children instructed in the Christian faith, built and enlarged churches, and took an

Constantinople (now Istanbul, Turkey) was Constantine's new capital and patriarchal city in early Christendom.

active part in the affairs of the church.

Though Constantine was not baptized until late in life, the church considered him a Christian ruler. Yet the alliance of church and state under Emperor Constantine brought many problems to the church and laid the foundation for rivalry between church and state that was to plague society for more than a thousand years. This simultaneous alliance of church and state and the struggle between them was an important factor that led to corruption in medieval Christendom.

In the eyes of the sixteenth-century Anabaptists, Constantine was anything but a blessing for the church. Many Anabaptists believed that under Constantine the apostolic church ended, experiencing a fall into sin. As the church closely cooperated with kings and governments, it became secular and worldly, more concerned with power and wealth than with spiritual values.

Augustine sets direction for the church

Augustine (354-430) is one of the most important leaders in church history. He stands on the threshold between the early church and the church of the Middle Ages.

Augustine's conversion shows vividly the attraction Christianity held for many people. But his activities and writings also point to weaknesses and contradictions within the church. These developed into a need for reform.

Born in North Africa of a devoutly Christian mother, Monica, and a father who became a Christian late in life, Augustine received Christian instruction when young. His mother did not have him baptized as a child because she, like other parents, believed that baptism washed away all sins committed before the rite was administered. Thus many waited for baptism until the passions of youth had passed.

In his teens Augustine lived with a woman who, before he was eighteen, bore him a son they named Adeodatus, "given by God." But Augustine found that the pleasures of life could not satisfy him. He tried a variety of intellectual and philosophical pursuits, yet felt empty. Much later he wrote that the human soul cannot find rest until it finds God.

Augustine became a teacher in North Africa, Rome, and eventually Milan, where he learned to know Ambrose, the bishop of that city.

Suffering from self-doubt and disgust because he could not control his sexual desires, Augustine was once in a garden when he seemed to hear the voice of a child telling him to "take and read." As he looked around, he found Paul's letter to the Romans. His eyes fell on the end of the thirteenth chapter: "Let us live honorably, . . . not in reveling or drunkenness. . . . Instead, put on the Lord Jesus Christ, and make no provision for the flesh, to gratify its desires."

Augustine felt God was speaking to him about his personal life. He was converted, and Ambrose baptized Augustine and his son at the same time on April 25, 387.

As a Christian, Augustine was able to control his sexual desires, but he still found pride and other human weaknesses a problem. He returned to Africa, where he became the bishop of Hippo and wrote his important books. His *Confessions* became one of the greatest autobiographies in world literature, and *The City of God* remains a landmark in the philosophy of history.

In his writings Augustine became a great defender of the church. When Germanic tribes destroyed Rome in the fifth century, Christians were blamed for the calamity. Augustine argued that Christianity represented the city of God, which in the end would conquer the city or kingdom of the world. While Augustine had the ultimate end in mind, the Roman Catholic Church soon emerged as the victor over all other religions and aspects of life. In 800, when the pope crowned Charlemagne emperor, the Holy Roman Empire was born.

Augustine's view of human nature later influenced reformers such as Martin Luther. Augustine emphasized the depravity of human nature, insisting that the human will was not free and that only God's grace through faith could redeem the individual. According to Augustine, God even chose or predestined those who would be saved and those who would be lost.

Wishing to support Christian emperors, Augustine argued that under certain conditions Christians could and should serve in the army. According to Augustine, certain wars were just—for example, a country's effort to defend itself against aggressors. The theory of the just war was later more fully developed by Thomas Aquinas and others.

Anabaptists did not accept Augustine's views on war, nor did they follow some of his other beliefs. For example, the Anabaptists did not emphasize the depravity of human nature as much as Augustine and Luther did. Anabaptists believed that individuals can respond to the grace of God and are responsible for their own actions.

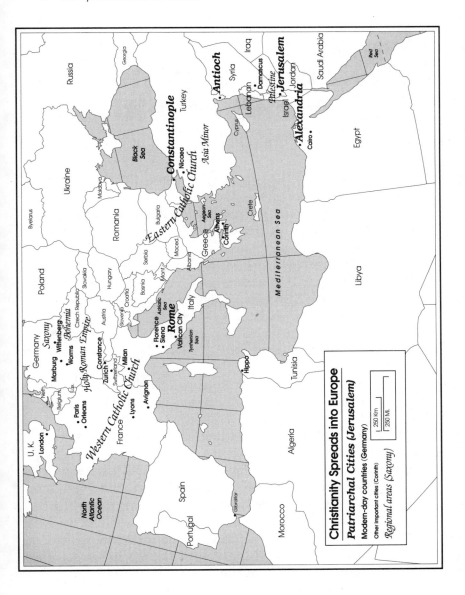

Christianity Spreads into Europe

Patriarchal Cities (Jerusalem)

Modern-day countries (Germany)

Other important cities (Corinth)

Regional areas (Saxony)

250 Km

250 Mi.

2

The church gains power and wealth

Rich in things, yet poor in soul

A story is told about the wealth and spiritual poverty of the medieval church. A cardinal was walking with the pope through Vatican City in Rome, admiring its architecture, gardens, works of art, and general wealth.

The pope referred to a story in Acts 3 where Peter and John had no money to give a poor beggar unable to walk. Instead, they healed him in the name of Jesus. The pope observed: "We can no longer say with Peter, 'I have no silver or gold.' As successors of Peter, we have become rich and powerful."

The cardinal smiled ironically and replied: "Neither can we say, 'In the name of Jesus Christ of Nazareth, rise up and walk.' "

True or not, the story illustrates what happened to the church founded by the poor and humble Jesus. With its recognition by the Roman emperors as an important religion within the empire, the church in time became the largest landholder in Europe. The clergy, from the pope to the bishops, became powerful leaders in society.

The story of how this happened is both fascinating and discouraging. Yet we shall see that the witness of Jesus and his kingdom did not die out altogether. A reawakening came in the sixteenth century. [1]

The church defines right belief

The Gospel writers record few words from Jesus about the organization and administration of the church. Indeed, only twice does the word *church* appear in the Gospels. Roman bishops later took one saying of Jesus that mentions the church and made it into something Jesus had not meant.

When Peter declared Jesus to be "the Son of the living God," Jesus responded: "You are Peter, the Rock; and on this rock I will build my church, and the powers of death shall never conquer it. I will give you the keys of the kingdom of Heaven; what you forbid on earth shall be forbidden in heaven, and what you allow on earth shall be allowed in heaven" (Matthew 16:17-19, New English Bible).

This passage does not say anything about a series of successors to Peter or about his authority with regard to the "power of the keys." In fact, at the end of John's Gospel, we read of Jesus commanding Peter to tend and feed the sheep. This command also applied to the other disciples and to all succeeding shepherds or pastors.

Jesus never instituted powerful church leaders who would lord it over their flocks. Humility, love, and the welfare of those who accepted the Christian message were to be the concerns of leaders in the church.

However, practical, social, religious, and political considerations and factors soon changed and sometimes distorted the early vision of Jesus for his church. In repsonse to needs, a tighter organization and special emphases in teaching emerged in the church. Paul's letters describe many of these changes. Some people in the church had physical needs. The poor received care from deacons appointed by the church. Elders and pastors looked after the spiritual needs of their members and interpreted the gospel to them.

False teachings, heresies, caused confusion in the early church. Heated debates questioned whether or not Jesus was man, God, or both. The question of whether or not God was in three persons (the Trinity) became a major theological problem. The church had to face questions about whether the Fall into sin had corrupted the human individual completely, or whether there was still freedom of will to respond to the grace of God.

When Roman emperors came to help the church, powerful church leaders tried to determine which views and doctrines were orthodox or correct and which were not. Those who lost the debates were often called heretics because they dissented from established church dogma. They were banished, persecuted, or put to death by church and state officials.

Trying to agree about the Trinity

The present form of the Apostles' Creed, recited in many churches today, probably did not exist before the sixth century. The essential core, however, has a much earlier origin. Bishops and other church leaders wrestled for a long time about how to express their belief concerning God. Eventually they agreed on what they considered the belief of the apostles. The creed begins, "I believe in God, the Father almighty. . . . I believe in Jesus Christ, God's Son, . . . who was . . . born of the Virgin Mary. . . . I believe in the Holy Spirit, . . . the resurrection of the body."

Formulating the church's belief in the Trinity proved most difficult. To Christians it was clear from the writings of the New Testament that Jesus was both human and divine. But how Jesus related to God and the Holy Spirit was much less obvious. Church fathers such as Tertullian, Origen, and Augustine wrestled with this doctrine and eventually gave it the shape we have today: There is but one God, but this God is in three persons—Father, Son, and Holy Spirit. Exactly how the three persons are interrelated is a mystery.

Arius (250-336), a leader in the church of Alexandria, Egypt, did not accept the formulated doctrine of the Trinity, maintaining that "the Son has a beginning but that God is without beginning." The church became divided over the issue. Because of concern about division and factions within his empire, Emperor Constantine eventually stepped in. To deal with the issue, about three hundred bishops attended a council in Nicaea, Asia Minor, in 325.

Supported by the emperor, the orthodox bishops triumphed over the Arians and established Christ's co-existence with God from all eternity. Deviation from the Nicene Creed was punishable by death. The council ordered Arius's books destroyed, and his supporters were banished. Right belief and unity in the church and empire came at a high price. Moreover, the church, with the support of the state, became a persecutor of "heretics."

Another struggle about dogma or teaching began with disagreement between Augustine and Pelagius, a British monk. When Pelagius came to Rome at the end of the fourth century, he was shocked by the loose living of many Romans. He insisted that if people tried to keep the commandments of God and live a Christian life, they could do so. Augustine disagreed, stating that the human individual was so corrupted through sin that only God's grace through faith could redeem and transform the sinner.

Questions concerning human sinfulness and free will have been vigorously studied in the church through the centuries. These questions became important during the Reformation when Reformers such as Martin Luther and John Calvin did not fully agree with the Anabaptists.

In their struggle for right beliefs in the early church, orthodox bishops emerged victorious, influential, and powerful. Especially prominent were the bishops of Jerusalem (because of its historic association with Jesus), Antioch in Syria (where the followers of Jesus were first called Christians), Alexandria in Egypt, Constantinople (the new capital of Emperor Constantine), and Rome.

Saint Peter's Basilica, the leading church of Roman Catholic Christendom, is named for Christ's disciple Peter, from whom the popes claim succession. It stands within the boundaries of the Vatican City in Rome on the Vatican Hill, the site where by tradition Peter was buried after being crucified.

The Roman bishop becomes pope

By the beginning of the fifth century, the bishops of Rome began to attain greater prestige, influence, and power. Several factors led to this. Rome was the capital of the western part of the empire. According to tradition, Peter and Paul had worked and died for their faith in Rome. When the city fell to the Germanic tribes in 410, the bishop of Rome provided comfort and stability to Roman society. Eventually the bishop of Rome took the title of *pope*.

Pope Leo I, known as "the Great," held office from 440 to 461 and was an influential and forceful leader. He insisted that Christ had commissioned Peter to become the rock foundation of the church and the doorkeeper of the kingdom of heaven. The popes thus thought of themselves as Peter's successors, with authority to "bind and loose" in spiritual matters. The pope's powers increased, until in the nineteenth century the popes assumed "infallibility." This is the assumption that popes cannot err when they make official pronouncements in matters of faith.

The popes also claimed that they were superior to emperors and other rulers. After all, earthly rulers were only responsible for their subjects' physical and material well-being, whereas the popes were responsible for the salvation of people's souls. Pope Innocent III, who ruled between 1198 and 1216, compared the pope to the sun and the emperor to the moon: just as the moon derives its light from the sun, so the emperor receives his authority and power from the pope. The emperors, of course, challenged these extraordinary claims. The result was a power struggle between church and state that lasted for centuries.

The church divides

The struggle for power among the bishops and quarrels about correct belief and practice eventually led to a break between the Western (Latin) church and the Eastern (Greek) church. The church at Constantinople refused to acknowledge the claims of the Roman popes, and the Western church viewed the Eastern church with suspicion.

Tensions between the two came to a head in the ninth century. The Church of Rome added one word to the Nicene Creed—*filioque* (and the Son)—which changed the teaching about the Trinity. Before the new phrasing, the Holy Spirit came "from the Father" only, but after the addition, "from both the Father and Son." The Easterners regarded the change as a false teaching.

There were other differences. In the Eastern church, priests married and grew beards; in the Western church, priests were celibate (unmarried) and shaved.

In 1054 the pope's representative, Cardinal Humbert, went to Constantinople to smooth out differences. However, Eastern Patriarch Michael Cerularius snubbed him by not receiving him. Consequently, Humbert excommunicated Cerularius, and Cerularius excommunicated Humbert!

Western crusaders in the thirteenth century completed the division between the two churches. They raided and destroyed Eastern churches and installed Latin bishops over them.

When Sultan Mohammed (Mehmed) II captured Constantinople in 1453 and changed the city's name to Istanbul, the Eastern church preferred the "turban of the sultan to the crown of the pope." Attempts at union were unsuccessful, and the division remains to this day. The Russian Orthodox Church is part of the Eastern church. When Mennonites migrated to Russia in the eighteenth century, the strict Russian Orthodox church did not allow them to evangelize among its members.

Monks and nuns seek to follow God

With the power of the popes and clergy on the increase and the great prestige and wealth of the church, Christian faith and morals began to decline. The earliest indication that all was not well in Christendom came from men and women who felt they needed to separate themselves from the world to live for Christ.

Concerned individuals began to leave their occupations, sometimes good positions, for places and lives in the desert. From the third and fourth centuries on, monks and nuns, either as individual hermits or in communities, withdrew from the world to devote themselves to a life of contemplation and submission to the rule of Christ.

The most famous of the early monks was Anthony of Egypt (250-356), who was born into a well-to-do Christian home. One day in church he heard Jesus' words from the

Some people called him Simon the Saint. Others said he was a pillar in the church. And a few said he needed to come down from his pillar and go get a bath and a haircut.

Gospel: "If you wish to be perfect, go, sell your possessions, and give the money to the poor; . . . then come, follow me" (Matthew 19:21).

Anthony sold his land and distributed the proceeds among the poor, keeping only enough for the care of his sister. He withdrew to a ruined fort on a mountain and lived there for some twenty years, seldom seen by anyone.

Anthony was an intelligent, wise, and humble man who worked with his hands. Emperor Constantine and two of his sons wrote to him, asking for and receiving Anthony's counsel. Anthony died when he was 105.

Simeon Stylites, a fifth-century hermit, lived on a pillar

east of Antioch for thirty years. People brought this "pillar saint" food and drink, and he is said to have dripped with vermin. His fame spread and he preached to many people, including high state officials who came to see him. Some were converted from paganism. These extreme ascetics were often called "athletes of God" and were reputed to perform miracles of healing.

Jerome (347-420) was a famous monk in the western part of the Roman empire. A gifted and diligent scholar and a master of languages, Jerome translated the Bible into Latin, called the *Vulgate*. He formed an especially close friendship with Paula, one of the wealthy Roman women interested in

The Verona monastery is in northeastern Italy. A cloister, from the Latin word *claustrum* (hidden), is a covered walkway along the walls of an interior courtyard. Cloisters were prominent design elements in early monasteries, cathedrals, and churches, and were used as passageways between the enclosed areas of a structure.

the ascetic life. Together they visited the holy places where Jesus had lived, and near Bethlehem they decided to stay and live their monastic life. Jerome built a monastery, while Paula erected convents and a hospice for pilgrims.

Monasteries and nunneries became popular during the Middle Ages. They became oases of holiness and scholarship. Monks and nuns vowed to remain poor, virtuous, and obedient to the monastic rules, modeling the "perfect" life for the rest of society. Many medieval reformers came from the monasteries. It is significant that Martin Luther and some Anabaptist reformers had been monks.

The best leaders money can buy

By the fourteenth and fifteenth centuries, the church was in serious trouble. Persons with money could buy high church positions. This practice is called "simony," a term derived from the New Testament where Simon the Magician offered the apostles money in exchange for spiritual gifts (Acts 8:9-13). Unqualified persons often filled bishoprics and other church positions. They were friends and relatives of those in power. Such nepotism, derived from nephew, contributed to shallowness, materialism, and greed in the church. It was difficult to change these evils.

The struggle for power and wealth in high places, including the papacy, led to a rapid spiritual decline. Pope Innocent VIII (ruled 1484-1492) was in urgent need of income, so he sold church positions and created new offices for money. Some of the cardinals he appointed were worthy men, but one was the son of his brother and another the thirteen-year-old son of a powerful man from Florence, Italy. Several of the cardinals lived in luxury in the style of secular princes: they hunted, gambled, entertained lavishly, and had mistresses. Outstanding among them was Rodrigo Borgia, nephew of Pope Calixtus I.

Rodrigo Borgia, a Spaniard, became Pope Alexander VI in

1492, the year that Columbus sailed to the New World. Though an able administrator, Alexander VI shamelessly advanced members of his own family into positions of power and prestige. By his mistress he had four children; by other women, he had two more children.

His son Caesar received lucrative positions when he was only seven years old. Later Caesar became bishop, then archbishop, and eventually cardinal, acquiring huge possessions from his benefices. There were also rumors about the pope's shameful acts with his daughter Lucretia.

Literature of the time reflected the secular and immoral life of the church clergy. An Italian writer, Giovanni Boccaccio (1313-1375), wrote a book of one hundred stories, *The Decameron,* which portrayed the seamy side of the lives of clergy, monks, and nuns. Boccaccio vividly describes adultery, whoring, and other vices. Christian humanist Desiderius Erasmus (1466-1536) wrote *Julius Excluded,* the story of how the sixteenth-century Pope Julius II was excluded by Saint Peter from heaven because of his sins and his materialistic life.

Even the monasteries, former centers of holiness, began to decay spiritually and morally. The records tell of widespread lethargy, luxury, and clear immorality. We read of unmarried daughters and sons of the nobility entering the monastic life for unspiritual reasons. Having no inner call to the cloistered life, they disregarded the monastic rules and ideals, kept private incomes, and lived comfortable or even luxurious lives. Monks were often lazy, spending much of their time in hunting, in frequenting taverns, and in frivolous and obscene talk. Sometimes monks and nuns mingled and they reportedly had their babies killed, before or after birth.

The decline of the popes' influence had begun long before Alexander VI and Julius II. In 1309 the seat of the papacy moved to Avignon in southeastern France because of the unstable political situation in Italy and the corruption so prevalent in Rome. Then the popes had their spiritual authority challenged and came under the influence of the French kings.

In 1377 Pope Gregory XI, under pressure, went back to Rome, thus ending the "Babylonian Captivity" of the church. But the move did not solve the problem. There were then two popes, one in Rome and one in Avignon, each condemning the other. At one time there were even three popes, with rulers and church people taking sides for one or the other. Many Christians lost respect for the church over the confusion in leadership.

Early reformers emerge

Sincere men and women, including secular and spiritual rulers, viewed with alarm the deteriorating conditions in church and society. However, it was not easy to decide how the church should deal with the problems. Neither rulers nor popes had the authority to implement reform. Remembering the success of the Council of Nicaea in the fourth century, many thoughtful people suggested that a general council might end the division within the church and bring about much-needed reform.

Councils convened in the fourteenth and fifteenth centuries, meeting from time to time in different places. The Council of Constance (southern Germany, 1414-1418) ended the "Great Schism," or division in Christendom (1378-1417). However, it failed to deal with moral corruption in the church because of the opposition to reform by the many church leaders who benefited from their positions of power and material wealth.

On one thing the members of the Council of Constance could agree—the prosecution of heretics. A heresy, according to the church, was a belief that was in opposition to the official teaching of the church. The church believed the Albigensians and Waldensians were heretical groups. Individ-

C. G. Hellqvist

John Hus was burned at the stake, July 6, 1415, at Constance (Germany).

uals such as John Wycliffe of England and John Hus of Bohemia were considered dangerous to the faith and life of orthodox Christians.

John Hus (1373-1415), a devout university professor and preacher in Prague, became a reformer a hundred years before Martin Luther. He sharply criticized church leaders and popes who failed to live Christian lives. Hus argued that no leader who lived in deep sin was really a pope or bishop. He supported other reformers, notably John Wycliffe, preached against the sale of indulgences, and held that God and his conscience were more important to him than the declarations of popes and councils.

Hus was sentenced to death. After prolonged imprisonment, he was demoted from the priesthood, and on July 6, 1415, burned at the stake. His voice fell silent, but his ideas and concerns for the Christian faith and church bore fruit in the sixteenth century.

Mystics follow another way

John Hus and John Wycliffe were not the only persons working for reform. The so-called mystics, male and female, emphasized the inner Christian life, union of the soul with God, and practical holiness. While remaining members of the church, they did not take all that seriously the functions of the clergy, institutions, or even the sacraments. In their spirituality and actions, mystics like Catherine of Siena, Joan of Arc, Nicholas of Cusa, and Thomas à Kempis stood for the essence of the Christian faith and life.

Catherine of Siena (1347-1380) came from a deeply religious home. Early in life she dedicated herself to Christ. She refused to get married, saying that she was a bride of Christ. Catherine spent much time in meditation, prayer, and serving the poor and the sick. Many believed she had miracle healing power. She wrote hundreds of letters of spiritual counsel to ordinary people, prominent churchmen, and even to the pope. She helped to reconcile enemies and warring factions. Catherine of Siena represented the best of late medieval spirituality and piety.

Similar to the mystics were the Brothers and Sisters of the Common Life in the Netherlands and Belgium. Following Jesus and before the Anabaptists, the Brothers and Sisters combined some of the principles of monasticism with the non-monastic life. They worked with their hands and held their possessions in common. This community valued books and contributed to the revival of education. Their emphasis on following Jesus resulted in devotional writings; the most famous is *The Imitation of Christ,* by Thomas à Kempis. Even today this book inspires many readers.

Waldensians contribute to reform

As a result of worldliness in the church, several groups emerged whose aim was to reform the church, or failing that, to live apart from the world. Among these groups were the Franciscans, followers of Francis of Assisi (1182-1226); the Lollards, followers of John Wycliffe (1324-1384); and the Waldensians. These and other groups contributed significantly to the success of the Protestant Reformation in the sixteenth century.

The Waldensians began with Peter Waldo, a rich twelfth-century merchant of Lyons, France. He was impressed with the brevity and insecurity of life and asked a theologian how to get to heaven. The Bible scholar told Waldo to sell all he had and give to the poor (Luke 18:22). Waldo studied the New Testament and decided to live and preach as Jesus did. His followers called themselves the "Poor Men of Lyons," while others called them the Waldensians.

Bishops and the pope opposed their preaching and living. The pope excommunicated the Waldensians in 1184 because of their belief that they ought to obey God rather than human authority (Acts 5:29). However, their numbers multiplied and they spread in their native France and into Spain, Italy, and Germany.

The Waldensians continued to live according to the New Testament. They memorized Scripture, preached the simple life of Jesus, and remained generally poor. Waldensians refused to obey the pope and bishops and declared that the church of Rome was corrupt. Their community held that women and other laypersons could preach, that masses and prayers for the dead were useless, and that purgatory had no biblical foundation.

Waldensians declared that bishops and priests who lived Christian lives should be listened to, but that sacraments administered by unworthy priests were not valid. They rejected oaths, even in law courts, and believed that all taking of human life was against the law of God.

The Waldensians were humble folk. Even their enemies agreed that they were industrious, labored with their hands, and gave to the poor, were temperate in eating and drinking, did not frequent taverns and dances, dressed simply, and regarded the accumulation of wealth as evil. Yet the Catholic Church and the civil authorities persecuted them as heretics.

Some historians believed that the Waldensians were the forerunners of the Anabaptists of the sixteenth century. Anabaptists were similar to the Waldensians in their beliefs and practices, but no direct historical link has been established between the two groups.

The church persecutes heretics

As we have seen, many factors prevented the church from reforming its leaders and members. Instead of dealing with the root causes of the spiritual and moral decline in society, church and state united in persecuting "heretics" and deviant groups like the Waldensians. Accused heretics were considered guilty of the charges against them until proved innocent. To get the desired information or a confession of guilt from the accused, authorities interrogated, imprisoned, and tortured them. When the church decided that the accused was guilty as charged, the condemned person was handed over to the state for execution.

While persecution took place throughout Europe, forced conversions and executions of people reached a climax in Spain during fourteenth and fifteenth centuries. The Catholic Church compelled Muslims and Jews to accept Christian baptism or face expulsion or death. Many of these non-Christians "converted" rather than face the alternative. When officials discovered that the new converts continued in their traditional beliefs and practices, the authorities gave them harsh treatment.

The persecuting arm of church and state was the Inquisition. Such men as Ximenes and Torquemada, who had the zeal of reformers, developed the fifteenth-century Inquisition in Spain. They contributed little to much-needed church reform. On the contrary, the Inquisition represented the church's failure to deal with its problems. It also reflected the degenerated condition of the church.

The Grand Inquisitor

A most vivid literary description of the Inquisition is a chapter in Dostoyevsky's novel *The Brothers Karamazov*, titled "The Grand Inquisitor." In this nineteenth-century Russian novel, Jesus returns after fifteen hundred years and walks the streets of a city. People recognize him, come to him with their needs, and he blesses and helps them.

When the Grand Inquisitor is informed that Jesus has returned, he is angry and troubled. He has Jesus arrested and imprisoned. In prison the Inquisitor tells Jesus that he should not have come back, for the church had done well without him; in fact, it had "corrected" his work by giving people material comforts. Actually, the Inquisitor admits, the church is no longer following Jesus but the devil.

The Inquisitor tells Jesus that he deserves to be executed, but in the end he orders Jesus to leave and never come back. Jesus does not speak a single word. He simply kisses the old Inquisitor and leaves. Dostoyevsky's literary portrayal of what the medieval church had become captures well what many sincere people felt and believed at the time. Many were hoping and praying for a genuine reformation of the church.

■ ■ ■

3

Reformers shake the church

A thunderstorm changes history

On a hot, humid day in July 1505, a young student approached a village in the German region of Saxony. The sky became overcast, there was a sudden shower, and then a crashing storm. A bolt of lightning split the black clouds and knocked the traveler to the soaking ground. Terror-stricken, he cried out, "St. Anne, help me! I will become a monk!"[1]

For Martin Luther (1483-1546) it was a life-changing experience. Instead of becoming a lawyer, the career for which he had trained at the university, he entered a monastery. He studied theology and church history, and in time became a successful Reformer of the church. Luther was a leader in the Protestant Reformation, which was so thorough and wide-ranging that some have called it a revolution.

Luther was not the first Reformer of the medieval church. As we saw in the previous chapter, there were men and women long before Luther's time who tried to reform the church. They were not as successful as Luther. Yet without their preparatory work, Luther and other Protestant reformers would not have achieved their goals. In the sixteenth century, time was ripe for a thorough reform.

What made the Reformation possible?

Spiritual bankruptcy and moral corruption within the medieval (Middle Ages) church were not the only factors that eventually led to the Protestant revolution. Nationalism, economics, and humanism were also powerful factors that made the sixteenth-century Reformation possible.

The Catholic faith united medieval Europe, even though society divided along many lines. The Holy Roman Empire and the Catholic Church, presided over by the emperor and the pope, united the different countries, regions, and peoples. Some leaders compared this unity to the seamless garment of Jesus for which the soldiers under the cross cast lots.

Feelings of *nationalism* emerged and developed in the latter part of the Middle Ages. People began to think of themselves as French, German, or English first, and as Catholics second. The Hundred Years' War (1337-1453) between England and France illustrates this shift well. Joan of Arc, the Maid of Orleans, who led the French against the English, made it clear that she, a French woman, was fighting the foreign English. France belonged to the French, she insisted, and she demanded that the English stay in England.

Similarly, the Germans began to view the Italian popes as foreigners who exploited the German people, milking the "German cow" for "Peter's pence," the money that had to be paid to Rome. When Luther emerged as a Reformer, many German nobles hailed him as a national hero.

Since regions divided along national lines, Reformation leaders and groups could expect support from their people and rulers. Moreover, the Catholic Church and the emperor could no longer count on strong united action against the Protestant Reformers. Luther received support from his prince, the Elector of Saxony, and other powerful German princes.

European *economics* also changed toward the end of the Middle Ages. In medieval times, whoever had much land was rich and powerful. The church was the largest landholder in Europe. With the voyages of Columbus and other explorers in the fifteenth and sixteenth centuries, gold and other precious metals replaced land as the most valuable commodity and created a well-to-do middle class, sophisticated and independent.

Businesspeople, lawyers, teachers, bankers, and other professionals rose to prominence, and with their cash they acquired great influence and power. Thus, the banker Jacob Fugger of Germany lent money to church leaders, kings, and princes, influencing politics and church affairs.

Fugger's money also financed the election of Emperor Charles V (ruled 1519-1556), the Catholic secular head. The electors and other princes decided in favor of Charles V because they saw him as a generally weak ruler who would be unable to curb their own power and influence. This division and weakness within the Holy Roman Empire enabled Luther and other reformers to introduce needed changes and to oppose the clergy who stood in the way of reform.

Finally, *humanism* helped prepare the way for the Protestant Reformation. Humanists were scholars who emphasized human values and the power of reason; promoted education and scholarship; went back to the classical Greek, Latin, and Christian sources; and worked toward the reformation of the church. They criticized the clergy, undermined superstition, and questioned the authority claimed by the popes.

Erasmus, for example, was one of the greatest Christian humanists of all time. While remaining a Catholic, he supported Luther, was a friend of Swiss Reformer Ulrich Zwingli, and was sympathetic toward the Anabaptists. Without the work of the humanists, the Protestant Reformation would not have succeeded.

A monk finds grace

When Luther entered the monastery in 1505, his father did not like it. His parents wanted him to practice law, not become a churchman. But Luther was determined to devote

Through Fire and Water

Martin Luther, German leader of the Reformation.

his life to the church and find peace for his soul.

Some people have claimed that Luther's vow in the thunderstorm was made out of fear alone. More likely, it was the culmination of long thought.

Luther's choice of a monastic order shows that he was serious about his decision. He entered the Augustinian order, one of the strictest groups at the time. As a monk, Luther prayed, worked, punished himself for his sins, and with tears sought to find a gracious God. Unlike many nuns and other monks, Luther's efforts to find grace and forgiveness seemed in vain. His superior pointed the struggling monk to grace in Christ, but whenever Luther thought of Christ, he imagined him as a stern judge ready to punish sinners. For Luther, God was an angry judge, not a gracious Father.

While in the monastery, Luther studied theology to become a teacher in the Catholic Church, eventually earning a doctorate. The newly established University of Wittenberg appointed Luther professor; he lectured on books of the Bible.

One day, while preparing for his lectures, Romans 1:17 seemed to leap from the page: "The one who is righteous will live by faith." This was a quotation of Habakkuk 2:4. Similar passages in Paul's letter to the Romans spoke of faith and becoming "just." Luther was familiar with those texts but had not given them much thought.

From that moment on, Luther knew what Christian faith

was all about. Salvation comes from a gracious God in Christ, and a person receives this grace by faith only. It is not human doing or good works that redeem and make the sinner just, but God's free grace and love in Christ. Luther was free, forgiven, and happy, and his life took on new purpose and meaning.

Forgiveness for sale

There was a vacancy in the archbishopric of Mainz. This large diocese in Germany offered the potential of a large income for a worthy archbishop. The Catholic Church offered Albert of Brandenburg (1490-1545) the position if he would pay his own installation fee. But Albert was not a qualified candidate. He was too young, and he already held two bishoprics. Nevertheless, buying positions was nothing new. Pope Leo X (ruled 1513-1521) asked Albert to pay twelve thousand ducats, "for the twelve apostles," he said.

Albert made a counteroffer of seven thousand, apparently for the seven deadly sins. In the end they settled on ten thousand, perhaps for the Ten Commandments! Albert borrowed the money and paid for the archbishopric of Mainz.

To raise the money to pay for the loan, the pope permitted the proclamation of an indulgence, the remission of some of the penalties for sins—for a fee. Half of the proceeds from this "holy trade" went to Albert—a fact not mentioned to the indulgence buyer—and the other half to the construction of the St. Peter's Cathedral in Rome.

The indulgence seller, John Tetzel, traveled through German territories, promising that as soon as the money dropped in his box, the donor's relatives and friends were released from purgatory. Never before had the gospel and the grace of God been so cheap. Money took the place of repentance.

Martin Luther, who recently had gone through agony of soul to find salvation, was shocked and angry. In response, he walked to the Castle Church in Wittenberg on the last day of October 1517 and fastened ninety-five theses or statements on its door.

Written in Latin, the theses stated that the grace of God, not human works, forgives sins and redeems the sinner. Some statements expressed criticism of the popes, even ridiculing papal claims. Eager students translated the theses into German, and Luther, the courageous monk and professor, became known throughout Germany and beyond. The Protestant Reformation had begun.

Luther's red-hot pen

Through the next years, Luther preached, taught, and wrote about the need for a thorough Reformation of the church. He kept several printing presses busy, and in 1520 he published three booklets which were quite radical in tone and content.

The first was addressed *To the Nobility of the German Nation,* appealing to the princes and nobles to consider the plight of the church and to do something to help. Since the popes and councils had failed to reform the church, Luther argued, the princes might be more successful. The popes have no more spiritual authority than ordinary Christians, according to Luther. Since all baptized Christians possess the Holy Spirit, they are their own priests and are responsible to God only. Thus, clergy and laypeople are equal before God.

There were other radical statements in this booklet. If we fight the Turks, Luther asked, why don't we fight the popes who are robbing us? The clergy should be free to marry. Pilgrimages to Rome and other "holy places" are useless. Universities are "gates of hell" if they don't train young people in godliness. Congregations should have the right to appoint their own pastors.

The booklet was a firebrand. Some of Luther's partners

The Ninety-five Theses

On October 31, 1517, Martin Luther nailed ninety-five points or statements to the Castle Church door in Wittenberg, intended for discussion among his colleagues. The statements were written in the Latin language. Here are a few of them:

1. Our Lord and Master Jesus Christ wishes that our entire life should be one of repentance.

2. The pope's indulgences don't remove guilt from a sinful person.

3. Indulgences are evil because they divert people from feeling sorry for their sins and from true salvation in Christ.

4. The person who repents is forgiven by God without indulgences.

5. The pope would do better to sell St. Peter's Basilica (church) in Rome and give the money to the poor.

6. If the pope has the power to release people from purgatory, why in the name of love doesn't he do away with purgatory altogether?

7. Why doesn't the pope build the church of St. Peter with his own money?

8. Peace and forgiveness come to a person through faith in a gracious Christ.

■ ■ ■

feared that it would cause a revolution. The idea of the priesthood of all believers, it was feared, might lead to the breakdown of all authority, law, and order. Luther, however, stood by what he had written. In fact, he announced that he had "another song against Rome."

The next "song" was also a book, *The Babylonian Captivity of the Church*. Here Luther attacked five of the seven sacraments of the Catholic Church, keeping only baptism and the Lord's Supper. Luther eliminated confirmation, ordination,

History doesn't tell us what Martin Luther thought when he heard about the Diet of Worms, but he agreed to check it out anyway.

marriage, penance, and anointing with oil before a person dies, arguing that while useful and good they are not necessary for salvation. Christ had not made these important church practices into sacraments, according to Luther.

In *The Freedom of a Christian*, another booklet, ironically dedicated to Pope Leo, Luther explained the gospel. The Law in the Old Testament, according to Luther, condemns sinners, whereas the gospel in the New Testament presents

Christ, who fulfills the demands of the Law and brings about salvation. Redeemed people become inwardly free. They are not slaves to anyone. Yet in day-to-day life and in society, Christians must submit to governments and the laws of the country as others do.

These and other writings of Luther became influential among both Luther's followers and other radical groups, including the Anabaptists. In fact, Luther's courage became an example to many individuals and groups concerned with the Reformation of the church. Moreover, the content of Luther's writings indicated the direction in which the Reformation was to move.

"I will not retract anything"

While Luther encouraged other Reformers, the Church of Rome became worried about Luther's influence upon the masses. As a result Pope Leo X sent Luther a solemn letter of warning or decree, called a "bull." The bull of 1520 compared the German Reformer to a "wild boar" that had invaded the vineyard of the Lord. Listing forty-one errors in Luther's writings, the bull said: "The books of Martin Luther which contain these errors are to be examined and burned."

It took the papal bull three months to reach Luther. When it arrived in Wittenberg toward the end of the year, Luther, his colleagues, and his students made a bonfire outside the city and burned the bull and other books on medieval theology. With this symbolic act, Luther broke with Rome and turned from his Catholic past. Like John Hus before him, he expected martyrdom for his actions.

The Diet of Worms, an imperial gathering of church and state officials, met in the spring of 1521. Its agenda included an examination of Luther's writings and the possible condemnation of the Augustinian monk. Luther was invited to attend. The emperor promised safety as he traveled. His friends warned him of danger in attending the Diet. But

Luther replied that even if there were as many devils as tiles on the roofs of Worms, he would still go there. When he arrived in the city, people greeted and cheered him as a hero.

When Luther came into the large hall where the Diet met, he saw his books spread out on a table. Luther received two questions in the presence of Emperor Charles V and the dignitaries: Are the books on the table yours? Are you ready to retract the errors in them? He was to answer simply yes or no, without "horns and teeth"—that is, without malice.

Luther answered that his books were not all of one kind. Some were about Christian faith and life, and some attacked the abuses in the church and the evil lives of popes. How could he retract anything from them without harming the truth and continuing the corruption within the church?

Finally Luther declared, "Since then Your Majesty and your lordships desire a simple reply, I will answer without horns and without teeth. Unless I am convinced by Scripture and plain reason—I do not accept the authority of popes and councils, for they have contradicted each other—my conscience is captive to the Word of God. I cannot and I will not recant anything, for to go against conscience is neither right nor safe. God help me. Amen."[2]

As Luther left the hall, German knights and nationalists cheered him. The Catholic party and the emperor, however, condemned Luther and put a price on his head.

On his way back to Wittenberg, Luther was "kidnapped" by horsemen and taken to the Wartburg Castle, where he was kept in hiding. The Elector of Saxony, Frederick the Wise, had thus arranged for Luther's safety. While at the Wartburg, Luther translated the New Testament into German and wrote on Reformation issues.

He returned to Wittenberg in the spring of 1522. In Luther's absence, his colleagues Andrew Carlstadt and Philip Melanchthon had continued the Reformation work there.

The peasants rebel

It soon became evident that Luther's ideas had released forces that even the Reformer had not foreseen. Principles like the "priesthood of all believers" had freed people to think for themselves, to read and interpret the Bible, and to take responsibility for their own lives.

Luther found that his followers often understood the Bible differently than he did. For example, Luther held that the heart of the gospel was the free grace of God received by faith. However, his colleague Carlstadt believed that works of love were just as important as faith. On this point the Anabaptists agreed with Carlstadt.

In society, especially among the common people, the Reformation was greeted as the beginning of necessary changes. The peasants had suffered for centuries under oppressive overlords and rulers. From time to time, they rebelled, but generally their lot did not change.

When the Reformation exposed corruption in the church, peasants expressed their own grievances and demanded justice. After all, they argued, since the nobles are Christians too, they surely will agree to treat their subjects fairly and justly. They soon discovered the nobles had no intentions of changing.

Radical leaders such as Thomas Müntzer (1488-1525), a former follower of Luther, supported the peasants. At first the demands of the peasants, as expressed in their *Twelve Articles*, were most reasonable and phrased in biblical language. Like Luther before them, the peasants were willing to withdraw any article that did not have scriptural support. But matters soon got out of hand. Bands of peasants began to attack castles and monasteries and rose in bloody revolt against their overlords.

Luther believed the peasants had misunderstood and warped his message. When he wrote against the pope and church, Luther argued, he had spiritual corruption and oppression in mind, not social, economic, or political conditions. He had proclaimed inner freedom in Christ, not abolition of serfdom and changes in the social order. More seriously, according to Luther, the peasants had no legal or moral right to rebel against their legitimate rulers. Rebellion was against God's order and punishable by law.

Luther sides with the nobles

At the height of the peasants' rebellion in the mid-1520s, Luther sharply criticized them in a pamphlet titled *Against the Murderous and Thieving Hordes of Peasants*. Luther accused the peasants of breaking their oaths to their lords and taking up arms against divinely instituted governments.

Luther called rebellion inexcusable, for it led to the breakdown of all law and order. "Therefore," he advised the princes, "let everyone who can, smite, slay, and stab, secretly or openly, remembering that nothing can be more poisonous, hurtful, or devilish than a rebel. It is just as when one must kill a mad dog; if you don't strike him, he will strike you, and the whole land with you."[3]

The nobles did not need Luther's encouragement. The well-armed nobles butchered some one hundred thousand peasants. They tortured and executed those who tried to flee. The rulers remained unrepentant. Luther believed they had fought in a "just cause," whereas the peasants had acted in "bad conscience"; hence, the peasants deserved death in body and soul. Luther did not retract anything he had written against the peasants. According to Luther, they got what they deserved.

Why did Luther take the side of the nobles against the peasants? According to some historians, Luther was worried that people might hold him responsible for the war.

Some people of Luther's time suggested as much. "You, Luther, refuse to acknowledge the insurgents," Erasmus wrote, "but they acknowledge you, and the instigators of this war claim the gospel as their guide." In opposing the peasants, Luther sought to clear himself from all responsibility for the war.

Second, Luther worried that the Peasants' Revolt might undo the Reformation. He feared that the spiritual issues of his work would degenerate into mere social and economic changes, which he believed missed the whole point of reform. Moreover, Luther believed that a victory for the peasants would lead to the breakup of all institutions and result in social chaos. Some historians have even suggested that Luther allied himself with the nobles because he needed them in his work of reform.

Common people turn from Luther

The peasants' crushing defeat disillusioned them about the great Reformer and his cause. Luther had attracted the common people until 1525. The oppressed believed that the newly discovered gospel would reform the spiritual areas of life and improve their social and economic conditions. Luther dashed the hopes of many peasants when he sided with the nobles.

Many common people turned away from Luther and his message and began to listen to the more Radical Reformers, including the Anabaptists. Anabaptism emerged early in 1525 and began to spread rapidly throughout Europe.

There is good reason to believe that radical preachers, including some Anabaptists, used the peasants' defeat as effective propaganda in advancing their message. These preachers spoke of practical Christianity, justice for all people, community and sharing one's goods, and following Jesus in all areas of life. The common folk listened, and many accepted the Anabaptist gospel. Luther had thus played into the hands of the Anabaptists.

Unfortunately, the connection between the Peasants' Revolt and the Anabaptists colored Luther's view of the

Radical Reformers in general and Anabaptism in particular. Thomas Müntzer and Andreas Carlstadt, leaders among the common people and Luther's opponents, influenced the Anabaptists with their writings. Even though these men never became Anabaptists, Luther and other mainline Reformers saw them as founders of Anabaptism. For Luther, this connection was proof that Anabaptists could not be trusted. He thought that even the peaceful Anabaptists were devils in disguise.

No handshakes between Luther and Zwingli

Luther was not the only Reformer. Quite independent of Luther, yet influenced by his writings, was Ulrich Zwingli (1484-1531), the leading Reformer of Switzerland. Zwingli's personality and work were not as colorful as Luther's, but in Switzerland's Reform movement and in the history of early Anabaptism, his role was as important as Luther's.

By the end of the 1520s, the emperor and the old church still threatened the Reformers. At the Second Diet of Speyer in April 1529, the Catholic majority ruled that in Lutheran lands, Catholics must be tolerated. However, in Catholic lands, liberty would not be extended to the Lutherans. Nineteen territories, led by Philip of Hesse, protested this arrangement. The protesters became known as *Protestants*.

At this Diet, Catholics and Protestants agreed that Anabaptists were not a legal religious group and should be persecuted.

In an effort to unite the German and Swiss Protestants against their common Catholic enemies, Philip of Hesse invited Reformation leaders from Wittenberg, Strasbourg, Basel, and Zurich to come to his picturesque castle in Marburg to discuss issues that divided them. Luther, Zwingli, and other Reformation leaders accepted the invitation. In October 1529, they met for the Marburg Colloquy.

The point of contention was the meaning of Christ's

words from the Last Supper, repeated in the Lord's Supper: "This is my body," and "This is my blood." Luther argued that these words must be taken literally, meaning that Christ was *bodily* in the bread and wine (known as "real presence").

Zwingli maintained that Jesus' words meant that the bread and wine represented the Lord's body and blood. Zwingli agreed to accept Christ's *spiritual* presence in communion but not his bodily presence. Luther remained unmoved. He drew a circle with chalk on the table and wrote, "This is my body." The debate did not result in handshakes. The Protestant reformers agreed to disagree, to the great disappointment of Prince Philip.

The Romanesque Grossmünster, where Ulrich Zwingli started the Reformation in Zurich in 1519.

Zwingli leads reform in Switzerland

Who was this Ulrich Zwingli who opposed Martin Luther on the Lord's Supper and the Anabaptists on baptism? What Luther as a Reformer was for Germany, Zwingli was for Switzerland. Yet the two men were different. Zwingli was more rational, cooler, in his work as a Reformer. Zwingli had gradually, without great spiritual stress, realized that he was called by God to work for Reformation in the church.

Zwingli had a happy childhood, growing up with no great sense of sin. When he became a priest, he did not observe the clerical obligation of chastity. After he broke with the Catholic Church, Zwingli married the woman he had lived with off and on.

Having studied at several universities, Zwingli was attracted to the humanists of his time, especially to Erasmus, with whom he corresponded and who became his friend. Through the eyes of humanism, Erasmus and Zwingli saw the corruption in church and society.

Zwingli's fame as a preacher increased when in 1519 he became the people's priest at the Central Church (Grossmünster) in Zurich, a wealthy city in Switzerland. Preaching on the Gospel of Matthew, he attacked abuses in the church and Switzerland's practice of sending mercenaries to fight for other countries. As a chaplain in such a mercenary force in Italy, Zwingli had seen how this practice corrupted Swiss men. Under Zwingli's leadership, the civil authorities of Zurich ruled that priests should be free to preach in accordance with the Word of God.

By 1523 the Reformation in Switzerland was well under way. Zwingli came out against monastic vows, clerical celibacy, praying to saints, purgatory, viewing Catholic mass as a sacrifice, and teaching that salvation can be earned by doing good works.

When Zwingli preached that salvation comes by faith, the council of Zurich supported him. Priests and nuns became

Ulrich Zwingli, leader of the Reformation in Zurich, Switzerland.

married; images, relics, and even organs were eliminated from the church; monasteries were seized and turned into schools; the mass was replaced with a German church service. Working closely with the civil government, Zwingli forged an even closer union of church and state than that achieved in Luther's Germany.

Other Swiss states accepted the reform measures that came from Zurich. In a debate in 1528, Zwingli, assisted by his colleagues, proposed many of the basic beliefs in the Reformed Church. Among the main articles were: Christ is the head of the church; the Word of God is the final authority in the church; Christ alone is our righteousness; the Bible does not teach the bodily presence of Christ in the Lord's Supper; there is no biblical foundation for the veneration of saints, for intercession for the dead, for purgatory, or for holy images; and marriage is natural and open to all, including the clergy.

While Protestant states or cantons accepted the Reformed Church, the Catholic cantons remained opposed, even hostile. Armed hostilities broke out. In 1531 when Zurich attempted to force Protestant preaching upon neighboring Catholic cantons, the Catholics went on the attack.

In this War of Cappel, Zwingli accompanied the Zurich forces as chaplain and was killed in battle, sword in hand. Luther was convinced that God punished Zwingli because he had not accepted the real presence in communion and had fought with the sword.

Redrawing the map

By 1530 the religious map of Europe had changed. In 1500 the Roman Catholic Church, however much in need of reform, still existed as it had for over a thousand years. Now Protestant churches were taking shape throughout Europe. The original desire for reform had resulted in the breakup of old religious institutions, beliefs, and ways of life. New institutions and ways of worshiping God were established. These changes did not take place peacefully. Strife, even bloodshed, accompanied the transformation.

Out of this struggle, a third movement arose—the Radical or Anabaptist Reformation, beginning in 1525. Though opposed by Catholics and Protestants, Anabaptists believed their Reformation was more thorough than the Magisterial Reformation of Luther and Zwingli, who used magistrates and other government officials to enforce change in the church. To the development of Anabaptism we now turn.

How do you know when your church is faithful?

Menno Simons needed to reply. A Reformed pastor had bitterly attacked the Anabaptists, calling them conspirators, a devilish sect, and a false church.

Menno responded by listing six ways to tell whether a church is truly following Christ. Menno published his defense in 1554. Do you think his description of the faithful church still applies today?

1. The true church holds to the Word of God as its only standard for belief and practice. When Constantine legalized Christianity in the fourth century, dramatic changes soon followed. It wasn't long until customs and traditions held as much authority as Scripture. Menno argued that practices and beliefs need to emerge from teachings in the Bible.

2. A faithful church practices baptism and communion in the way the early Christians did. Baptism and communion have always been the church's two primary signs of grace. The early church baptized young people and adults upon confession of their faith. The Lord's Supper was a time of celebration and fellowship around a table. But Menno believed that sixteenth-century church sacraments had become "mere elements, words, and ceremonies." The Anabaptists wanted to celebrate baptism and communion like believers in the first and second centuries.

3. Christ's followers show love for their neighbors. Catholic Emperor Charles V had issued an order for Menno's arrest, offering one hundred gold guilders as reward. The state church also wanted to capture Menno. To avoid imprisonment, Menno moved about secretly, accepting support from other Anabaptists in homes, barns, and caves. In the eyes of the state church, apparently, love for one's neighbor did not include renegade preachers such as Menno Simons.

4. A faithful church expects persecution—the "pressing cross of Christ." Menno knew that from history. The early disciples suffered Nero's wrath, and third-century Christians felt the emperor's sword. The Anabaptists, however, bore torture and death at the hands of a state church that called itself Christian.

5. The true church boldly confesses Christ "in the face of cruelty, tyranny, fire, and the sword." Menno first preached in a Catholic parish. His personal conversion, about ten years later, transformed his ministry. Despite the persecution he faced as an Anabaptist preacher, he chose to proclaim Christ as the only foundation for the church. Members of Christ's kingdom in each generation bravely confess Jesus above any political or religious power.

6. A faithful church brings forth the fruits of Christ. Christians show Christ's character through their daily lives. They separate themselves from the values and practices of the present age. They strive to love and serve God completely. And they invite others to join the community of faith.

The debate with Gellius Faber, Reformed pastor of Emden, must have saddened Menno. He grieved over disputes among Christians. In a letter three years later, he said, "There is nothing upon earth which my heart loves more than it does the church." Yet his desire for faithfulness to Christ forced him to respond.

What about today? Do we love the church enough to analyze its strengths and weaknesses?

Do members of your church try to apply the teachings of the Bible to daily life? Are baptism and communion meaningful signs of grace where you worship? Do Christians you know demonstrate active, nonviolent love? Has anyone suffered for a clear witness to Jesus? Do you and your friends display the fruits of Christ? Are Christians from any background welcome to join your congregation?

Nearly 450 years ago, Menno took up quill, ink, and paper in response to Gellius Faber. Now it's your turn to reply. How do you know when your church is faithful?

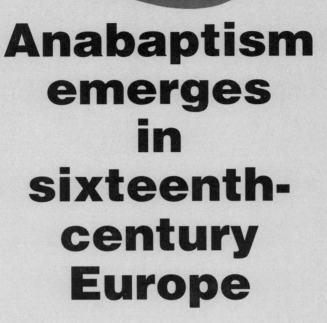

Anabaptism emerges in sixteenth-century Europe

4

The Swiss Brethren break with Zwingli

"Baptize me!"

It was on a Saturday, almost certainly the evening of January 21, 1525, in the house of Felix Manz and his mother. A group of some fifteen young people, single and married, had gathered for Bible study, prayer, and discussion of faith-and-life issues. Suddenly a young man wearing a blue jacket got up, walked over to Conrad Grebel, one of the leaders, and said, "Baptize me. Baptize me in the name of God with the true Christian baptism."

George Blaurock's request surprised Conrad Grebel and the others. Baptize an adult who had been baptized as an infant many years ago? Moreover, Conrad Grebel had no authority from the church to perform church functions. Most important, to rebaptize anyone was against the law. The authorities could fine them, expel them from the city, even kill them for breaking the law.

Blaurock was still kneeling, waiting for baptism. Grebel then reached for one of Frau Manz's kitchen dippers, partially filled it with water, and baptized Blaurock in the name of the Father, the Son, and the Holy Spirit. Blaurock then, upon the request of the others in the room, baptized each one.

"And so," we read in the old account of this event, "in great fear of God, together they surrendered themselves to the Lord. They confirmed one another for the service of the gospel and began to teach the faith and to keep it. This was the beginning of separation from the world and its evil ways."[1]

Today it is not unusual for Mennonite young people, often in their teens, to ask for baptism and join the church. Five hundred years ago, however, no one took believers baptism for granted. In fact, a person who decided to take the step of obedience to Christ in baptism knew that it meant breaking the law and facing banishment and persecution.

Why, then, did people like the group in Manz's house submit to adult or believers baptism? Was baptism that important, and was the price of baptism not too high? To answer these questions, we must look at what led to that first baptism in 1525.

Young radicals rebel against their teacher

As we have seen in the previous chapter, Ulrich Zwingli was the most powerful Reformer in Zurich, Switzerland. He fearlessly preached the Word of God, criticized abuses in the old church, and took decisive action toward reforming the church. He removed images from the churches, abolished the Latin mass, introduced German church services, and monks, nuns, and priests began to marry.

In all these reforms, the city council supported Zwingli, although the city fathers cautioned Zwingli not to proceed too rapidly lest the common people find the changes too radical and too soon. Like Luther in Germany, Zwingli did not wish to alienate the people or oppose the council.

Zwingli's friends, associates, and followers were less cautious than their leader. For Conrad Grebel, Felix Manz, and their friends, the Reformation did not proceed fast enough nor according to the clear teaching of the Word of God. Zwingli's regard for the city council did not sit well with his more radical followers. They criticized and even ridiculed Zwingli for always running to "my lords" to ask their opin-

Thanks to his beliefs on baptism, Conrad Grebel found himself in hot water with the authorities more than once.

ion on matters that pertained to the church and faith. The radicals believed that only the Word of God should be consulted and acted upon. In spiritual matters the magistrates should have nothing to say and certainly not interfere.

Zwingli's way of dealing with matters of reform was holding debates (disputations) in which the Reformers, the city leaders, and the people participated. Such debates dealing with changes and innovations, however, were often more of a farce than genuine attempts at resolving differences of opinion.

In all the debates held between 1523 and 1525, Zwingli was declared the winner and the Radical Reformers the losers. In other words, the magistrates not only meddled in spiritual matters, but they also decided how faith issues were to be resolved. The need for separation of church and state became obvious to the Radicals, who were disappointed with the Magisterial Reformation.

The Radicals choose believers baptism

Early in 1525 the debate about infant versus adult (believers) baptism was of great importance for the Reformation movement and the emergence of the Anabaptists. For the Swiss radicals, the question was very real. Reading other Reformers, notably Thomas Müntzer, Andrew Carlstadt, and the New Testament, they became convinced that there was no biblical basis for baptizing infants.

The Radicals decided not to baptize their own children. However, after the debate of January 17, Zwingli and the council decided that all infants must be baptized and that adult rebaptism was not acceptable. A few days later, as we have seen, Conrad Grebel and his friends performed the first believers baptism among themselves.

For the Anabaptists (rebaptizers), faith had to come before baptism, following the words of Jesus in Mark 16:16. "The one who believes and is baptized will be saved." Since infants cannot testify to a conscious faith, according to the Anabaptists, they ought not to be baptized. When they become teenagers and adults, they can choose to follow Christ. Some Anabaptists ridiculed infant baptism, calling it "a dog's bath." Obviously the Catholic and Protestant society did not find this attitude acceptable.

Why was the issue of baptism so important in sixteenth-century Europe? At that time most people believed that baptism not only removed the guilt of sin from the infant, but also made the baby a member of the church. To postpone baptism till later in life would divide society into Christians and non-Christians. For Zwingli and other mainline Reformers, adult baptism would result in a large part of society remaining pagan. Especially Zwingli believed in a Christian society (*corpus christianum*), a Christendom where all baptized people were part of the church.

Anabaptists, on the other hand, believed that faith was to be received voluntarily. Baptism and church membership were only for those who repented of their sins and made a personal decision to follow Jesus (discipleship). Anabaptists believed that unbaptized children were safe in Christ and thus could wait until they were old enough and able to respond to God's grace. When the Radicals practiced their beliefs on baptism, they became targets of hatred from the rest of society.

The first Anabaptist leaders

Catholics had their pope, Lutherans had Martin Luther, and the Reformed had Zwingli. The Anabaptists had no one leader at the top. Even *Menno Simons*, from whom Mennonites get their name, was one among many leaders of the Anabaptist movement. This made Anabaptism diverse, even fragmented, but it also exemplified the Anabaptists' strong belief in "the priesthood of all believers." In the church, according to the Anabaptists, all members are equal.

Who were the first leaders of Swiss Anabaptism? According to some Anabaptist historians, *Conrad Grebel* (c. 1498-1526) was the acknowledged leader of the Swiss Brethren. Grebel performed the first baptism, as we have seen, and Grebel in the name of his radical friends wrote important letters to Thomas Müntzer and Martin Luther. Grebel was only twenty-eight years old when he died of the plague, thus undoubtedly escaping a martyr's death.

George Blaurock (c. 1492-1529), who requested baptism of Grebel and whom we met at the beginning of this book, was a fearless and successful evangelist, proclaiming the gospel and baptizing people. *Wilhelm Reublin*, born between 1480 and 1484, died a natural death after 1559. An effective leader at the beginning, Reublin later renounced Anabaptism and then served the authorities who had persecuted him and his friends. *Michael Sattler* and *Balthasar Hubmaier*, both martyred for their faith, influenced Anabaptism with their writings. We shall meet them and their work later.

"Into your hands, Lord"

Felix Manz (c. 1498-1527), who became one of the first Anabaptist martyrs, was the son of an unmarried mother. His father was a Catholic clergyman who before the Reformation served at the Central Church in Zurich. An intelligent young man, Manz studied Latin, Greek, and Hebrew in Zurich and later attended the University of Paris.

When Zwingli began his reforming work, Manz was among those who supported him. Before long, however, Manz and his friends disagreed with Zwingli on matters of reform, especially on the question of believers baptism versus infant baptism.

The Schipfe, site of Felix Manz's drowning on the Limmat River.

Manz and Blaurock faced repeated arrest and imprisonment for their preaching and baptizing among the Swiss
populace. Sometimes they escaped, and sometimes their
captors set them free in the hope that they would stop their
evangelistic activity. Toward the end of 1526, the two leaders
were again arrested and taken to Zurich.

Since Blaurock was not a citizen of Zurich, the authorities
flogged him and banished him from the city. Manz's charge
was setting up a separate church, teaching that a Christian
could not become a magistrate nor use a sword, and baptizing. His sentence decreed death by drowning. Zwingli, his
former teacher and friend, supported the sentence.

On January 5, 1527, many people followed Manz's procession to the Limmat River, the place of execution. Manz's
mother was in the crowd, encouraging her son to remain
strong in the faith. The executioner bound Manz's hands
together, pulled them over his knees, and pushed a stick
through under his knees and above his arms. Thus immobi-
lized, Manz was pushed into the cold water, but not before
he sang out, "Into your hands, Lord, I commend my spirit."

Young Anabaptists think for themselves

The Swiss Brethren saw themselves as another reform
movement, the beginning of a third way between Catholics
and Protestants. They knew, however, that they were indebted to the two other traditions for much of what they came to
believe and how they tried to apply the gospel to their life.
They also knew that the Catholics and the Protestant Reformers rejected their way and persecuted them.

In their struggle to develop Christian communities, Anabaptists reached out to other sympathetic Reformers, hoping
to find support. In communicating with other Reformers,
they showed a remarkable independence of thought and
belief. This is all the more surprising, considering the youth-
fulness of the early Anabaptist leaders. Most of them were

young people in their twenties and thirties, an age when ideals, courage, and radical action often outweigh caution and practical considerations.

As early as September 1524, even before the Anabaptists established their congregations, Conrad Grebel and his friends wrote two important letters to German Reformers who had influenced their thinking. Their letter to Müntzer exists today, and through it we learn much about the Swiss Brethren. The letter they wrote to Luther did not survive, but there are indications of what it contained and that the Grebel group was bold enough to criticize the great German Reformer.

A letter to Thomas Müntzer

Dated September 5, 1524, Grebel's letter to Thomas Müntzer begins, "To the sincere and true proclaimer of the gospel, Thomas Müntzer, . . . our true and beloved brother with us in Christ." The letter deals with such things as the worship service, the Lord's Supper, baptism, and music in the church.

While Müntzer's ideas about reforming the church were in agreement with the Swiss Brethren, Grebel and his friends objected to certain of Müntzer's innovations. German hymns, for example, which Müntzer had introduced, had no scriptural basis.

Grebel said, "We find nothing taught in the New Testament about singing, no example of it." On the basis of Ephesians 5:19, the Grebel group believed that Christians were to sing to the Lord in their hearts only. In this the Swiss Brethren were influenced by Zwingli, who also removed music from the worship service.

Of greater concern to the Grebel group was Müntzer's belief that Christians may defend themselves with the sword. "The gospel and its adherents," Grebel wrote, "are not to be protected by the sword, nor are they thus to protect

A short distance east of Zurich is the Cave of the Anabaptists (Täuferhöhle), a secret meeting place and hideout during times of persecution.

themselves. . . . Neither do they use worldly sword or war, since all killing has ceased with them."

In a postscript to the letter, Grebel came back to the question of the sword. The Swiss heard that Müntzer had preached "against the princes, that they are to be attacked with the fist." "Is it true?" Grebel asked, hoping that the Reformer whom the Swiss admired wasn't a "warlord."[2]

As far as we know, the letter never reached Müntzer. In the spring of 1525, during the height of the Peasants' Revolt the authorities executed Müntzer as a rebel and leader of the peasants. The letter, however, tells us much about the Swiss

Brethren. They had never met Müntzer personally. They knew him from his writings only, particularly those which dealt with baptism. They looked up to Müntzer, who like them sought to reform the church and met opposition from powerful mainline Reformers. The Swiss Brethren thus reached out for support in their own trials and difficulties, trying to establish links with other like-minded Reformers.

Sadly, the Swiss Brethren soon found that Thomas Müntzer did not share their beliefs. Müntzer's use of the sword against the "godless" was contrary to what the Swiss Anabaptists believed. For the Swiss Brethren, nonresistance or Christian pacifism was an important article of their faith. The letter also shows that while the Grebel group was influenced by other Reformation figures, they were fairly independent in their understanding and interpretation of the Word of God. For them, the Bible was most important.

The Grebel group wanted to keep Christian worship free of anything contrary to the gospel or not stated specifically in Scripture. By the way, it is good that Anabaptists didn't follow Conrad Grebel in his opposition to singing hymns in church. Anabaptists and later Mennonites sang many hymns in times of persecution and praised their Lord in congregational meetings.

In their letter to Müntzer, the Grebel group stated that they had written to Martin Luther as well. "So I wrote to Luther too," Grebel writes, "on behalf of my brethren and yours, and have exhorted him to cease from the false sparing of the weak."[3] Grebel meant that Luther should not use the weakness of Christians as an excuse for not working more courageously toward reform. According to Grebel, Luther like Zwingli was more concerned about pleasing people than following the Word of God. Again we see that the Swiss Brethren, while appreciating the work of other Reformers, followed an independent course.

Luther apparently never responded to Grebel's letter. From

someone in Wittenberg, the Swiss learned that Luther had received the letter but that he didn't quite know how to answer Grebel. The Reformer may have been positively impressed with the Swiss Brethren, but before long, Luther was among those who persecuted the Anabaptists.

Importance of the Schleitheim meeting

By 1527, only two years after the first believers baptism, it had become clear that Catholic and Protestant society would not allow Anabaptism to spread and become dominant. Some Anabaptist leaders had tried to establish Anabaptism on a larger scale in society, the way Luther and Zwingli were establishing territorial churches.

Balthasar Hubmaier (1480-1528) was at first fairly successful at establishing Anabaptism in Waldshut, a town of about 7,000 citizens in southern Germany. Hundreds of persons were baptized, and Anabaptism became the dominant faith in this town. When Austrian forces attacked Waldshut, Hubmaier had to flee, and the old Catholic faith was reintroduced. Anabaptism on a larger territorial scale had failed.

It gradually dawned on the early Anabaptists that as re-

The Schleitheim Brotherly Agreement, written by Michael Sattler and other Anabaptists, 1527.

The Benedictine monastery of St. Peter, located in the Black Forest of Germany, where Michael Sattler was prior (second in charge) before his conversion to Anabaptism.

jected and persecuted believers, they would remain in the minority, and many people would hate their church. They also believed on the basis of the gospel that small Christian communities were to let their light shine in a dark world. Thus individual believers gathered in congregations were to model for the world what it means to be true disciples of Jesus.

This vision of a separated Christian community was first drafted in 1527 in a document called Brotherly Union, the Schleitheim Confession. The writer was Michael Sattler (c. 1490-1527), a former prior in the Benedictine monastery of St. Peters in the Black Forest east of Freiburg, Germany.

Sometime during the Peasants' War, Sattler decided to leave the monastery. He married Margaretha and eventually joined the Anabaptists. As an Anabaptist leader, Sattler became as important as the other leaders we have mentioned. The film *The Radicals* vividly portrays the life, work, and death of Michael and Margaretha.[4]

The meeting at Schleitheim, a small town in northern

Switzerland, took place secretly on February 24, 152
gathered group discussed and debated issues regarding the
Christian faith and church. In the end they agreed to accept
a document containing seven articles for their guidelines.
In the introduction, the group warned against "false
brothers . . . who have turned away from the faith." These
persons were not named, but historians believe the reference
is to persons like Hans Denck, Balthasar Hubmaier, and
Hans Hut—Anabaptist leaders who did not share some of
the beliefs and practices of the Swiss Brethren. The document then stated the articles the group agreed to accept and
live by.

Seven convictions of Swiss Anabaptism

1. *Concerning baptism.* Baptism is administered to all [who]
have repented "and [who] believe truly that their sins are
taken away through Christ." Infant baptism is rejected as
"the greatest and first abomination of the pope." Baptism is
for those who request it without any pressure from others.

2. *Concerning the ban.* Matthew 18 is the basis for dealing
with a fellow member who slips and falls into error or sin.
Counsel begins in private, and only later does the erring
member come before the congregation. If the person does
not repent, the ban or excommunication must follow.

3. *Concerning the Lord's Supper.* Those who wish to take
part in communion "must beforehand be united in the body
of Christ, that is, the congregation of God, whose head is
Christ, and that by baptism." The emphasis here is on the
oneness of members with Christ and that only "children of
God" may take part in the Lord's Supper.

4. *Concerning separation.* Separation from the world is part
of following Jesus. By worldliness is meant "popish and
repopish" (Catholic and Protestant) works, idolatry, Catholic
or Protestant church attendance, winehouses, and other
"carnal" things. Christians must also separate themselves

from "diabolical weapons of violence—such as sword, armor, . . . and all of their use to protect friends or against enemies— by virtue of the word of Christ: 'You shall not resist evil.' "

5. *Concerning shepherds.* The shepherds or pastors "take care of the body of Christ." If the shepherd suffers exile or martyrdom, "at the same hour another shall be ordained to his place, so that the . . . little flock of God may not be destroyed, but be preserved by warning and be consoled." Thus the pastor's role of preaching, teaching, and counseling is important in building the congregation.

6. *Concerning the sword.* God established governments that use the sword, but they are "outside the perfection of

Zollikon house where Swiss Anabaptists formed their first congregation in the last week of January 1525.

Christ." Governments use the sword to punish the wicked and to protect the good. In the Christian community, violence has no place, even for self-protection. In renouncing the sword, Christians follow their Lord, who was "meek and lowly of heart."

Because Christians have renounced all sword power, it is not fitting for them to serve as magistrates or hold governmental office. Rulers are part of the kingdom of this world, whereas Christians live according to the rules of the kingdom of God, for their "citizenship . . . is in heaven."

7. *Concerning the oath.* This article teaches that Christians do not swear to validate the truth of their statements. Their life and speech ought to be simply yes and no, "for what is more than that comes from evil," according to Jesus' words.[5]

Michael Sattler's life in the monastery influenced the writing of the Schleitheim articles. Such Anabaptist ideals as separation from the world and the Christian community as a model of Jesus' way had roots in Benedictine monasticism.

Not all Anabaptists accepted the Schleitheim articles. In 1527, Balthasar Hubmaier wrote "On the Sword," in which he argued that Christians must at times use the sword in defense of their government or country. Later, Menno Simons did not draw the line as sharply between the kingdom of God and the kingdom of the world. He believed that it was possible for a Christian to be a ruler, although he rejected the sword and all violence for Christians. Nevertheless, the Schleitheim Confession stands as a clear statement of what the Swiss Brethren believed and attempted to live. Those articles became the basis for all subsequent Mennonite confessions of faith.

Michael Sattler's cruel death

In May 1527, the Austrian authorities captured Michael Sattler, his wife, Margaretha, and about twelve other Anabaptists, who were tried as heretics. The charges against the

Anabaptists, were these: by disobeying the law against Anabaptism, they were dangerous enemies of the empire; they denied that Christ was really in the Lord's Supper; they rejected infant baptism; and they refused to swear an oath of loyalty to the government.

Sattler's captors applied two specific charges to him alone: he had abandoned the monastic order and married, and he declared that Christians should not to go to war, not even against the hated Turks. This last charge was especially serious. Both church and state considered the Turks dangerous enemies who threatened to destroy Christendom. Only traitors would refuse to fight the Turks. It was treasonous and a serious crime for the Anabaptists to assert their peace position.

In his defense, Sattler spoke clearly, with conviction and courage, basing the reasons for his beliefs on the Word of God. He said he had left the monastery because, according to the apostle Paul, the monastic position was unchristian, deceptive, and dangerous to one's faith. From his own experience in the monastery, he knew what kind of life monks lived. They were vain, deceptive, grasping, and they took sexual advantage of married women, girls, and maidservants.

As to the second charge, Sattler admitted that he had taught nonresistance on the basis of God's commandment: "You shall not kill." He even admitted to having said that if war were right, he would rather fight against so-called Christians who persecute and kill God's people than against Turks. Turks do not know Christian faith, he said. But so-called Christians claim to know Christ and still they persecute his witnesses.

The judges were angry. The secretary of the court snapped at Sattler, "You rascal of a monk, shall we argue with you? You archheretic, I say, if there were no hangman here, I would hang you myself and be doing God a good service."

Sattler's verdict read as follows: Michael Sattler shall be committed to the executioner, who "shall take him to the square and there first cut out his tongue, then forge him fast to a wagon, and there with glowing iron tongs twice tear pieces from his body, then on the way to the site of the execution five times more as above, and then burn his body to powder as an archheretic." [6]

When Sattler heard this sentence, Margaretha comforted and supported him. In the presence of the crowd, she expressed great joy at her husband's courage in the face of death.

They carried out the sentence as read. It is impossible to describe Sattler's pain and suffering, but he remained true to Christ. He prayed for his persecutors and called on the people to repent and turn to God. Sattler was bound to a ladder with ropes, a bag filled with powder was tied around his neck to hasten his death, and he was then thrown into the fire.

As the flames engulfed him, Sattler prayed, "Father, I commend my spirit into your hands." The authorities executed several other Anabaptists that day, and eight days later they drowned Margaretha in the Neckar River. A noble lady tried to persuade her to renounce her faith and stay at her court. But Margaretha declared that she would rather be true to her Lord and her husband than live in safety and luxury.

In spite of persecution, Anabaptism spread rapidly among the masses. Persecution could not stop people from embracing the faith. One of the rulers, after executing 350 Anabaptists, exclaimed, "What shall I do? The more I kill, the greater becomes their number!" Catholics and Protestants feared that Anabaptism might become the dominant faith in their regions.

The significance of a vision

In December 1943, Harold S. Bender presented an important paper to the American Society of Church History. He entitled it "The Anabaptist Vision." In this paper Bender dealt with the contributions that Anabaptists made to society and the vision they had for the Christian church. As a historian, Bender wanted to present the Anabaptists fairly and sympathetically. As a theologian and church leader, Bender hoped that twentieth-century Mennonites would catch the vision seen by their spiritual forbears.

According to Bender, the Anabaptists contributed greatly to American Protestantism and to democracy in general. Among these contributions he listed "the great principles of freedom of conscience, separation of church and state, and voluntarism in religion." The Anabaptists were the first to clearly state these principles. Further, they "challenged the Christian world to follow them in practice." The Anabaptists in a real sense completed the Reformation that Luther and Zwingli had begun.

Quoting Heinrich Bullinger, Ulrich Zwingli's successor in Zurich, Bender described what the Swiss Brethren taught: "One cannot and should not use force to compel anyone to accept the faith, for faith is a free gift of God. It is wrong to compel anyone by force . . . or to put to death anyone for the sake of his erring faith. It is an error that in the church any sword other than that of the divine Word should be used.

"The secular kingdom should be separated from the church, and no secular ruler should exercise authority in the church. The Lord has commanded simply to preach the gospel, not to compel anyone by force to accept it. The true church of Christ . . . suffers and endures persecution but does not inflict persecution upon anyone." [7]

Bender's summary of the Anabaptist Vision

1. *Christianity as discipleship.* While Luther emphasized the inner experience of faith, the Anabaptists stressed both faith and the expression of faith in life. "The great word of the Anabaptists was not 'faith' as it was with the reformers, but 'following' [Christ] (*Nachfolge Christi*)."

2. *A new concept of the church.* Luther and Zwingli kept the medieval idea of a large church with membership of the entire population from birth. The Anabaptists rejected infant baptism and formed a church of converted members who voluntarily joined the body of Christ.

3. *The ethic of love and nonresistance.* This belief excluded all warfare, strife, violence, and the taking of human life. Not only did this principle apply to war and other forms of killing, but also to human relationships in family, between individuals, and in society. In creating a new Christian community, the Anabaptists followed Jesus' teaching and example as described in the Gospels.[8]

Critics of Bender's Anabaptist vision said that his view of Anabaptism was perhaps too limited and exclusive. Bender often seemed to imply that the Swiss Brethren were the most faithful Anabaptists, thus slighting other individuals and groups with somewhat different visions. In stressing that Zurich was the cradle of true Anabaptism, Bender often paid less attention to the movement's other centers and failed to appreciate that other Anabaptist groups emerged independently from the Swiss Brethren. The next chapters will examine how several of these groups contributed their faith and visions to the worldwide Mennonite family.

■ ■ ■

Reformation or restoration?

Luther, Zwingli, and other mainline Reformers were Reformers in the true sense of the word. They struggled to reform the badly flawed, even corrupt, medieval church. As Reformers, they revived true Christian faith and introduced the principle of the priesthood of all believers. They removed abuses connected with the sale of indulgences and the veneration of saints and images. As Magisterial Reformers, they kept infant baptism, the idea of a territorial church, and the close relationship between church and state.

For the Anabaptists, reforming the old church was not enough. Instead, they wanted to restore the church as it had existed in apostolic times. They believed that when Emperor Constantine in the fourth century elevated Christianity to a high place within the empire, the church began to decline spiritually and morally, becoming quite worldly as time went on. This loss of faith and the abuses that crept in were due to the marriage of church and state, the emerging wealth of the church, and churchmen struggling for power, position, and influence.

In going back to the example of Jesus, the faith of the early church, and the standards of the New Testament, the Anabaptists were most radical. Historians have called them Radicals or Radical Reformers, and their movement is known as the Left Wing of the Reformation.

In their fearless witness to the truth, they were a serious irritant to the old church and society. No wonder they were feared and hated. But as Bender and other historians have shown, the Anabaptists' separation of church and state, voluntarism in religious faith, and belief that each should be free to worship God according to one's conscience—all these have greatly influenced modern democracies.

5

Anabaptism develops in Holland

A fool for Christ

God must have a great sense of humor. The apostle Paul says, "It pleased God through the foolishness of preaching to save those who believe" (1 Corinthians 1:21, KJV). The preachers God uses are not always perfect men and women but humans who are often weak, eccentric, even foolish. Melchior Hofmann was no doubt a "fool for Christ," a peculiar man whom God used to take the Anabaptist gospel to northern Europe.

Melchior Hofmann (c. 1495-1543) was born at Schwäbisch-Hall in southern Germany. He received a good elementary education and later learned the trade of a furrier. He was an avid reader of the medieval mystics, the Bible, and Luther's writings. Luther's work left a deep impression on Hofmann. He became a zealous follower of the Reformer.

In the 1520s Hofmann made business and preaching trips to the Baltic states, Sweden, and Denmark. His charismatic personality and eloquence moved his audiences to action against images and other abuses in the church. Officials of towns and countries often had him arrested, imprisoned, or driven out of their regions. Luther supported Hofmann at first, but then turned against him.

The Anabaptists attracted Hofmann by their biblical faith, disciplined living, and expectation of Christ's return. In 1530 he preached in the Netherlands and East Friesland with

Strasbourg's single-spired red sandstone cathedral was a welcome sight for many Anabaptists who were tolerated here for several decades.

great success. At Emden he baptized some three hundred persons and established an Anabaptist congregation. People called his followers Melchiorites, and Menno Simons eventually became one of them. Hofmann influenced Dutch Anabaptism more than anyone else. A productive writer, he published many books that influenced the Anabaptist movement in northern Europe.

His teaching about the end-time brought Hofmann into difficulties. In the spring of 1533, he went to Strasbourg, announcing that Christ was about to set up his kingdom in that city, after a terrible slaughter of unbelievers. Moreover, Hofmann claimed that he was the promised Elijah who was to appear just before the end. In Strasbourg he would await Christ's second coming, he told the city fathers, even in prison if necessary. The city council obliged the prophet, imprisoned him, and did not allow him to write anymore. He died in prison in 1543.

The Münster madness

Hofmann rejected all violence and stressed holy living. He cannot be held responsible for the Münster tragedy. Hofmann's emphasis on the end-time and the imminent return of Christ, however, contributed to the beliefs and practices of a group of Anabaptist fanatics who used violent measures to establish their kingdom in Münster, a city in northwestern Germany, in 1534.

Those Anabaptists in Münster exchanged their earlier peaceful life and ethical standards for violence and sexual immorality. Instead of following Jesus, they sold out to leaders who led them into error and destruction. They baptized men and women by force, drove out of the city those who resisted them, practiced polygamy (plurality of wives), and killed their opponents—and all this in the name of Christian faith. Both guilty and innocent Anabaptists faced cruel punishment when the madness was over. What led to these tragic events?

In the early 1530s, the citizens of Münster were restless. The city was in the grip of Reformation fever. In 1531, a former priest, Bernhard Rothmann, who had visited Wittenberg and other Reformation centers, encouraged religious unrest. Preaching Lutheran ideas, he had great influence on the city. Melchior's followers were also active. Before long, Rothmann embraced the Anabaptist faith and promoted adult baptism. The stage was set for the appearance of fanatical prophets.

Early in 1534 two self-styled prophets arrived in Münster. One was *Jan Matthys*, a baker from Haarlem in the Netherlands. Melchior Hofmann had baptized him, but they had different beliefs. Matthys believed it was time to destroy the unbelievers and to prepare for Christ's kingdom on earth. The other prophet was *Jan van Leyden*, a tailor, merchant, and innkeeper. He was a gifted yet power-hungry young man. These prophets and their followers gave Anabaptism a bad name for many years to come.

With these two leaders in town, things happened rapidly in Münster. The Anabaptists seized the city hall and installed Bernhard Knipperdolling as mayor. They expelled anyone who refused their baptism. Many male citizens fled, leaving wives and children behind to look after their property until they could return.

Messengers went out to proclaim that Münster was the "New Jerusalem," where all persecuted Anabaptists could live in peace and safety. Many Anabaptists flocked to Münster, believing that Christ's kingdom was about to be established.

The local Catholic bishop organized an armed force of Catholics and Protestants and laid siege to the city. After a vision and in a foolhardy inspiration, Jan Matthys and a few of his followers decided to go outside the city and fight their enemies. The Catholic forces killed Matthys and his men. A woman, Hille Feicken, also went out in an attempt to kill the bishop as Judith in the Apocrypha of the Old Testament had beheaded Holofernes. The Catholics killed her too.

A terrible massacre

Jan van Leyden was then the only ruler of Münster; he called himself "King David" or "King of Zion." He married Matthys's widow, "Queen Divara," and introduced polygamy. Men competed for wives, wanting as many as possible; women had little say about their personal preference.

"King David" had seventeen wives. He charged one wife, Elizabeth, with adultery and insubordination, killed her with his own hands, and trampled her body with his feet. Those men who at first opposed polygamy and the "king's" innovations were punished, usually with death.

Besieged by their enemies, the Münsterites lacked food and other supplies. Jan van Leyden tried to keep up their morale and spirits with theatrical performances and diversions. Finally on June 25, 1535, someone from within be-

These three iron cages on the tower of St. Lambert's church in Münster once held the bodies of radical Anabaptist leaders put on public display.

trayed the city, and the bishop's army gained entrance. A terrible slaughter and bloodbath followed, with Anabaptist men and women fighting bravely to the end.

Jan van Leyden, Bernhard Knipperdolling, and Bernhard Krechting were captured, tortured, displayed in various parts of the country, and then put to death. The Catholic officials hung their corpses on the tower of St. Lambert's church as a warning to all Anabaptists and their sympathizers. The iron cages are still hanging on the tower of the church today.

The Münster episode had negative results for the Anabaptist movement. Society and rulers did not separate the peaceful Anabaptists from the Münster fanatics. Anabaptists suffered even worse persecution than before. The Münster episode became an excuse for killing all Anabaptists in attempts to wipe out the movement.

In reality the Münster Anabaptists were a mockery of true Anabaptism. The only thing the Münsterites and peaceful Anabaptists had in common was adult baptism. The Münsterites had violated all Anabaptist ideals, including love and nonresistance, voluntarism in matters of faith, separation of church and state, high moral standards, and discipleship.

Menno Simons pointed out how wrong it was to hold the Anabaptists responsible for the offenses of the Münsterites because both practiced adult baptism. That was as unreasonable as to accuse the Lutherans of crimes committed by some of the popes because both practiced infant baptism.

Menno Simons becomes an Anabaptist

After the Münster catastrophe, Menno Simons (c. 1496-1561), a Catholic priest in Holland, joined the Anabaptist movement. In many ways, it was the worst time to become an Anabaptist. After Münster, hatred and persecution of Anabaptists increased, and the movement was in danger of spiritual disintegration. Through God's leading, Menno Simons embraced the Anabaptist faith exactly at this difficult time and helped to bring Anabaptism back to its earlier intentions and ideals.

Menno was born about 1496 in the Dutch village of Witmarsum. Menno entered the priesthood at the age of 28. He received his training in a monastery, thus becoming well acquainted with the monastic life. He knew Latin, some Greek, and he studied the church fathers. Menno did not read the Bible much before his second year as a priest. His first parish was near his parental home at Pingjum, where he served as village pastor with two other priests. He loved his easygoing life, playing cards, drinking, and pursuing leisure.

Menno's doubts concerning the Catholic church began in his first year as a priest while celebrating the mass. He wondered whether the bread and wine in communion actually changed to the flesh and blood of Christ. Tormented by his doubts, he finally turned to the Bible for answers. Menno soon concluded, "I did not get far in it before I saw that we had been deceived."

Menno struggled between the teachings of the Bible and the practices of the church. He found help in some of Luther's writings. Luther taught him that Scriptures should have the first place in a person's life and be the final authority in matters of faith. Still a priest, Menno began to preach from the Bible, becoming known as an "evangelical preacher."

The church in Pingjum where Menno Simons served as a priest. The tower dates back to the sixteenth century.

Soon the question of baptism troubled Menno. When Melchior Hofmann introduced Anabaptism to East Friesland in 1530, the rebaptizers were persecuted by the authorities. A follower of Hofmann, Sicke Snyder, died a martyr's death in Leeuwarden, near Menno's home. "It sounded strange to me," Menno wrote, "to hear of a second baptism."

He again "searched the Scriptures diligently and considered the question seriously but could find nothing about infant baptism." Then he read the church fathers, Luther, and other Reformers who argued in favor of infant baptism. But "each one," Menno concluded, "followed only his own mind." By 1531 Menno was convinced that believers baptism was biblical and that infant baptism had no support in Scriptures. Yet Menno still kept his position as priest in the Catholic Church, enjoying a life of ease.

During the early 1530s, the Dutch and North German Anabaptists became militant and began to deviate from their earlier faith principles. While still a priest, Menno tried to convince them that they were wrong. An Anabaptist group organized an armed defense at the Old Cloister near Bolsward, Holland, and on April 7, 1535, the authorities defeated them. Among those killed was a Peter Simons, who may have been Menno's brother.

Then in July of the same year, the "New Jerusalem" at Münster came to a disgraceful end, with many Anabaptists killed. All this made a great impression on Menno, who felt responsible for these deceived people. As Menno later wrote: "The blood of these people . . . fell so hot upon my heart that I could not stand it, nor find rest in my soul. . . . I saw that these zealous children, although in error, willingly gave their lives . . . for their doctrine and their faith. And I was one . . . who had disclosed to some of them the abominations of the papal system. But I . . . continued in my comfortable life . . . simply in order that I might enjoy physical comfort and escape the Cross of Christ."[1]

Menno knew what he had to do. Tearfully he asked God to forgive his sins, create within him a clean heart, and bestow upon him "wisdom, spirit, and courage" for a new life in Christ. In January 1536, Menno renounced all "worldly reputation, name, and fame." He submitted to stress and poverty, and left his home community and parish to start an "underground" existence. Among the lowly and persecuted believers, Menno found a new spiritual home and his most important life's work.

Menno leads the Anabaptists

A group of six to eight persons visited Menno shortly after his conversion, "men who sincerely abhorred not only the sect of Münster, but the cursed abominations of all other worldly sects." These delegates from the Anabaptist communities urged him "to put to good use the talents which I, though unworthy, had received from the Lord." Menno's skills in organization and leadership, his pastoral concern, and his ability with the pen were just what the scattered Anabaptist congregations needed.

Menno accepted the call from God and his people, and from that moment his life changed radically. In 1536, in the province of Groningen, Holland, Obbe Philips ordained Menno to the ministry. Menno began to travel throughout the Netherlands and northern Germany, organizing and teaching the congregations.

A few bits of information about Menno's family have come down to us. His wife's name was Gertrude, and the couple had at least two daughters and a son. Since Menno was a hunted man with a price on his head, it was dangerous for his family to be connected with him and to be known by the authorities. So Menno wrote as little as possible about his family and their whereabouts. It must have been very hard for his wife and children to move from place to place, often hiding in damp and cold places, constantly afraid that

"Menno Hut" in northern Germany, where Menno lived, wrote, and worked in relative security during his final years. In front of the cottage stands the linden tree supposedly planted by Menno himself.

they and Menno would be arrested as Anabaptists.

Menno responded to charges that his followers were revolutionary Münsterites by appealing to rulers and governments to distinguish between the fanatics and the peaceful Anabaptists. He pleaded with officials to allow his followers to believe and live by their consciences. In all his writings on the subject, Menno demonstrated that Anabaptists were peace loving, that they obeyed governments on the basis of God's Word, that they sought to live according to the gospel, and that they were often better Christians than either the Catholics or Protestants.

Mennonites are named after Menno

Menno's leadership in northern Europe bore fruit. Rulers began to identify differences between the violent Anabaptists and the peaceful followers of Menno. In 1543 and 1544, Charles V, emperor of the Holy Roman Empire, pressured Countess Anna of Oldenburg (East Friesland) not to protect the Anabaptists in her region but to punish them harshly. When the countess ignored his counsel, the Catholic church excommunicated her as an offender against divine and imperial majesty because she protected people declared to be

As a priest, Menno Simons said he enjoyed an easygoing life of playing cards and drinking. He gave it up when God called him to conversion and a life of organizing and teaching the new Anabaptist congregations springing up in northern Europe.

enemies of God and the emperor.

She then issued a decree that the Anabaptists were to leave the country and that anyone who sheltered them would be punished. In this 1544 document, the term "Mennist" occurs for the first time. Countess Anna differentiated between the violent Anabaptists and the peaceful followers of Menno, thus giving "Mennonites" their name. The name stuck, and eventually the Swiss and South German Anabaptists adopted the name as well. Countess Anna never enforced the mandates strictly; until her death in 1562, she remained favorably inclined toward the Mennonites.

Menno Simons continued to travel, write, and publish. He came to live in Holstein in northern Germany, an area between Hamburg and Lübeck, in the village of Wüstenfelde near today's Bad Oldesloe. In the Menno Hut, which still stands today, he had his own printing press and living quarters. The most important book he published is the *Foundation-Book* (1539), in which he deals with the faith and life of Christians, supporting his teaching with numerous references to the Bible.

All of Menno's writings begin with 1 Corinthians 3:11: "For no one can lay any foundation other than the one that has been laid; that foundation is Jesus Christ." On this foundation Menno tried to build faithfully the spiritual house of Mennonites. After his death in 1561, his followers honored him by erecting a small monument at his burial place. The village of Wüstenfelde was destroyed during the Thirty Years' War (1618-1648), but the church Menno helped to build still stands.

As a leader, Menno Simons was compassionate and respectful of members in the congregations, calling them "brothers" and "sisters" in his letters. He was not the serious elder he is sometimes made out to be. In some of his letters, he referred to himself humorously as "the one who is lame" and "the cripple who loves you." Some scholars believe that

Menno tales and tricks

There are some "Menno tales" and "Menno tricks" that have come down to us, stories about so-called white lies or half-truths. We don't know whether they are true, but they illustrate in part Menno's human-ness. Here is one such story:

Menno was riding on a stagecoach. Instead of being in the coach, he was riding up front, up high, with the driver. The authorities dashed up on horses to arrest Menno if they could find him. They asked, "Is Menno Simons in that coach?" Menno turned around and yelled into the coach, "Is Menno Simons in there?" And the occupants said, "No, he's not in here." Menno told the authorities, "They say Menno's not in the coach." So he lived to die in bed.[2]

■ ■ ■

Menno suffered a stroke that left him disabled. Several pictures, painted after his death, portray him with a crutch.

Oh, those church rules!

Menno Simons and his fellow elders such as Dirk Philips and Leenaert Bouwens focused regularly on the moral purity of the church. Especially after the catastrophe of Münster, it was important that society see their followers as upright, honest, and clean-living disciples of Jesus. The apostle Paul's image of the church "without spot or wrinkle" was one of Menno's favorite passages. At congregational and conference meetings, church leaders often discussed discipline, the ban, and shunning or avoidance.

In the second half of the sixteenth century, Mennonite elders held meetings in Emden, Wismar, Strasbourg, and other centers. At all of these meetings, they discussed and debated questions of how Christians were to live in the world. The meetings usually ended with participants agree-

ing on some articles of faith and life, which they then submitted to the congregations for acceptance or further discussion. For example, at meetings in Emden and Wismar (1547,
1554) they adopted the following regulations:
   • Mennonites were not to marry outside the community
of faith.
   • Adultery was the only ground for separation between
husband and wife.
   • Marital partners should avoid a spouse who had
sinned, not sharing "table and bed."
   • Only in cases of extreme necessity could one carry on
business relations with a banned member.
   • Young people needed to have the consent of their parents to marry.
   • Members should not apply pressure to debtors,
although just debts could be collected.
   • Weapons could not be carried in military service.
   • Only members ordained by the proper elders of the
congregation could preach in the congregations.

A woman opposes the ban

When leaders attempted to enforce these rules, a storm
arose throughout the Dutch and northwest German congregations. In Emden the Mennonite leaders banned a member
named Rutgers for committing some sin. The leaders also
ordered his wife, Swaen (meaning swan), to avoid or shun
her husband. Swaen protested, saying that when she married her husband, she promised to love him and be faithful
to him until death.

Elder Bouwens insisted that Swaen deny her banned husband "table and bed" or she too would be excommunicated.
Swaen had friends in Emden and elsewhere, and soon the
case divided the communities—those who took Swaen's
side and those who supported the strict elder.

Both sides appealed to Menno Simons. Menno wrote to

Etching by Jan van Luyken in *Martyrs Mirror*

Anneken Hendriks was tortured and burned to death in Amsterdam, Holland, 1571. Her mouth was filled with gunpowder to prevent her from speaking and to hasten her death.

the congregation at Emden, asking them to be less strict in the application of the ban. "Excommunication is instituted for reformation and not for destruction," he counseled. In this case, Menno felt, a strict application of marital avoidance would harm members and destroy the unity of the church.

However, the strict Dutch leaders didn't listen to Menno. Bouwens had Swaen excommunicated and threatened Menno with disciplinary action. At a later meeting on the issue, the "hard banners" won Menno over to their side. Before his death Menno confessed that the matter of church discipline had been the most difficult part of his ministry.[3]

Menno Simons the Reformer

Menno's place among the Reformers of the sixteenth century is unique. In some ways he cannot be compared with Martin Luther for the Lutherans, or Ulrich Zwingli and John Calvin for the Reformed tradition. These mainline Reformers occupy center stage in church and world history. In their work and writings, they initiated and shaped large religious movements whose members today number in the millions. The volume of Menno's writings, for example, pales in comparison with Luther's works of some sixty volumes in English translation. Menno's *Complete Writings* contain less than one thousand pages.

Menno's task was more difficult than that of the other Reformers. The Magisterial Reformers had the support of powerful rulers who even went to war to defend their cause and to force Protestantism on territories and countries. But Menno renounced all violence and state support. With other Anabaptists, he appealed to the hearts and minds of people to follow the humble Jesus.

As pastor of his persecuted followers, Menno organized congregations and defended the peaceful Anabaptists before the authorities with his writings. He purified members from the infections of Münster and brought Anabaptism back to its earlier beliefs and principles. Without Menno's ministry, Dutch Anabaptism might not have survived.

Early divisions among Dutch Mennonites

Under the Spanish-Catholic Duke of Alva, Dutch Mennonites were severely persecuted. At least fifteen hundred Dutch Anabaptists, both men and women, suffered martyrdom in the sixteenth century. In the second half of the century, things changed for the better. In 1572 when Prince William I of Orange introduced religious freedom for all, including Mennonites, he made the Netherlands the first country in Europe that stopped martyring Anabaptists.

The Mennonites were grateful to Prince William. Two leaders representing the Dutch Mennonites brought William 1060 guilders as a token of their appreciation for the protection and privileges they enjoyed. They asked the prince to use the money for peaceful purposes.

Unfortunately, the decades of bitter persecution had not united the Dutch Mennonites into a cohesive body of believers. They often argued about the ban, dress codes, and ethics. They were strong individualists and serious Bible readers, and took full responsibility for their souls' salvation and their Christian walk. Hence, Mennonites tried to follow their consciences in all areas of life. Linguistic and cultural differences also tended to divide the groups. Thus, by 1600 there were four distinct groups among the Dutch Mennonites.

1. The *Frisian* Mennonites were native to Friesland in the north, the province where Menno Simons was born. The elders exercised considerable influence and authority in the congregations. They selected the ministers, baptized, administered the Lord's Supper, and dispensed church discipline, including the ban, shunning, and marital avoidance. Names such as Dirksen, Friesen, Funk, Harms, Janzen, Martens, Pauls, Quiring, and Unger derive from the Frisian Mennonites.

2. The *Flemish* Mennonites came to Friesland from Flanders (Belgium), where they had suffered persecution. Because many of them were weavers and had contacts with the French, the Flemish had "higher" culture and wore finer clothes than the Frisians. They were also less rigid in the application of the ban than the Friesians. Moreover, their congregational life was fairly democratic, with the elders having less power than the Frisian elders.

Since it was difficult for them to affiliate with the Frisians, the Flemish formed their own congregations. To maintain their separate identity, they even rebaptized persons from other Mennonite congregations who wished to transfer their membership to their body. Names which derive from the Flemish Mennonites are Classen, Dyck, Epp, Harder, Neufeld, Penner, Regehr, Reimer, Thiessen, Warkentin, and Wiens.

3. The *Waterlanders* were the most tolerant and open to change among the Dutch Mennonites. The name comes from the areas in which they lived, in and near Amsterdam and in the coastal regions. The Waterlanders opposed the "hard banners," believing that marital avoidance was too harsh. In this they disagreed with Menno, Bouwens, and Dirk Philips.

While quite traditional at first, this group eventually adopted a tolerant attitude toward non-Mennonite society. They were much more open than other Dutch Mennonites in the areas of marriage with non-Mennonites, admission of persons from other churches without rebaptism, participation in government, and openness to the culture around them. They were also the first to promote education, build schools, and appoint educated and salaried ministers.

Hans de Ries (1553-1638) was an outstanding leader among the Waterlanders. He wrote a confession of faith (1610), composed hymns for the congregations, and compiled a book of martyr stories. Later the martyr stories developed into the famous *Martyrs Mirror,* compiled by Thieleman J. van Braght (1660). De Ries was an able defender of the faith, actively opposing those who denied the divinity of Christ and the Trinity. He also worked hard to bring about greater cooperation among the various Mennonite groups.

In the seventeenth century, the Waterlander Mennonites became quite integrated into Dutch society. They entered many professions and occupations, became well-to-do, and made diverse business and cultural connections. There were writers and artists among them, and many entered the medical profession.

There is a persistent tradition that the great painter Rembrandt was a member of the Waterlander congregation in Amsterdam. We do know that Rembrandt had friends among Mennonites, painted their portraits, and was sympathetic toward their faith and life.

4. The *Upper Germans* were Mennonites who had come from South Germany during times of persecution. They occupied a middle position between the Frisians, Flemish, and Waterlanders in thought and practice. In 1555 and 1557, the German and Swiss Anabaptists met in Strasbourg to discuss the views and practices of the Dutch Mennonites, particularly their interpretation of the ban and avoidance.

They then sent a delegation of three men to Menno and some of the Dutch congregations to learn their views on the matter and to establish harmony between the German and Dutch Mennonites if possible. But their well-intentioned efforts ended in disappointment and more confusion. The German congregations in the Netherlands remained separate from all the other Mennonite communities.

The Waterlanders never did adopt the name "Mennonite." Dutch Mennonites today still go by the name *Doopsgezinde* (baptism-minded). The other groups, especially the Frisians and the Flemish, adopted the Mennonite name and followed Menno's teaching more closely than the Waterlanders.

The Frisians and Flemish, being more conservative than the Waterlanders, were among the first to leave the Netherlands for Poland, Prussia, and ultimately for Russia and America. Nevertheless, the *Doopsgezinde* congregations, the former Waterlanders, continued to assist their fellow believers whenever they experienced hardships. Mennonites throughout the world are much indebted to the generosity of their Dutch forebears.

6

Radical reform comes in South Germany and Moravia

Flasks of magic potion?

Anabaptism spread like wildfire in Austria and South Germany. Often Anabaptist evangelists needed only a few hours to establish a new congregation. One evening they would preach the gospel in one place, baptize those who wished to become members, and establish a new congregation. The next evening they would be in another place to do the same.

The opponents of Anabaptism were shocked at the rapid spread of the movement. Unable to explain the success of the Anabaptists, some people believed that their preachers carried little flasks of magic potion to put a spell on the audience.

One of the most successful Anabaptist preachers was Hans Hut (? - 1527), known as the apostle of the Anabaptists in Upper Austria and South Germany. A native of Thuringia, Central Germany, Hut was a bookbinder and book salesman. Attracted by the Reformation, he soon spread the new Lutheran faith in Würzburg, Bamberg, Nürnberg, Passau, and as far as Austria.

One city council described Hut as being the chief leader of

the Anabaptists, well educated, clever, rather tall, a peasant with light brown cropped hair and a blond mustache. He was dressed in a gray or sometimes black riding coat, a broad gray hat, and gray pants.[1]

Like many other radical Reformers, Hut's first doubts were about baptism of infants. Wittenberg theologians could not answer his questions about infant baptism. He came to the conclusion, on the basis of Matthew 28:19-20, Mark 16:16, and Acts 19:3, that the New Testament had nothing to say in support of baptizing babies.

Hut also wondered why Lutheran preaching did not result in a more disciplined life. He refused to have his newborn child baptized, saying that baptism should not take place until the baptismal candidate understood what faith and Christian discipleship meant. Friends eventually persuaded Hut to join the Anabaptists. On May 26, 1526, Hans Denck baptized him.

Hans Hut worked with great dedication and zeal for the Anabaptist cause. He went on preaching tours, baptized many people, and sent other evangelists in all directions to proclaim the gospel. The difficult times in which he lived, including the Peasants' Revolt and the threat of Turkish invasion, convinced Hut and many others that the end-time and the second coming of Christ were near.

With glowing words, Hut preached about God's judgment, the great tribulation to come, and the safety of believers in Christ. He also taught that governments are from God and that Christians should be subject to them. Hut based his views about the return of Christ and the end-time on the Bible, not on mere speculation. His enemies, however, charged that Hut was politically motivated and that he was a rebel against governments.

At Nikolsburg, Moravia, Hut was the leader of those Anabaptists who renounced violence. Another Anabaptist, Balthasar Hubmaier, believed that in some instances Christians could and should defend their government with the sword. Hut insisted that under no circumstances were believers to use weapons. He noticed cruel treatment of the peasants in 1525 and of leaders like Thomas Müntzer who believed that the "godless" should be destroyed. All this convinced Hut that violence was not the way of Christian disciples. That position did not make him popular with some state officials.

There is some confusion about how Hut died. According to his son Philipp, "Hut was racked [tortured] in the tower and then released. He lay like one dead."[2] When Hut's torturers departed, they left a candle in his cell that ignited straw on which he was lying, suffocating the helpless prisoner. A day later they burned his body at the stake. A daughter of his was drowned for her faith in Bamberg.

Many of Hut's writings and songs have survived; some are in the *Ausbund,* the earliest collection of Anabaptist songs, still used in Amish worship services. One of his songs is entitled "Let Us All Sing Heartily."

"They are daily beheading some"

Two important Anabaptist conferences met in 1527. One took place in February at Schleitheim, on the border between Switzerland and Germany. The other meeting, known as the Martyrs' Synod, took place on August 20 in the South-German city of Augsburg. Later historians called this conference a Martyrs' Synod because most of the delegates to the meeting died martyrs' deaths.

More than sixty representatives from South Germany, Austria, and Switzerland came to discuss Anabaptist teachings and ways of spreading the gospel throughout Europe. The Schleitheim gathering of Anabaptists wrote their decisions down and later published them. No written statements of the Augsburg conference have been found.

Other writings by some of the participants at the meeting tell us what happened at Augsburg. The delegates discussed strategies of evangelism and the course of Anabaptist activity. After the meeting these Anabaptists went out in twos and threes in all directions to proclaim their faith and discipleship in Christ. Most of them met death within a short time. Among the delegates at the synod were Hans Denck, Hans Hut, Jakob Wiedemann, and others. Hans Denck, the gentle and learned Anabaptist leader, was the chairperson of the gathering. Noticeably absent were Felix Manz, Conrad Grebel, and Michael Sattler. Officials had drowned Manz in Zurich, Grebel had died of the plague during his exile, and Sattler had been burned at the stake. George Blaurock was fleeing from his persecutors in the mountains of Switzerland, and Balthasar Hubmaier was active in Moravia and elsewhere.

Thus, between the meetings of Schleitheim and Augsburg, a mere six months, prospects for the young Anabaptist movement had not improved. In the next hundred years, thousands of Anabaptists followed their early leaders in death.

As soon as the authorities of Augsburg learned about the conference in their city, they took severe measures to punish the participants. Four days after the synod, the city council made arrests, tortured the prisoners, and sent messages to other cities warning them that the hated Anabaptists were coming with their heresies.

Early in 1528, a cruel decree against the Anabaptists authorized a band of four hundred armed horsemen, so-called Anabaptist hunters (*Täuferjäger*), to capture them and bring them to trial. A citizen of Augsburg wrote: "It is such a misery that the whole city of Augsburg is saddened. They are daily beheading some, at times four or six, and at times ten persons."

Too gentle for cruel times?

Hans Denck (c. 1500-1527), the moderator of the Martyrs' Synod, was a shining light among the South German Anabaptists. While he accepted most Anabaptist teachings about baptism, the Lord's Supper, and the church, he believed that the inner reality of the Christian faith was more important than outward ceremonies and institutions.

Some have described him as a "spiritualist" among the Anabaptists. He believed that there is a part of God within each individual, and that this "divine light" can respond to God's call and grace. With Luther and the Anabaptists, Denck held that the believer is redeemed by the grace of God, but he also insisted that faith needed to result in works of love. His motto was "No one may truly know Christ except one who follows him in life."

Denck's reading of medieval mysticism influenced his religious life. He had studied closely a collection of writings known as *German Theology,* which Luther had republished in 1518. University educated, Denck became a teacher and schol-

The Chronicle of the Hutterian Brethren **is a major source of their earlier history. The handwritten original is in South Dakota.**

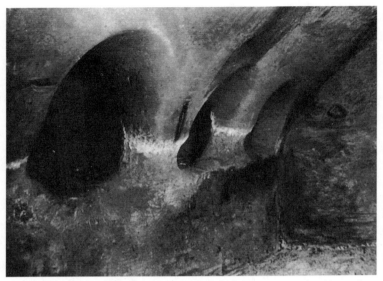

To protect themselves during times of persecution, the Hutterian Brethren in Moravia built underground hiding places.

ar. Denck is best known for his writings on love and the commandments of Christ. The love of God in Christ stands in the center of his faith and life. Denck's love and tolerance extended to his opponents and enemies.

An effective debater, he expressed sorrow for having hurt his opponents in heated discussions. *The Mennonite Encyclopedia* says, "He is one of the few personalities of the sixteenth century who never indulged in controversy except with a heavy heart; not a trace of abusiveness or unfairness is to be found in his writings."[3]

But Hans Denck was a hounded man. Driven out of Nuremberg (Nürnberg) and other cities, he had to leave his wife and children behind. However, the bright flame which burned within him could not be extinguished. Through teaching, counseling, preaching, debating, and writing, Denck laid a good foundation for Mennonite spirituality and Christian discipleship.

Denck was one of those tolerant Anabaptists who wished to include all sincere believers, whatever their religious persuasion, in the church of Christ. His contemporaries knew him as "the famous Hans Denck" and as a highly talented youth. Today some Mennonites consider him a model Anabaptist. Not yet thirty, Denck died, like Conrad Grebel, of the plague in November 1527.

To carry a sword or a stick

The Hutterites live in closed communities, hold all things in common, and take their name from an early leader, Jakob Hutter (hatmaker). Hutter served his people for only two years, between 1533 and 1535. Yet in this short time, he left an indelible mark on his community, which to this day holds him in highest esteem.

What Menno Simons did for Mennonites, Jakob Hutter did for Hutterites. When several leaders could not agree, Hutter united the group. When they were in danger of disintegration, he brought discipline into the group and established a solid spiritual foundation for its future. But we are getting ahead of ourselves. We need to tell the story of how the Hutterite communities began.

In their distress the Anabaptists of South Germany, Switzerland, and Austria were looking for places of refuge where they could live in peace and make a living. One such place opened up in Moravia, a region in southern Czechoslovakia (now the Czech Republic). There on the Nikolsburg estate, owned by the Lords of Liechtenstein, the persecuted Anabaptists found a home, protection, and ways of making a living.

The Liechtenstein brothers favored the Reformation, and in Nikolsburg a Lutheran congregation had already spread reform ideas. When Anabaptists, including Balthasar Hubmaier, came to Nikolsburg, their missionary activity bore fruit. One of the ruling nobles, Leonhard von Liechtenstein, received adult baptism and thus joined the Anabaptists. Nikolsburg and its surrounding areas soon had many Anabaptist communities.

With an Anabaptist nobleman as ruler, the question arose whether his Anabaptist subjects were required to pay taxes for defense and to serve in the military. There was soon a division concerning issues of government and the sword. Hubmaier believed that Christians ought to pay taxes and even defend their government with the sword. He wrote a booklet, *On the Sword*, arguing his position. The ruler, Leonhard von Liechtenstein, agreed with him.

Jakob Wiedemann and Hans Hut disagreed, showing from the Gospels and the example of Jesus that Christians were to have nothing to do with violence in any form. Those who sided with Hubmaier were called *Schwertler* (sword-bearers), while those who followed Wiedemann and Hut were

Home of Jakob Hornd'l, the potter in a typical Moravian Hutterite village, well preserved by the Czech government.

A school in Sobotiste, Slovakia, a former Hutterite settlement.

called *Stäbler* (staff-bearers).

The tension between the two groups came to a head in 1528. King Ferdinand of Austria pressured the Liechtensteins to persecute the Anabaptists and to contribute money and supplies to the war against the Turks. When Leonhard opposed King Ferdinand and even threatened to use military force against him, the nonresistant Anabaptists decided—and were even ordered—to leave Nikolsburg. Wiedemann and a group of about two hundred adults and many children packed their possessions and left Nikolsburg.

Outside the gates, under the open sky, they deliberated about what to do next. *The Chronicle of the Hutterian Brethren* describes what happened: "They took counsel together in the Lord because of their immediate need and distress and appointed servants for temporal affairs. . . . These men then spread out a cloak in front of the people, and each one laid his possessions on it with a willing heart—without being

Today there are over fourteen thousand Hutterites in Canada and the United States. These Hutterite young women are from the Pembina Colony, Darlingford, Manitoba.

forced—so that the needy might be supported in accordance with the teaching of the prophets and apostles."[4]

Hutterite origins

This is how the Hutterite practice of holding all things in common began. It grew out of their material needs at the time and the practice of the first Christians as recorded in

Acts 2:44-45: "All whose faith had drawn them together held everything in common: they would sell their property and possessions and make a general distribution as the need of each required" (paraphrased). It is this communal living and sharing all their material possessions that sets the Hutterites apart from other Anabaptist-Mennonites.

The Wiedemann group then moved north and settled in Austerlitz, which belonged to the four noble brothers of Kaunitz. Though Catholic, the Kaunitz brothers were sympathetic to the peaceful and industrious Anabaptists and allowed many persecuted Anabaptists to settle in their territory.

There was, however, not much peace within the groups themselves. Suspicions arose about whether leaders actually gave up all their possessions. There were power struggles between some leading men. Questions about ethical matters resulted in conflicts and quarrels. These internal difficulties brought Jakob Hutter to the Austerlitz and Auspitz communities. Though he did not have much formal education, Hutter was a charismatic leader and a successful organizer and preacher.

A rebel becomes an Anabaptist

We do not know when Hutter became an Anabaptist nor when and where he was baptized. He came from South Tyrol in Austria, where he had learned hatmaking. It is possible that his name derives from his trade. There is some evidence that before his conversion to peaceful Anabaptism, he participated in peasant revolts.

Following the failure of armed uprising in South Tyrol, Hutter may have gathered around him surviving rebels and organized a Christian community of goods at Welsberg. When authorities discovered and scattered the group in 1529, Jakob Hutter was among those who managed to escape. In 1532 officials issued a warrant for his arrest. The

A courageous woman

While many Anabaptist men and women came from among the common people, there were also noble persons, including noble women, who joined the Anabaptist ranks. *Helene of Freyberg* is one of the most prestigious women among this group. Her home was the ancestral castle of Münichau near Kitzbühel in Tyrol, Austria. Kitzbühel, a town of 2,000 inhabitants, was an important center of Anabaptists. Helene was married and the mother of three sons.

In 1528 she came in contact with Anabaptists and accepted their faith. From then on, she sheltered many Anabaptist preachers in her castle and became active in house fellowships. The authorities in Innsbruck soon learned of her activities and threatened her, stating that "if she does not recant [her faith], she has to be brought before the judges." About 1530 she fled, leaving her husband and sons behind.

From then on, Helene's life was that of an exile and

Helene gladly accommodated Anabaptist preachers in her castle, but there were times when it all got to be a bit much.

missionary. She first went to Constance and later to
Augsburg. In 1538 her husband died, after which her
sons supported her and intervened on her behalf before the authorities. She befriended many Anabaptist
leaders and corresponded with them.

The Anabaptists called her a "lay leader." Her greatest contribution was providing shelter for Anabaptists,
establishing house churches, and mediating between
Anabaptist and Reformation leaders. "Although we
have no record that she preached publicly, she was
extremely active in private settings, teaching and leading citizens and commoners alike."[5] We do not know
where and how she died.

■ ■ ■

warrant included the following details about him: "Jakob
Hutter, . . . a person with a black beard, who wears a black
woolen military coat, a blue doublet, white trousers, and a
black hat." Another source states that Hutter "is said to be
carrying a gun."[6]

Whatever his involvement with the rebellious peasants be-
fore his conversion to Anabaptism, Hutter was a peaceful
Anabaptist leader when he came to the assistance of the
Austerlitz communities. For two years he labored faithfully in
Moravia, teaching, cleansing, and organizing the communi-
ties.

In 1535, at the height of the Münster rebellion, the Anabaptists suffered severe persecutions everywhere. The Austerlitz group almost disintegrated. Officials executed Wiedemann and many of his fellow believers in Vienna. According
to the Hutterian *Chronicle*, over two thousand men and
women died at the hands of the executioners. King Ferdinand placed a price of forty guilders on Jakob's head. On a
night in November 1535, Jakob and his wife were captured
and taken to Innsbruck for trial.

King Ferdinand decided to deal harshly with Hutter to frighten those who might follow him or other Anabaptist leaders. The *Chronicle* graphically describes Hutter's torture and execution on February 2, 1536: "They tied a gag in his mouth, . . . tortured him, and caused him great agony. . . . Yet they were not able to change his heart or make him deny the truth. . . . Full of hatred and revenge, the priests imagined they would drive the devil out of him.

"They put him in ice-cold water and then took him into a warm room and had him beaten with rods. They lacerated his body, poured brandy into the wounds, and set it on fire. . . . After he had suffered all their cruelty and yet remained firm and upright, a Christian hero steadfast in faith, these wicked [men] . . . condemned him and burned him alive at the stake."[7] Though Hutter's wife managed to escape from prison, the authorities executed her about two years later.

Anabaptist women leaders

Anabaptist women worked side by side with men in proclaiming the gospel, baptizing new believers, and teaching congregations the way of Christian discipleship. Authorities persecuted these women leaders, and many of them suffered cruel fates. According to the *Martyrs Mirror*, about one-third of all Anabaptist martyrs were women.

Many of these women were married and had children. Yet family ties did not prevent them from working as missionaries and accepting the punishment that other Anabaptist leaders received. In southern Germany and Austria, particularly in the Tyrol region, about 40 percent of Anabaptist martyrs between 1527 and 1529 were women.

Women in Austria contributed significantly to the spreading and strengthening of Anabaptism. For example, administrators in Salzburg captured Ursula Binder in 1527, and punished her for promoting Anabaptist teachings. In the village of Wells, two sisters spread Anabaptist ideas and peddled books as Hans Hut had done.

In another area an Anabaptist woman "made six new Christians in a short time." One named Dorothea Maler persuaded several women to join the Anabaptist movement. An unnamed woman ranked among the key leaders. She supposedly had baptized eight hundred people.

Pilgram Marpeck steers between extremes

South German Anabaptist leader Pilgram Marpeck (c. 1495-1556) was in close touch with the Helene of Freyberg circle. He was as important for South-German Anabaptism as Jacob Hutter was for the Hutterites and Menno Simons was for the Dutch Mennonites. A native of Tyrol, Austria, Marpeck had received a scholarly education. His many writings give evidence of his knowledge of Latin and theology. An engineer by profession, he designed water works, aqueducts, and means of transporting logs on flumes and rivers. He was also a mining judge. Before his conversion to Anabaptism, he earned a good salary and owned two houses.

At first Lutheranism attracted Marpeck, but soon the "Wittenberg gospel" disappointed him. Marpeck came to believe that Luther's teachings did not lead to an improvement of life but to "carnal freedom." Then he accepted baptism and joined the Anabaptists.

When as a judge Marpeck refused to condemn Anabaptists, authorities suspected him of belonging to their group. Forced to leave the Tyrol, he traveled to Strasbourg, Augsburg, and other centers. Wherever he went, he debated, wrote, and taught Anabaptist teachings. Anabaptists soon recognized him as an effective teacher and leader. Other Reformers judged him a dangerous heretic.

Marpeck steered effectively between two positions: an emphasis on inward spirituality on one hand; and an emphasis on outward things such as water baptism, ethics, and church organization on the other hand. He believed that while the Holy Spirit works in each believer, the Bible contains the Christian's standards for living. Yet Marpeck cautioned his fellow Anabaptists not to become too literal and legalistic about such external practices as baptism, the Lord's Supper, church discipline, and dress codes. For Marpeck, freedom in Christ and the leading of the Holy Spirit were important.

In his views, Marpeck was close to his fellow South German leader Hans Denck. However, more than Denck, Marpeck stressed the necessity of establishing visible church communities to model Christian faith in society.

Like Menno Simons in the north and Jacob Hutter in Moravia, Marpeck wanted to unite the various groups of the South German Anabaptists. For this purpose, meetings were held in Strasbourg (1554, 1555) and elsewhere. Approximately six hundred Anabaptists attended these conferences, discussing matters of church discipline, how Jesus became human (incarnation), the sinfulness of human nature, and other issues.

The records do not show how successful these attempts at unity were. However, Marpeck's influence and leadership through his many writings had a lasting impact on numerous congregations, some of which had five to six hundred members. Marpeck was fortunate to die a natural death. His usefulness as an engineer no doubt saved him from a violent end.

How different were the Anabaptists?

By now you may have wondered about the real differences between the Anabaptist faith and the beliefs of other Christians. You might even ask whether there were compelling reasons for persecuting Anabaptists and for Anabaptists to accept suffering and death for what they believed.

After all, you might think, all Christian groups believed in God, in salvation through Christ, in the church, and in an afterlife. As we have seen, Anabaptists accepted the Apostles' Creed with all other Christians and were part of the theological tradition of the church. Why then did the other churches persecute Anabaptist believers?

Here are some of the main points on which Anabaptists disagreed with the beliefs and emphases of the mainline churches, both Catholic and Protestant:

1. *Concept of church.* The Roman Catholics had long assumed that a territorial church to which all baptized persons belonged was quite acceptable. The Wittenberg and Zurich Reformers developed variations of this traditional view, also accepting the concept of *corpus christianum*—the "Christian body" or "society" within a territory. Infant baptism was the means by which people became part of the territorial church. Moreover, according to these theologians, the true church existed where the Word of God was preached and where the sacraments were administered faithfully.

Anabaptists broke with this traditional view of the church. According to the Schleitheim Confession and other documents, the Anabaptists thought of the church as a gathered congregation of believers who came to it voluntarily through baptism upon confession of faith. Adult baptism separated believers from the world and united them into Christian communities for the purpose of following Jesus and modeling the Christian faith in an unchristian society. This radical view of the church contradicted the traditional view. Hence, Anabaptists were hated and persecuted.

2. *Church and state and religious liberty.* Anabaptists believed the faith of Christians should be voluntary and free. This meant that governments had no right to interfere in spiritual or church matters as had happened, in varying degrees, in Protestant society. Anabaptists separated church and state, something that modern democratic governments have accepted. Because of this belief, many viewed them as rebels against all institutions and governments.

There was little tolerance and religious liberty in the sixteenth century. Both Catholics and Protestants persecuted those who did not believe as they did. Many believed they were doing God a favor by persecuting "heretics."

Anabaptists also believed that their faith was right and that others were in error. However, Anabaptists did not persecute and kill others for their faith. They used only the ban or other forms of discipline in their congregations. They believed faith was a gift of God and therefore was free. No state or church had the right to interfere by force in a person's religious life. With their suffering for what they believed, Anabaptists paved the way for later tolerance in religious matters.

3. *Salvation and the Christian life.* Anabaptists accepted Luther's view that Christians are redeemed by the grace of God through faith. Contrary to the German Reformer, however, the Anabaptists stressed that works of love and a Christian lifestyle had to follow faith. In this they agreed with Catholicism, which emphasized the importance of "good works" in the lives of believers. Luther tended to separate works from faith, whereas in Anabaptism faith and discipleship were closely linked. Time and again Anabaptists maintained that both Catholic and Protestant Christians failed to live up to their confessions of faith.

4. *Nonresistance or pacifism.* Medieval and Protestant Christians were not pacifists. Augustine, Thomas Aquinas, and other church leaders had taught that Christians could participate in "just wars." The peaceful Anabaptists rejected the sword and all violence. For them, Jesus' teaching and example were the norm of faith and conduct.

It must be stressed, however, that the Anabaptist peace position extends to all areas of life, not just to war. Nonresistance "is not simply a matter of refusing to bear arms in wartime, although that is certainly included. Rather, it is a totally new life orientation in which all human relationships are

governed by patience, understanding, love, forgiveness, and
a desire for the redemption, even of the enemy."[8]

5. *Mission.* The Catholic and Protestant churches certainly
believed in evangelism and mission. But they relied more on
the institutional church and even governments to promote
their religion than on individual believers. Anabaptists were
zealous evangelists, witnessing as individuals about the love
of Jesus and what it means to be a disciple of Christ. They
endured severe persecution for this public witness.

Luther, for example, believed that "heretics" could believe
what they wished, but as soon as they publicized their faith,
they had to be stopped. Yet Anabaptists could not remain
silent. They were a light seeking to illuminate the darkness
around them and to attract people to their communities.

Roland Bainton, a non-Mennonite historian, summarized
how Anabaptists differed from both Catholics and Protestants and what they contributed to the Christian church and
society: "Anabaptists anticipated all other religious bodies
in the proclamation and exemplification of three principles
which are on the North American continent among those
truths which we hold to be self-evident: the voluntary
church, the separation of church and state, and religious liberty."[9]

Bainton goes on to explain that these principles, so important to us today, had been neglected by the medieval church
after Emperor Constantine united church and state in the
fourth century. In their attempt to restore the apostolic
church, the Anabaptists appeared to other Christians to be
innovative and radical. Their view and practice of New Testament faith laid the foundation for the historic peace
churches today.

Is your life a witness
to the Spirit, water, and blood?

Michael Sattler had to decide. Would he leave his comfortable life at St. Peter's monastery and join the Anabaptists?

Like many people of his time, Michael was troubled by the loose living of many monks and priests. In addition, his study of the Bible made him doubt much of what he had been taught about baptism and other church practices.

Anabaptists, Michael knew, baptized adult believers. Baptism was a sign of a person's changed life in Christ.

Michael learned that Anabaptists often wrote and talked about the three signs of baptism: Spirit, water, and blood (1 John 5:6-8). In addition to being baptized with water, people who truly believed were expected to live in a way that showed the Holy Spirit at work in them. And all believers had to be ready to suffer, even die, for their faith.

Did Michael have the courage to join them? Was he willing to accept financial uncertainty and the likelihood of persecution?

Sometime in 1525, Michael left St. Peters and headed for Zurich. Outside the monastery he celebrated Jesus as Lord and told others the good news. His intent was to live in the Spirit's power and follow Christ wherever that might lead.

Michael's water baptism did not come immediately. In his pursuit of the truth, he lived for some time just north of Zurich with the Anabaptist Hans Küntzi. There Michael learned the weaver's craft so he could support himself. During this time he also learned about the beliefs of the Anabaptists. By the summer of 1526, Michael joined the Swiss Brethren and made their faith his own.[1]

Michael's desire to join the church was tested by others in the Anabaptist community of faith. Conrad Grebel, Felix

Mantz, and others gave witness to the Spirit's work in Michael's life. In addition, Michael's testimony in the congregation helped to show his sincerity and commitment.

At the Schleitheim gathering in 1527, Michael helped the Anabaptists summarize their beliefs. In the first of seven articles, he wrote that baptism is for people who have repented and who truly believe their sins have been taken away. Baptism is a public witness for "all those who desire to walk in the resurrection of Jesus Christ."

Leaving the monastery with no financial security, marrying Margaretha, and following the Spirit's call were Michael's ideas of walking in the resurrection. He soon learned that he was never alone among the Anabaptists. In fact, Christ's resurrection power blossomed in his life as he worshiped, asked questions, and shared his struggles with others.

Michael gave witness to the baptism of blood when he was executed, just three months after the Schleitheim meeting. The baptism of blood symbolizes the Christian's ongoing battle against sin and the possibility of persecution or death for one's faith. Following Christ's example on the cross, many Christians through the centuries—including several thousand Anabaptists—died for their beliefs.

The threat of martyrdom still confronts some Christians in the worldwide Anabaptist family today. Yet each of us, regardless of nationality, birthplace, or family background, faces Michael's decision. Will you leave the past behind to discover a living faith, to join others who choose to follow Christ regardless of the cost? Is your life a witness to the Spirit, water, and blood?

Central Europe

⊙ National Capital
Regions
Cities and towns

100 km
0 ————— 100 Miles

Denmark

Baltic Sea

North Sea

Friesland ·Emden
:Pingjum ·Oldenburg
Witmarsum
Waterland

·Bremen

Lubeck.
Wismar
· Wüstenfelde
·Hamburg

Elbe River

⊕ Berlin

Poland

⊙
Amsterdam
Netherlands

·Münster
· Bielefeld

Rhine River

Germany

· Wittenberg

Flanders
⊕ Brussels

Belgium

·Cologne
·Marburg

Bonn·

·Eisenach   Leipzig

·Erfurt

·Frankfurt

Lux.   **Palatinate**.·Worms
·Frankenthal
Monsheim ·Mannheim

Prague
⊙

**Czech
Republic**

· Bamberg
· Würzburg

· Nürnberg
·Schwabisch Hall

Moravia Austerlitz
Nicolsburg·.·

Strasbourg

·Rottenburg

Danube River

·Augsburg   Passau·.

France   **Alsace**

St. Peter
·Freiburg
Schleitheim
Waldshut·
·Basel   ·Zurich

Tyrol

Munich

· Innsbruck

· Salzburg

·Kitzbühel   **Austria**

⊕ Bern
Switzerland

Swiss
and South
German
Mennonites

7

Seeking peace and finding division, 1600-1750

Jailbreaking preacher

Hans Landis worked quickly in the dim moonlight which filtered into his prison cell. He had been locked up in Zurich, Switzerland, for nearly four months—first in a castle and then in the city hospital. Before dawn on the morning of New Year's Eve, 1608, Landis made his escape.

Using a metal tool which friends had smuggled into his cell, Landis pried and pulled at the chains which bound him. Eventually breaking his bonds, he quietly slipped away. Stealthily he made his way outside and hurried through the dark, across the farms and fields which surrounded Zurich.

Landis knew exactly where he would go. He had important work to do. Although Landis was a Swiss farmer, it was his activity as a Mennonite preacher that landed him in jail. It was precisely his church work that called him back to his people.

Landis had been in jail before, charged with holding secret worship services. He and his congregation were among the spiritual descendants of the Anabaptist Swiss Brethren. Like them, Landis taught and practiced believers baptism. He also took seriously Christ's call to discipleship and the way of peace. But Anabaptist faith and activity was highly suspect—as was Landis's preaching against the corruption of

Old man Hans Landis had a knack for escaping from jail—with a little help from his friends.

the state church and the Zurich government. No wonder his ministry upset local officials!

Out of jail and back at home, Landis resumed his pastoral tasks. In addition to his preaching, Landis worked with other members of his church to care for the poor. His congregation maintained a special fund to provide interest-free loans to the needy. The Mennonites also owned a section of farmland which they used to grow grain for distribution to the poor.

Neighbors welcomed the congregation's charity and refused to turn Landis over to Zurich officials. But government authorities were irritated with the Mennonites' generosity, since it made their own attempts at public welfare look feeble and halfhearted. They could no longer ignore this jailbreaking preacher.

Seventy—and still escaping

By the winter of 1613, officials arrested Landis once more. The authorities told him to leave Zurich's territory and never come back. But Landis refused to go. More than seventy years old, he was determined to spend the rest of his life serving his congregation and neighbors. Besides, he argued, since "the earth is the Lord's" (Psalm 24:1), no human government could expel him from his farm.

Angrily, the officials decided to send Landis as a slave to ship owners on the Mediterranean Sea. But while Landis sat in jail awaiting deportation, someone slipped him a metal file. In three days he had sawed through his chains and escaped from prison again. Weeks later, he was back in his home community preaching, teaching, and assisting the poor.

Furious, the Swiss authorities arrested him again. This time they watched him more closely. On September 29, 1614, the court sentenced Hans Landis to death. Not wanting to take any more chances with this minister who had repeatedly escaped their grasp, they arranged for his execution the next day. Although in the past Landis had taken every opportunity to escape from prison, when death came he was not afraid to face it. "I have long looked forward with joy to this hour," Landis said as he was led away.

When the executioner asked Landis if he had any last words, the old pastor replied, "I know not what more to say, than that I wish that all people would come to a knowledge of their sins and repent, that they might be saved; this I would wish for everyone."[1]

Then the executioner beheaded him. The Swiss Mennonites mourned the death of Hans Landis and even wrote a hymn with forty-six verses about his martyrdom.

Although the state had finally done away with this influential Mennonite leader, civil authorities were wary of Landis's widow, Margereta Hochstrasser Landis. They feared she would encourage the Mennonite congregation and allow it to continue gathering for worship in the Landis home. Several months after her husband's execution, officials ordered Margereta to join the state church or turn over her farm. When she refused to surrender her Anabaptist faith, authorities locked her in solitary confinement in the Zurich hospital.

An invitation to ruined farms

Hans Landis was the last Swiss Mennonite martyr. After 1614 government officials decided that killing the Mennonites only made heroes out of them. Executing key leaders did not stop congregations from growing. Beheading defenseless people was becoming a public embarrassment.

The Swiss provinces adopted a new approach to discourage the Anabaptists. Officials began using economic discrimination and threats of deportation, hoping to make their lives so uncomfortable that they would either join the state church or leave Switzerland. Authorities—especially those governing the territory around Bern—imposed a series of heavy taxes and penalties on the Anabaptists. For example, laws barred Mennonite children from inheriting land from their parents. Such regulations made economic survival difficult, and some Mennonites began thinking of leaving Switzerland.

But while Swiss authorities tried to get rid of the Mennonites, some other Europeans welcomed the Anabaptists with open arms. Wealthy landowners in the *Palatinate* and the *Alsace*—regions bordering the Rhine River north of Switzerland—wanted Mennonites to come and settle as tenant farmers on their estates. These nobles had suffered heavy losses during the terribly destructive Thirty Years' War (1618-1648). During that lengthy conflict, armies roamed across central and western Europe, ruining fields, looting villages, and burning farms.

When the war ended, estate owners scrambled to find farm families willing to tackle the difficult job of replanting and rebuilding. Perhaps the Mennonites would accept the agricultural challenge in exchange for religious freedom.

By the 1650s, Swiss Mennonites were moving down the Rhine valley and settling in the Palatinate and the Alsace. In 1664 the Palatinate's ruler,

In the Palatinate, with the Rhine River in the valley below.

Karl Ludwig, issued a decree promising a measure of religious toleration for Mennonites.

The Swiss refugees could enjoy limited religious freedom, but they could not meet in large groups or build church buildings. Nor were they allowed to win converts from among their state-church neighbors. Despite these restrictions, the Palatinate seemed to be a safer place to live, and Swiss refugees continued to migrate there. In 1671, for example, when the governments of Zurich and Bern renewed their harsh attacks on the Anabaptists, 700 Mennonites left Switzerland and moved to the Palatinate.

A love-hate relationship

During the seventeenth century, the Swiss and South German Mennonites faced various challenges. Hostile governments, wars, and difficult migrations took their toll. Yet these external threats were not the only challenges they faced. The church also experienced disagreements and tensions *within* its fellowship.

By the 1690s, the Swiss and South German Mennonites were in a troubling predicament. Their non-Mennonite neighbors increasingly accepted and respected them. Instead of labeling Mennonites as dangerous subversives, popular opinion now frequently regarded the Anabaptists as upstanding models of charity and morality. However, civil authorities and state-church officials renewed their efforts to stamp out the Mennonites. New taxes, fines, and threats of imprisonment still targeted their congregations.

The Mennonites felt caught in this love-hate tension with

The Rhine River in the Palatinate region.

larger society. Their religious heritage and faith commitments had taught them to remain somewhat separate from the larger, hostile world. But what should they do when that part of the world seemed friendly and sympathetic toward them? What did separation mean in that kind of world? Could the church remain faithful to its calling if its members increasingly felt at home in larger society?

Days of division

In response, some Mennonites sought renewal by stressing group commitment, discipline, and an emphasis on separation from the world. They found a worthy spokesperson in Jakob Ammann. A Swiss-born Mennonite preacher, Ammann lived and ministered among Mennonites who had moved north into the Alsace.

In general, Ammann advocated a more deliberate church life. For example, he argued for a more frequent celebration of the Lord's Supper. He also emphasized the importance of group discipline and urged Mennonites to avoid or shun those who were excommunicated from the church. Avoiding flagrant sinners kept the church's witness strong and clear, Ammann argued. Shunning could be redemptive.

By breaking certain normal relationships with the unrepentant, Christians confronted wrongdoers with the seriousness of their sin and called them back to God. Ammann found support for his teaching in a number of Scripture passages and in several Dutch Mennonite confessions of faith which were circulating among the Swiss and South German congregations.

Not all Mennonites agreed with Ammann's approach to church renewal. A Swiss elder named Hans Reist spoke for those Mennonites who felt that the church's witness in a friendlier world meant playing down separation and fostering more contacts with sympathetic and understanding non-Mennonite neighbors.

The Amish division from the Swiss Brethren began in the fall of 1693 when unsuccessful meetings were held in the Niklaus Moser barn between the followers of Jakob Ammann and Hans Reist.

Furthermore, Reist argued that Ammann and his supporters put too much emphasis on church discipline. Reist agreed that the church must bar unrepentant sinners from the communion table, but he did not think that they should be shunned in other day-to-day activities. To do so would only drive them away, he said.

In the fall of 1693, Ammann and several friends traveled

to Switzerland to confer with church leaders there. Sharp disagreements surfaced between the supporters of Ammann and Reist. Several times Ammann tried to arrange a meeting to discuss the dispute. The gathering never took place, because Hans Reist and a number of his allies refused to attend. They claimed that Ammann did not really want an open discussion. In frustration, Ammann excommunicated Reist and his supporters, calling them stubborn and arrogant. Angrily, the two groups parted ways.

Those who agreed with Ammann were nicknamed "Amish Mennonites," or simply "Amish." They differed from the majority of Swiss and South German Mennonites in several ways. The Amish upheld a more rigorous church discipline, including the shunning of unrepentant former church members. As a part of their celebration of communion, members of Ammann's fellowship also washed one another's feet, following Jesus' example of servanthood in John 13. Finally, the Amish kept simpler peasant-style attire and avoided showy and fashionable clothing styles.

Menno Simons Historical Library, Harrisonburg, Va.

A drawing from around 1600 showing "Anabaptist hunters" chasing Swiss Mennonites in the forest of Herrliberg, near Zurich, Switzerland.

Pietism

During the late 1600s and the 1700s, a widespread renewal movement known as *Pietism* profoundly affected many Christians in Europe and North America. Although Pietism was a broad and complex movement, most Pietists shared several common emphases. They stressed personal devotion and godliness, regular Bible reading, and prayer. Many Pietists met in small Bible study groups for nurture and encouragement. Pietists also emphasized the spiritual unity of individual Christians and placed less importance on the larger church or on differences between denominations.

Although the Pietist movement was especially influential in Lutheran and Reformed churches, it also affected Mennonites in a number of ways. For example, some Mennonites began reading Pietist devotional literature and singing some of the many hymns the Pietists wrote.

In the Netherlands, many Dutch Mennonites formed or joined Pietist-style Bible study groups. Further south, during the controversy between Jakob Ammann and Hans Reist, Reist's supporters seem to have had some Pietist tendencies.

Mennonites had much in common with a particular group of radical Pietists who shared Anabaptist practices such as believers baptism and the rejection of violence. These radicals, known in North America as the German Baptist Brethren (or Dunkers), immigrated to America after 1719 and settled in many of the same communities as the Mennonites. Their fellowship later developed into the Church of the Brethren, the Brethren Church, the Old German Baptist Brethren, and several other groups.

■ ■ ■

Several years after the Amish and Mennonite division, a number of Amish leaders felt that they had acted too rashly in excommunicating Hans Reist and the other Mennonites. The division between the groups was terribly painful, and they were sorry that it had occurred. They asked the Mennonites for forgiveness and a chance to talk again. But the Mennonites refused, and the split continued with hard feelings on all sides. In fact, some years later when shipping companies were transporting groups of Anabaptist immigrants down the Rhine River, they had trouble getting the Mennonites and Amish to ride together on the same boat!

Hiding in a haystack

In the meantime Swiss Mennonites continued to face persecution. In 1699 the Bern government established a special police force known as the Anabaptist hunters (*Täuferjäger*). Bern officials paid the hunters for each Mennonite they tracked down and caught. Finding a preacher or congregational leader earned the hunters a higher reward than catching a lay member.

Although apprehended Mennonites did not face execution, they did have to leave the territory of Bern and promise never to return. In some cases captured Mennonites obeyed and moved to the Palatinate or the Alsace. In other instances, banished men and women broke exile—like Hans Landis a hundred years before—and returned to their homes.

One Mennonite preacher who defied his sentence of exile was Benedikt Brechbuhl (1665-1721). Repeatedly banished from the territory of Bern, Brechbuhl stayed away for a time, but always returned to minister to his congregation. Fleeing from authorities in 1709, Brechbuhl hid in a neighbor's haystack. A search party looking for the runaway minister descended on the farm, determined to search every corner.

Eventually they came to the pile of hay and began poking their swords in it. Brechbuhl tried to hold still, but when the

Albert M. Best, Lancaster, Pa.

**A typical farmstead in the Emme River valley, Bern, Switzerland.
Benedikt Brechbuhl lived nearby and worked in this region.**

swords began to graze him, he came out. The searchers immediately arrested him, along with his neighbor and brother who had helped him hide.

Brechbuhl spent eighteen weeks in a dungeon. After that,
he spent time in a prison workhouse where he made wool
cloth, every day from four in the morning until eight at
night. Thirty-five weeks into his year-long sentence, the authorities decided to get rid of Brechbuhl and his fellow Mennonites by shipping them overseas to what would become
the American colony of North Carolina. The Bern government contracted a boating company to transport fifty-seven
Mennonites—including Brechbuhl—north on the Rhine and
across the Atlantic.

Dutch Mennonites to the rescue

But as Brechbuhl and his fellow prisoners floated down
the Rhine, Dutch Mennonites were busily working to foil the
Swiss government's scheme. Mennonites in the Netherlands

The father of Palatinate agriculture

Of course, not all Swiss and South German Mennonites left Europe for America. Some who remained in Germany became prosperous farmers and leading citizens. Among these were David and Maria Kändig Möllinger, who operated a farm near the German town of Monsheim.

Scholars have acclaimed David Möllinger (1709-1786) as an innovative farmer who was not afraid to try new things. He introduced new kinds of hay and beets and experimented with better livestock feeds. Möllinger was also among the first to fertilize his fields with ground limestone. In addition, he operated a distillery where he made vinegar and wine.

Möllinger popularized the practice of crop rotation. Farmers typically planted the same crops on the same land year after year. But this practice depleted the soil's nutrients. Instead, Möllinger annually rotated his crops, planting different grasses and grains in succession in each field. By shifting his crops, Möllinger replenished the soil naturally.

Over the years, dozens of farmers, scientists, and government officials visited the Möllinger home to learn the latest in agricultural science. One visitor remarked that he could not imagine "a more orderly, productive, and blessed farm." Some scholars even called Möllinger the father of Palatinate agriculture.

■ ■ ■

had enjoyed religious freedom and toleration since the 1570s and had become prosperous and respected merchants and farmers. Yet Dutch Mennonites had not forgotten about their Swiss and South German brothers and sisters.

Since 1660 the Dutch had offered financial gifts and loans

to hard-pressed Swiss Mennonites who wanted to move northward into the Palatinate or eastward into Prussia or Poland. But the case of Benedikt Brechbuhl and the others on the prison boat was different. These Swiss Mennonites did not want to immigrate—at least not then or under those circumstances. They were being forced to leave.

Since the Rhine flows through the Netherlands, the prison ship's captain had to stop at the Dutch border before going on. The Dutch Mennonites appealed to their own government, asking their officials to liberate the Swiss prisoners since Holland was a free country. The Dutch authorities agreed and forced the shipping company to release the Mennonites.

Laurens Hendricks, a local Dutch Mennonite pastor, met the freed prisoners when they got off the boat. Although somewhat amused by their old-fashioned Swiss clothes, he was convinced that they were "very zealous to serve God." Hendricks' congregation fed and cared for the former prisoners until they left the Netherlands. Some returned to Switzerland, while others moved to the Palatinate.

Leaving the Old World behind

Intervening on behalf of the Swiss prisoners demonstrated the Dutch Mennonites' concern for the physical and social needs of fellow believers. Mennonites in the Netherlands practiced many forms of mutual aid, caring for and sharing with others in the church. In some cases the Dutch worked with their country's ambassador to Switzerland and negotiated on behalf of their imprisoned or exiled sisters and brothers. At other times they offered financial aid.

In 1710 they organized a Commission for Foreign Needs to assist Mennonite immigrants with money and traveling arrangements. By then, increasing numbers of Swiss and South German Mennonites were deciding to leave Europe in hopes of finding a more peaceful life in North America.

Most Mennonite immigrants hoped to settle on the large tract of land governed by the English Quaker William Penn. His American colony called Penn's Woods, Pennsylvania, promised a haven of religious freedom. As a Quaker, Penn had suffered religious harassment in England. In Pennsylvania, he offered toleration for religious minorities of all kinds. As a pacifist, Penn promised that his colony would not have an army or militia. Understandably, Mennonites found the possibility of living in Pennsylvania attractive.

Before long, dozens of Mennonite families arrived in the Netherlands, seeking passage to America. Like thousands of other Germans, some Mennonites pulled up stakes for economic reasons. Each year making a living in Europe seemed more difficult. The terribly severe winter of 1708-1709—so cold that the mighty Rhine River actually froze over—ruined the fortunes of farm families all over the Palatinate. Other Mennonites left primarily to escape religious persecution. A few probably went in search of adventure, and many

Swiss-Mennonite names

According to C. Henry Smith, Switzerland was the native land of nearly all the Mennonites in America east of the Mississippi River. This includes the Palatines in Pennsylvania, the Amish of Illinois and Ohio, as well as the Swiss who came directly to America in the early nineteenth century.

Among many others, the following names are of Swiss origin: Amstutz, Augsburger, Brubaker, Bowman, Baer, Bechtel, Dirstein, Eby, Frey, Graber, Hostetler, Hauri, Hirschy, Kaufman, Krebiel, Landis, Lehman, Lichty, Musselman, Neff, Oberholzer, Reist, Schantz, Schlabach, Schlegel, Schowalter, Shenk, Steiner, Stucky, Staufer, Smucker, Troyer, Ummel, Wenger, Yoder, and Zuck.

■ ■ ■

sailed for a combination of reasons.

Soon the Dutch Mennonites and their Commission for Foreign Needs felt overwhelmed by the constant demands of the growing number of immigrants. Afraid they would not have enough resources to help everyone, the Dutch begged the Swiss Mennonites to be more reasonable with their requests and more organized in their travel plans. Nevertheless, the Dutch always found ways to help those in need. Many Swiss and South German Mennonite families who went to North America would not have been able to make it without the help of their Dutch sisters and brothers.

8

Mennonites settle in North America, 1683-1860

A dreamer comes to town

On an autumn day in 1694, an elderly couple hobbled into a small village north of Philadelphia. The man had become blind in recent years, and he walked with difficulty. After traveling for days, penniless and alone, they had finally arrived at their destination—the infant Mennonite community at Germantown, Pennsyvlania. Years of dreaming and moving from place to place were over. Pieter Cornelisz Plockhoy and his wife had finally found a home.

Plockhoy had always been a dreamer. Growing up in the Netherlands, this Mennonite knew the harsh realities of warfare and the oppression of the poor. But Plockhoy also had visions of a peaceful and just society and hoped to establish such a community in England. When his plans failed, he dreamed of beginning a Christian commonwealth in America.

In 1663 Plockhoy sailed from Amsterdam with two dozen Mennonite families and settled at *Zwaanandael* (Swan Valley), by the Delaware River (now Lewes, Del.). Plockhoy envisioned the settlement as a classless society based on Christian principles of justice and mercy. His group forbade slavery and shared their work and wealth as much as possible. They prayed that their dream might become a lasting reality.

But this first serious attempt at planting a Mennonite community in North America ended abruptly. A year after the Plockhoys and their partners arrived in Delaware, British troops, under orders to seize all Dutch colonies on the Atlantic coast, pounced on Swan Valley and scattered the colonists. An officer later bragged that his soldiers had destroyed the community to the last nail.

Lost and alone, the Plockhoys moved to a nearby English town. One day they heard that other Mennonites had sailed from Europe and were living in a new settlement in Pennsylvania. Hoping their dream was not dead after all, the Plockhoys set out to find this new attempt at an American Mennonite community. They eventually made their way to Germantown, where they spent the rest of their days living among brothers and sisters in the faith. After years of dreaming, they had finally found a home.

Arrivals on the *Concord*

The village of Germantown (today a part of the city of Philadelphia) was not a classless society nor was it a completely Mennonite town. In fact, Mennonites were always a minority there. But Germantown was home to the first *permanent* Mennonite community in North America. Decades earlier some Dutch Mennonites had settled on Long Island and what would become New York City, but apparently they never developed a stable church. Then there was Plockhoy's ill-fated Swan Valley settlement. Germantown, on the other hand, proved to be a lasting community even though its beginnings were quite modest.

In the fall of 1683, a small band of immigrants founded Germantown. The group had sailed together aboard the ship *Concord*. Considering the hazards of ocean travel at the time, the passengers enjoyed a relatively easy Atlantic crossing. The *Concord's* passengers included thirteen households—eleven families and two single men—from the Lower Rhine city of Krefeld. Although these immigrants were more Dutch than German, they called their new Pennsylvania settlement Germantown.

Only one of the immigrant couples, Jan and Mercken Schmitz Lensen, were Mennonites. Some of the others had been Mennonites at one time, but in recent years had converted to Quakerism.

The group set to work organizing their village and establishing businesses. Jan Lensen, for example, was a weaver, as were several others in the party.

In a decade, more Mennonite immigrants settled in Germantown. At first all the Germantown villagers—whether Quakers, Mennonites, Lutherans, or Reformed—worshiped together. As more settlers arrived, separate church groupings formed.

Before long a Mennonite silk merchant named Dirk Keyser (1635-1714) began leading Sunday morning services for

The Germantown Pennsylvania meetinghouse, built in 1770, is the oldest surviving Mennonite meetinghouse in North America.

Mennonites and a few other Germantown residents. Keyser's preaching consisted of reading aloud from a book of printed sermons originally presented by ministers in Europe.

By 1699 a distinct Mennonite congregation had formed in the village. Paper manufacturer Willem Ruttinghuysen (1644-1708) became the group's first minister. Earlier a successful papermaker in Europe, Ruttinghuysen established America's first paper mill. In 1708, shortly after his death, the Germantown congregation numbered thirty-four members. That year the group chose new leaders, celebrated its first communion service, and performed its first baptisms—receiving eleven more men and women into fellowship. In the midst of this activity, the church also decided to stop meeting for worship in homes and built a log meetinghouse along Germantown's main street.

Immigration waves and Native Americans

No sooner had the Germantown Mennonites reorganized than the trickle of German immigration to Pennsylvania swelled to a wave of incoming families. Beginning in 1709, large groups of immigrants arrived on the Atlantic shore. Of the thousands of Germans seeking refuge in Penn's Woods, only a few were Mennonites, but they were enough to greatly increase their church's numbers.

During the next fifty years, a few thousand Mennonites and some five hundred Amish immigrants found their way to North America. Some stayed in Germantown temporarily; a few remained in the village permanently. But most quickly moved on—some to the north, settling in areas like Skippack, or west to places like Lancaster.

Throughout the eighteenth century, Mennonites joined the general westward migration of European settlers. In the 1730s, Mennonites moved into western Maryland and Virginia's Shenandoah Valley. Within several more decades, frontier communities in central and western Pennsylvania also included Mennonite pioneer families.

The arrival and migration of Mennonite colonists was also a part of the larger story of the European conquest of North America. While the settlers thought of America as the New World, for Native people it was their old homeland. Before white settlers began arriving on America's shores, millions of Native Americans lived in what would become Canada and the United States. Yet by 1800, large percentages of them had died—many from new diseases brought from Europe.

It is difficult to know with certainty how the early Mennonite immigrants and their Native American neighbors got

The Germantown slavery protest

Germantown was the site of the first formal protest against slavery in America. In 1688, four Germantown residents drafted a petition decrying human bondage. Three of the writers were Quakers, and they directed their protest to fellow members of that group. Arguing from the golden rule, the petitioners declared, "We shall doe to all men, licke as we will be done our selves: macking no difference of what generation, descent or Colour they are."

The writers also charged that slavery was the same sort of evil as the religious persecution their ancestors had once faced. "In Europe there are many oppressed for Conscience sacke," they wrote, "and here there are those oppressed wch are of a black Colour." Should not Christians oppose one form of oppression as much as the other?

Then too, the petitioners figured, since slavery robs its victims of their freedom, it really amounts to stealing. So they concluded that "we who profess that it is not lawful to steal must, lickewise, avoid to purchase such things as are stollen, but rather help to stop this robbing and stealing if possible and such men [slaves] ought to be delivered out of the hands of the robbers, and sett free."

None of the petition writers were Mennonites, although three were of Mennonite background and one of them apparently joined the Germantown Mennonite congregation a few years later. Still, the document reflected the widespread Mennonite opposition to slavery. There are no definite records of any American Mennonites ever owning slaves, and a later Mennonite confession of faith written in Virginia declared that "as all are free in Christ, they must take no part in slaveholding."

At the same time, few Mennonites became involved in the abolitionist movement against slavery. Most seemed to assume that as long as they did not personally own slaves, their consciences were clear.

■ ■ ■

along. Only isolated incidents and family stories have filtered down through history. There are many tales of goodwill between the two peoples—Native Americans visiting Mennonite homes to talk or trade, and in some cases working as cattle herders on Mennonite farms. There are stories, too, of American Indians teaching Mennonite children to hunt and fish.

But distrust and violence was also a large part of the Native American experience of the European immigration. Caught in the international intrigue of French and British wars and pushed off their land by broken treaties, Native peoples sometimes resisted encroaching white settlers.

Observing nonresistance, several Mennonite and Amish households—such as the Jacob Hochstetler family of Northkill, Pennsylvania—died in Indian reprisals. In 1764 a group of Native Americans attacked the Page County, Virginia, home of Mennonite preacher John Roads. They killed John and his wife, Eve, and six of their thirteen children. Later it was discovered that the attackers were actually led and encouraged by a white man.

In at least one case, Mennonites tried to protect Native Americans from violence at the hands of other colonists. In 1763, a party of white settlers repeatedly raided the few remaining Indians in Lancaster County, Pennsylvania. Although the attackers almost wiped out the local Conestoga tribe, two elderly Indians survived, hidden in the farmhouse cellar of Mennonite farmer Christian Hershey. The two lived the rest of their lives on the Hershey farm.

Meanwhile, some other Mennonites tried to aid the Indians by contributing money to the Quaker Fund for Friendly Association—an account that supported honest negotiation and fair payments to Native peoples.

Fighting between white settlers and Native Americans was not the only concern of pacifist Mennonites. As rumblings of war between Britain and France grew louder and closer, the rising clamor of conflict concerned those who remained committed to the way of peace.

In the 1740s, church leaders made arrangements to have the massive *Martyrs Mirror* translated and reprinted for their congregations. They hoped that the stories of discipleship and nonresistance recorded in its pages would encourage the church to remain faithful to the gospel of peace.

In 1756, the Seven Years' (or French and Indian) War erupted, but it never resulted in military conscription, and most of the battles took place far from Mennonite homes. However, war would not always remain so distant, and before long the violence of revolution came much closer.

Peace, faith, and revolution

The American Revolution (1775-1783) was a deeply divisive conflict. Groups of American *patriots* vowed to win in-

Martyrs Mirror

Would you find a thick, fifteen-hundred-page book full of tales of death and torture inspiring? Many Mennonites do. *Martyrs Mirror* reminds them of the seriousness of Christian faith and the fierce opposition the church sometimes faces. *Martyrs Mirror* is a massive collection of early Christian and Anabaptist martyr stories.

In 1660, a Dutch Mennonite minister, Thieleman Jansz. van Braght (1625-1664), published the huge martyr book. He had spent years researching stories of Christians who suffered and died since the time of Christ. Van Braght hoped that the stories of steadfastness would encourage his church members in their faith. He worried that too many Mennonites in his day were becoming wealthy and lax in their Christian commitments.

Jan Luyken (1649-1712), a Dutch poet and artist, produced 104 copper etchings as illustrations for the second edition of *Martyrs Mirror* in 1685. His images were graphic reminders of the horrors of persecution.

In 1748, Mennonites living in Pennsylvania had the book translated into German. They worked with the monastic Seventh-Day German Baptist Brethren of the Ephrata (Pennsylvania) Cloister community to produce the huge volume. Facing the possibility of warfare in their new American home, the colonial Mennonites wanted the witness of history to remind them of Christ's way of love.

Ironically, pages from several unbound copies may have ended up as shot wadding in soldiers' guns! During the American Revolution, soldiers foraging for supplies arrived at the Cloister and demanded paper. The troops confiscated unsold copies of the martyr book which the Cloister brothers had kept in storage.

Later, Mennonites and Amish in France and Germany also wanted copies of the book. They arranged to reprint the Pennsylvania translation for their own use. English versions of the book appeared in the 1800s. It is still in print today and is found in many Mennonite and Amish homes.

In the 1970s and 1980s, Mennonites purchased several of the original *Martyrs Mirror* copper etching illustrations from a European art collector. They became part of an exhibit on the *Martyrs Mirror* story.

■ ■ ■

dependence from the British government even at the cost of blood. Other colonists were *loyalists* who pledged to stand by King George III and to oppose the patriots by force. For members of the *peace churches*—such as the Mennonites, Quakers, Brethren, and Schwenkfelders—it was not acceptable to fight against the king or use violence to defend the crown. For Christian peacemakers, warfare was off limits, even when commanded by a king or demanded by a revolution.

In 1775, as news of the war's first battles reached their communities, the Mennonites addressed the new patriot government with a petition. In the petition Mennonite preacher Benjamin Hershey (1697-1789) explained that although the peace churches had dedicated themselves to serve all people in any way that they could, they would not fight. Mennonites appreciated the freedom they had found in Pennsylvania, he assured the government. But Christian freedom extended only so far.

"We find no Freedom," Hershey declared, "in giving, or doing, or assisting in any Thing by which Men's Lives are destroyed or hurt."[1] Violence in the name of freedom was counterproductive, he said, since it only destroyed the very people and communities it claimed to help.

Neither the patriots nor the loyalists ever fully accepted the Mennonites' peace stance. The revolutionary government organized local patriot groups called Committees of Observation which tried to pressure people into supporting the revolutionary cause. These committees sometimes had trouble with Mennonites who refused to join in the war spirit.

John Newcomer, a well-known Mennonite gunsmith, built six-foot "long rifles" famous for their accuracy. When the Lancaster Committee of Observation ordered Newcomer to supply guns for George Washington's army, Newcomer refused. He had always advertised his guns as hunting rifles and never intended them to be weapons of war. The patriot committee was angry—who was this gunsmith to defy them and reject their contract? The committee fined Newcomer and ordered him never to make another gun. So far as is known, Newcomer gave up making his famous hunting rifles and thereafter supported himself as a wheelwright and blacksmith.

Death in Germantown

Although Newcomer felt the social and economic pressure of the war, in the fall of 1777 the reality of battle came terrifyingly close to the Mennonites living near Philadelphia. As troops maneuvered around the city, British soldiers camped on Mennonite farms, including that of minister and mill owner Mathias Pannebecker. They took all of Pannebecker's grain and flour and destroyed his milling equipment.

At the same time, Washington's troops camped on the farm of Mathias's cousin, Samuel Pannebecker. The patriot forces burned Samuel's wooden fences and took all of his grain, hay, and poultry. Families scrambled to hide food and livestock from looting soldiers on both sides of the conflict.

As tensions mounted, the American army launched a surprise attack, engaging the British at Germantown. For a time the battle raged around the Mennonite meetinghouse. A

British general fell mortally wounded from a shot fired from the meetinghouse cemetery. American troops carried one of their generals, hit in the thigh by an artillery shell, to a Mennonite farmhouse, where he bled to death.

The battle continued until Washington's troops retreated in defeat, but both sides had lost heavily. In silent testimony to the terror of that day, the Mennonite meetinghouse still bears battle scars and bullet holes.

In addition to the violence of the war itself, the revolution posed other problems for Mennonites. The patriot government ordered all men to denounce King George and swear loyalty to the new state. The Mennonites refused, not only because they opposed oaths, but also because to do so would be taking sides in the war. "It is against my conscience," said one man who refused the oath, "because we shall be at peace with everybody and forgive all."[2]

In one county, the sheriff arrested and imprisoned nine Mennonite men who would not swear. As punishment, the sheriff sold all of the jailed men's property at public auction, leaving their families with almost nothing.

Eve Yoder and Esther Bachman, wives of two of the men, appealed the harsh ruling. They sent a letter to the revolutionary legislature, protesting their husbands' imprisonment and the sale of their belongings. Moved by the women's requests, the state freed the men and compensated their families. Eve and Esther not only reunited their households; they also helped to set a precedent for religious freedom in the emerging nation.

Commitment and renewal

The war tested the strength of Mennonite convictions. For the most part, the church's committment to the Christian witness of peace remained strong. In the face of revolutionary zeal, a few Mennonite sons took up arms, but they were exceptions.

Home of first Mennonite minister in North America, Willem Ruttinghuysen (William Rittenhouse), of Germantown, Pennsylvania. He was also the first papermaker in North America.

As North American Mennonites lived out their beliefs, their convictions attracted others. Michael Ziegler (c. 1680-c. 1765), a German cloth weaver raised in a Lutheran home, came to Pennsylvania and settled among Mennonites in the Skippack community. Eventually he asked for baptism and joined his neighbors' church. Later he became one of their leading preachers.

But while Ziegler and others joined the Mennonites, some children from Mennonite families left the fellowship. David Rittenhouse (1732-1796), great-grandson of the Germantown minister and papermaker Willem Ruttinghuysen, became a famous astronomer, mathematician, and first director of the

U.S. Mint. Yet he had no time for his family's faith.

American Mennonites also faced new questions about salvation and discipleship. Throughout North America, a widespread revival movement sparked discussion about faith and life. Some churches began stressing that each Christian should have a powerful and sometimes emotional conversion. Such an experience, they claimed, was at the heart of Christianity and provided assurance of being in right relationship with God.

Mennonites did not know what to make of this new stress on conversion. Some wholeheartedly supported it and felt their church had become spiritually dull and cold. Other

Printing press in the Ephrata Cloister, Pennsylvania, on which the 1748 German edition of *Martyrs Mirror* was printed.

Hans Herr House

The Herr house, Lancaster County, Pennsylvania, was built in 1719. The Conestoga wagon was a significant part of the Pennsylvania German history and culture.

Mennonites, though, argued that faith was more than conversion—it was also daily discipleship. They feared that too much stress on the experience of *becoming* a Christian might take away from the equally important task of *living* as a Christian. Instead of an emotional conversion, they emphasized Christian faith as a day-in, day-out way of life.

Around 1780, out of such discussion and debate, a group of spiritually earnest men and women began meeting and formed a new fellowship. Several of the group were Mennonites, including one of the leaders, Jacob Engel (1753-1833). They stressed the importance of experiencing a profound Christian conversion. Yet they also emphasized the need for daily discipleship and group commitment. They believed that true faith should blend both of these emphases.

Neighbors nicknamed the group the River Brethren since they met near the Susquehanna River in eastern Pennsylvania. In many ways the River Brethren were like the Mennonites—both groups practiced believers baptism (the River

Brethren did so by immersion) and stressed simplicity in life and nonresistance to violence. The new group later adopted the name Brethren in Christ. The Old Order River Brethren and the United Zion churches are also descendants of the River Brethren movement. Within several generations, the River Brethren spread across the United States and into Canada.

Migration and mutual aid

Many Mennonite families moved westward during the first half of the nineteenth century. By 1860, congregations stretched from New York and Virginia to Kansas and Iowa. A major migration also took Mennonites to Upper Canada (later named Ontario). Although a few Mennonites settled on the Niagara Peninsula as early as 1786, not until 1800, did large numbers begin entering Canada.

A few of the early Ontario settlers may have been colonists disgusted with the American Revolution and wanting to remain under British rule. However, the large majority of those who moved to Ontario were attracted by the region's good, inexpensive farmland.

After 1800 Mennonites began settling in the area that became Waterloo County. A steady stream of immigrants arrived until the community discovered that the land they had purchased was still heavily mortgaged by the seller. Unsure of what to do, they appealed for help to fellow church members in Pennsylvania. Putting their tradition of mutual aid into practice, these congregations responded and provided money to pay off the land's debts and secure the young settlement's future.

By 1805, families were once again coming to the Waterloo area, and the community continued to grow. The settlement's central village was known as Ebytown, named for the areas' well-known Mennonite bishop and schoolteacher, Benjamin Eby (1785-1853). Ebytown was later renamed

Mennonite Archives of Ontario, 1987-1.2

Ebytown, Ontario, Mennonite meetinghouse, built in 1834. This early congregation became First Mennonite Church of Kitchener.

Berlin and is known today as Kitchener.

Mennonites were not only migrating within the United States and Canada. They were also arriving on North American shores in large numbers. After 1815, immigration rose dramatically as a new era of relative peace in Europe made travel across the Atlantic safe once again.

The promise of a better economic future in Canada or the United States lured many Europeans. But Mennonites had an additional reason to pack their bags. Increasingly, French and German governments required military service from all of their citizens. Not willing to compromise their commitment to peace, Mennonite families decided to leave. As a result, between 1815 and 1860 as many as one thousand Mennonites and three thousand Amish arrived in North America.

Verena Sprunger Lehman: a pioneering immigrant

Verena Sprunger Lehman (1828-1913) was one of the many nineteenth-century Mennonite immigrants to North America. She grew up in the Jura Mountains of Switzerland, where she met and married schoolteacher Peter Lehman

(1821-1899). Difficult economic conditions and religious intolerance drove some of Verena's relatives to think about leaving Europe. In 1852 Verena, Peter, and their two daughters joined her family in moving to America. The trip was long and difficult for the group of eighty-two people. After making their way to the French coast, they spent forty-one days at sea.

When the Mennonites landed in New York, swindlers took advantage of the group's inability to speak English and cheated them out of some of their money. Nevertheless, Verena and her family pressed on and eventually arrived in Wayne County, Ohio, where an already-established community of Mennonite immigrants offered them a place to stay. After resting in Ohio, Verena's family moved to a more permanent home near what would become the town of Berne, Indiana.

During their first several years in Indiana, Peter was seriously ill and unable to work. Verena labored to clear their land, establish and manage the farm, and keep the growing family fed and clothed. When Peter did get better, his responsibilities as the community's first minister took much of his energy. About the time the Lehmans were finally on their feet and established in Berne, Peter decided that they should move to Missouri. Once again Verena spent years carving a farm from the wilderness.

Later in their lives, Verena and Peter moved back to Berne. Able to rest from the backbreaking work of homesteading, Verena busied herself with raising flowers and knitting dozens of socks for students at a Native American school in Oklahoma. She also loved to sing and experimented with harmonizing and arranging hymns.

Verena's life may not have been typical of every Mennonite immigrant, but she did represent some things common to most of them. Like hers, journeys to North America were often long and tiresome. Having arrived, the immigrants benefited from their church's commitment to mutual aid and care, but few found life easy in North America. Many picked up stakes and moved several times, migrating further westward or turning back east. And for many, the strength they received from prayer and song carried them through their lives.

The keg with a mysterious leak

Pioneer woman Verena Lehman was at the forefront of the temperance movement which discouraged drinking alcohol. Although not all of Verena's family agreed with her firm stand against drinking, that did not faze her a bit.

One day she drove a nail into her husband's wine barrel. Some time later, after the wine had mostly drained out, she casually mentioned that—strangely enough—the keg must have somehow developed a leak.

Verena could hardly keep a straight face when she told her husband that his wine barrel had mysteriously sprung a leak and was nearly empty.

■ ■ ■

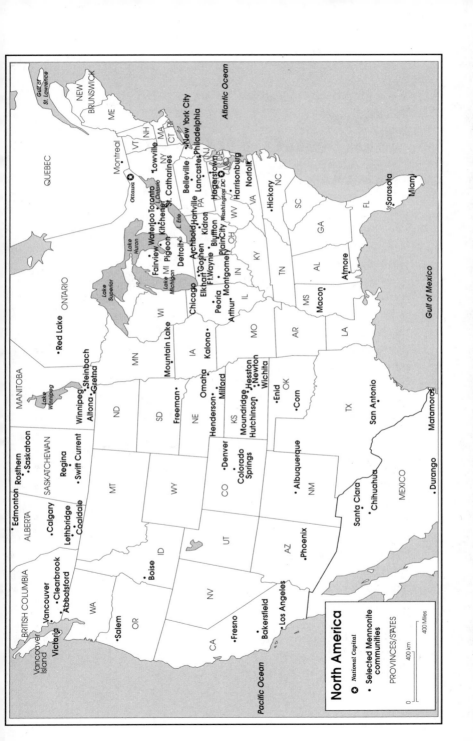

North America

✚ *National Capital*

• Selected Mennonite communities

PROVINCES/STATES

0   400 km

0   400 Miles

9

War and renewal, 1860-1940

The soldiers whose guns didn't work

During the first half of the 1800s, many Mennonites came to the United States to avoid the warfare and military conscription of Europe. However, soon after these immigrants arrived, hostilities broke out in America. During the American Civil War (1861-1865), both the southern Confederate states and the northern Union states drafted troops. Mennonites living in the North often avoided conscription by paying heavy exemption fees or hiring substitutes to fight in their places. Often those facing the draft in the South had fewer options.

Christian Good was one of several Virginia Mennonites drafted into the Confederate army at the beginning of the conflict. Within several months, his company of soldiers was on the front lines facing the enemy.

When the battle began, Christian and the other Mennonite soldiers refused to fire their guns. The commanding officer noticed Christian's disobedience first.

"Did you shoot when you were commanded to shoot?" the officer bellowed.

"No," Christian answered. "I didn't see anything to shoot at."

The officer pointed to the Union soldiers across the battlefield and again asked Christian if he saw anything at which to fire.

"No," Christian insisted. "They're people. We don't shoot at people."[1]

Noticing that Christian and his friends would not fight, other troops mocked that the Mennonites' guns must be "out of order." Even when an officer threatened to court-martial and execute anyone who refused to shoot, Christian and the other Mennonites held their fire. Eventually the Confederate army reassigned them to noncombatant duty.

Three renewal movements

The Civil War experience came as a shock to some Mennonites. In too many cases, Mennonite young men joined the army and—unlike Christian Good—participated in the fighting. Some ministers and parents wondered if the church had failed in its witness to the way of peace.

Meanwhile, other Mennonites were concerned with more subtle changes they noticed among their people. Some saw young women and men without deep Christian conviction routinely join their parents' church. Others believed that the church had grown wealthy and satisfied in its North American prosperity and had forgotten the needs of its neighbors. Others feared that many Mennonites were becoming increasingly individualistic and were ignoring the importance of the gathered church community. Could renewal come to such a people?

As many Mennonites began raising their concerns, several fresh streams of renewal began flowing across the church. Each stream, bubbling from within the Mennonite experience, watered a different part of the church. During the last half of the nineteenth century, these streams of renewal ran—sometimes quietly, sometimes in torrents—through Mennonite and Amish communities.

One stream became the *General Conference* (GC) Mennonite Church. A second represented the *Old Order* movement. A third stream produced a turn-of-the-century *awakening*

among Mennonite Church (MC) congregations. Each renewal movement was distinct and carried its own set of
strengths and weaknesses. Yet despite their diversity, all the
streams enriched the church.

Mission, education, and the General Conference

One of the first renewal movements flowed from the
vision of South German Mennonites who had immigrated to
Iowa before the Civil War. These settlers looked forward to a
time when Mennonite congregations from across North
America would unite and enlarge their united witness
through organized mission work and Christian higher education.

By 1860 these Iowans, along with a Pennsylvania minister
named John H. Oberholtzer (1809-1895), organized the General Conference Mennonite Church. Thirteen years earlier
Oberholtzer and other progressive-minded Mennonites
from his home state had formed a regional fellowship. Now
they joined the new General Conference body.

During its early years, the General Conference was not a
large group, but after 1874 it grew quickly. That year some
eighteen thousand Russian Mennonites began immigrating
to the American plains and the Canadian prairie. Many of
these settlers established congregations which joined the
General Conference and greatly increased its size.

Meanwhile, the General Conference quickly acted on its
education and mission goals. In the 1860s and 1870s,
General Conference congregations sponsored a secondary
school at Wadsworth, Ohio. Then in the 1880s, GC Mennonites in Kansas who had recently arrived from Russia established a number of academies; one became Bethel College in
1893. Other church-related schools followed.

By 1880, General Conference congregations were also
beginning to sponsor formal mission work. That spring the
family of Samuel S. (1847-1929) and Susanna L. Hirschler

The Magpie family were early Cheyenne Mennonites of Oklahoma.

(1861-1944) Haury moved to "Indian" territory in what later became Oklahoma. The Haurys began a school for members of the Arapaho nation. Their school was the first organized mission of any North American Mennonites.

In time, several Native American congregations grew out of the General Conference educational work. By the early twentieth century, Native people were helping lead these churches.

Establishing schools and planting churches among Arapaho—and later Cheyenne, Hopi, and Northern Cheyenne peoples—became a significant part of General Conference witness and services. In fact, within two decades of the Haurys' arrival in Oklahoma, more than one hundred GC Mennonites had served in mission outreach to Native Americans.

One outstanding missionary linguist was Rodolphe Petter (1865-1947). Petter spent his life studying Cheyenne language and culture. He translated much of the Bible and some Christian devotional writings into Cheyenne.

The stream of renewal which flowed through the General Conference opened new worlds of education and mission to American Mennonites. Both of these emphases stretched the church's horizons and broadened its vision. Soon Mennonite missionaries and educators were serving around the world.

Strength through the Old Order

While some Mennonites caught a fresh sense of God's Spirit through work in organized missions and higher education, another group of Mennonites and Amish found strength through a renewed commitment to community, group discipleship, and mutual aid. They became the Old Order Mennonites and the Old Order Amish. These people feared that many Mennonites were becoming caught up in materialism and individualism. In response, they called Mennonites to submit their personal wants and interests to the will of the larger church.

The Old Order folks rejected the many church programs which other Mennonites applauded. They were troubled by the spirit and methods of these innovations, believing that such activities worked against strong families and congregational life.

Old Order Mennonites objected to Sunday schools, for example, not because they opposed Christian education, but because they thought religious teaching was the responsibility of parents and of the entire church. Sunday schools took

David Hunsberger

The Old Order Mennonite meetinghouse near Linwood, Ontario.

Christian education out of the home, making the family less central, and it separated nurture from whole-group worship times. More subtly, Sunday school games, contests, and prizes encouraged competition and pride among children. In contrast, the Old Orders emphasized that God calls the church to live in a spirit of cooperation and humility.

In 1872 Mennonite bishop Jacob Wisler (1808-1889) organized an Old Order Mennonite congregation near Elkhart, Indiana. Eventually other Old Order Mennonite groups formed in Ontario (1889), Pennsylvania (1893), and Virginia (1901).

During the mid-1800s, many Amish also supported the Old Order movement within their church. Eventually about one third of them became the Old Order Amish. Most of the rest gradually merged with other progressive-minded Mennonites. The Old Order Amish continued traditional Amish practices such as holding worship in members' homes instead of constructing church buildings. This practice symbolized their belief that the church is a group of people rather than a place.

In the twentieth century, the Old Order Mennonites and Amish raised questions about the role of technology in human life. They believe that modern society's constant pursuit of bigger, faster, and newer things seriously jeopardizes healthy family and church life. As a result, Old Orders have chosen to curtail use of things such as cars and electrical appliances. Although at first glance their choices are not always clear to others, the Old Orders choose their way of life to build and maintain a cohesive, disciplined church.

A Mennonite awakening

Many Mennonites of Swiss and South German background did not drink from either the General Conference or the Old Order streams of renewal. These folks (earlier known as "old" Mennonites), had a different experience of revitalization. Around the turn of the twentieth century, these Mennonites, along with several thousand progressive

Archives of the Mennonite Church, Goshen, Ind.

Employees of the Mennonite Publishing Company, Elkhart, Indiana, 1886. John F. Funk is on the far left.

Saturday afternoon sewing class at the Chicago Home Mission, Illinois, with teacher Lina Zook, about 1897.

Amish Mennonites who joined them, experienced what they later called a spiritual awakening.

Some of these Mennonites saw renewal beginning in the pioneering work of Mennonite publisher John F. Funk (1835-1930). In 1864 Funk began issuing a regular church newspaper, *The Herald of Truth*, along with Mennonite doctrinal and devotional books. Partly through Funk's influence, these Mennonite congregations began thinking about new ways to pass their faith to the next generation.

They established Sunday schools for children, and many began holding their church services in English instead of German. Soon one of Funk's associates, John S. Coffman (1848-1899), introduced the practice of holding revival meetings. Revivalists such as Coffman preached a series of sermons for several evenings in sequence. Each evening, at the close of the service, they asked their listeners for a personal commitment. Frequently young people came forward to publicly commit themselves to Christ and the church.

As more youth joined the church, their energy and vision helped create a series of new activities. Beginning in 1887, several young people organized the first of many Mennonite youth groups devoted to Bible study and fellowship.

In 1893, Mennonite Church young people helped launch the Chicago Home Mission—the first Mennonite center for urban ministry. The mission's motto was "Where the sick are healed, the needy clothed, the hungry fed, and to the poor the Gospel is preached." Dozens of young men and women volunteered to make that motto a reality. The Mission offered a free medical clinic, evangelistic meetings, Sunday school, Sunday morning services, and a kindergarten for children ages three to six.

The Chicago Home Mission was one of many activities and programs which grew out of the awakening. Church colleges, Bible institutes, and foreign missions also stemmed from the renewal movement's energy and excitement. Only the coming of World War I slowed the pace of activity.

War fever

The First World War (1914-1918) tested Mennonite peace convictions in significant ways. In both Canada and the United States, war fever stirred deep patriotic emotions. Mennonites felt enormous public pressure to join in the war spirit and buy war bonds to help finance the conflict.

Patriotic neighbors often reacted angrily when Mennonites refused to take part in the public frenzy of hate and anti-German feeling. Some war supporters were especially suspicious of the Mennonites since many spoke German.

In a number of communities, groups painted Mennonite homes and church buildings yellow—to call the people cowards. In several cases in the United States, arsonists even torched Mennonite meetinghouses.

Governments also worked to muzzle the church's peace witness. In August 1918, U.S. federal agents raided the Mennonite Publishing House at Scottdale, Pennsylvania, and confiscated its supply of tracts explaining nonresistance to

Clara Brubaker: reaching out to rural neighbors

Clara M. Brubaker (1869-1958) was one of many young people who experienced the late nineteenth-century Mennonite awakening and dedicated her life to mission. As a young adult, she committed herself to ministry in the rural communities of Missouri's Ozark Mountains.

In 1897 Clara bought a piece of land near Birch Tree, Missouri, and donated it for the building of a community school. She then served there as teacher for many years. Clara also organized and taught local Sunday schools and spoke at Sunday school conventions. In addition, she carried on an active ministry of visitation, walking many miles through the Ozark hills to visit families, the elderly, and the sick.

Clara encouraged other Mennonites to become more involved in evangelism and service. Through the years she published seventy-eight articles in church periodicals. Many of these pieces called for more vigorous support of mission. Later in her life, she married fellow rural mission worker John R. Shank (1877-1958), with whom she continued her Ozark ministry.

■ ■ ■

violence. Meanwhile, Canadian postal officials barred some Mennonite periodicals from the mail.

By 1917 young men in both countries faced a military draft. Most Canadian Mennonites eventually received exemptions or permanent furloughs from the army. Even so, a few like Ernest J. Swalm (1897-1991), a Brethren in Christ conscientious objector (CO) from Duntroon, Ontario, spent time in prison for refusing to wear a uniform.

In the United States some COs had to report to army

camps and wait out the war's end. Many COs in the camps received harsh treatment: beatings, malnutrition, and neglect. In fact, two young Hutterites—Joseph and Michael Hofer—died from abuse they received in military custody. For those who spent time in military camps, and those who weathered the storm of public contempt on the home front, World War I was a sobering experience. It showed how unpopular the way of love could be.

Forced to buy war bonds

During World War I, the U.S. government sold special savings bonds to help pay for war costs. Many Mennonites refused to purchase the bonds, believing that they amounted to voluntary support of violence. Nevertheless, patriotic neighbors often tried to force Mennonites to contribute to the war effort.

In late spring 1918, in McPherson County, Kansas, a mob visited Daniel and Charles Diener, a father and son pastoring the Spring Valley Mennonite Church near Canton. The crowd demanded that the family buy war bonds, but the Dieners refused. Another night the mob returned and was more violent. Reluctantly, Daniel gave them a check for $50. However, the next morning he went to the bank and stopped payment on the check and instead made a donation of $75 to a Quaker relief organization.

Furious, the neighbors returned a third night, vandalized the men's homes, and then whipped, tarred, and feathered them. The mob threatened to kill the ministers if they did not buy bonds. Finally, the Dieners reluctantly agreed to purchase a few bonds.

■ ■ ■

Controversy and growth after the war

In the decades after the war, Christians across North America—including many Mennonites—faced both troubling controversy and new opportunities. In the 1920s conflicts erupted in many Mennonite communities over questions of doctrine and church life. Some church leaders debated the interpretation of the Bible. Others argued over whether Christians should wear fashionable or plain clothing. Still others disputed on biblical prophecy.

In some cases, the debates served as healthy discussions, but too often they turned into painful contentions. In frustration and anger, some congregations divided and members left the church. For Mennonites who experienced these deep conflicts, the postwar years were ones of pain.

But the 1920s and 1930s were also times of Mennonite mission activity, evangelism, and growth. After 1922 Mennonite congregations began sponsoring summer vacation Bible schools for neighborhood children. In 1938 congregations in eastern Pennsylvania established Camp MEN-O-LAN, the first of many church camps which opened later. As more Mennonites reached out to their neighbors, the church also crossed cultural and racial barriers.

In 1929 Chicago Home Mission volunteers Emma Oyer (1886-1951) and Anna Yordy (1885-1975) decided to learn to know neighbor families who had recently emigrated from Mexico. They visited Manuel and Ignacia León and invited the León children to Sunday school. Manuel and Ignacia expressed interest in attending church, but asked if the services could be in Spanish.

In 1932 the Chicago Mission asked a Mennonite missionary on leave from Argentina if he would begin Spanish-language worship. He agreed, and soon the Leóns and as many as seventy others were attending the Spanish services. A year and a half later, nine Mexican-Americans requested baptism and formed the first Hispanic Mennonite congregation (today Lawndale Mennonite Church). The group's pastor, David Castillo (1900-1986), became the first Hispanic Mennonite minister.

"The literal fulfillment of Scripture"

In the 1930s near Quakertown, Pennsylvania, members of the Rocky Ridge Mennonite Mission were also reaching out to neighbors of various ethnic and racial backgrounds. Several African-American families attended the congregation, including schoolteachers

Archives of the Mennonite Church, Goshen, Ind.

David, Elsa, and Anita Castillo. David was the first Hispanic Mennonite pastor (Chicago).

James H. (1888-1978) and Rowena Winters (1892-1970) Lark.

The mission's concern for and openness to all people drew the Larks to the church. "It was the literal fulfillment of Scripture that caused me to join Rocky Ridge Mission," Rowena later said. When she saw church members going into the community, "gathering up in their cars Italians, Poles, Dutch, American Negroes, and Germans, to take them to the house of the Lord," Rowena believed that she had found "a group of Christians who are really making their religion practical."[2]

In 1936 the Larks began helping with Mennonite summer Bible school programs in Virginia and later assisted in Illinois. In 1945 they moved to Chicago and began full-time urban ministry. A year later James was ordained as the first black Mennonite minister. The Larks spent the rest of their lives in church leadership.

James and Rowena planted or worked with congregations in Illinois, Ohio, Michigan, Missouri, California, and Kansas. They coupled evangelism and community development, promoting church-related neighborhood centers, recreation, and medical and educational facilities. In his eighties James was still serving the church as an interim pastor.

As the story of James and Rowena illustrates, the church's mission produces new missionaries. When the church takes the good news of God's love to others, it also receives. By 1940, more Mennonites of Swiss and South German background were beginning to receive the gifts and challenges which people like the Larks brought to the family of faith.

During their years in Europe and North America, Mennonites had given and received, shared with their neighbors, and helped one another. They had struggled to create homes

Archives of the Mennonite Church, Goshen, Ind.

James Lark and a group of children with the Chicago Home Mission, during the 1940s. James was the first African-American Mennonite minister.

and congregations, faced wars and threats of violence, and experienced renewal in a variety of ways. Although they deeply appreciated the ways God had moved in their past and through their tradition, they were increasingly aware of that same movement in the lives of others.

Harold S. Bender and Elizabeth Horsch Bender

Harold S. Bender (1897-1962) was an important twentieth-century Mennonite leader and scholar. A longtime professor and dean at Goshen (Indiana)

You've heard of someone being a "walking encyclopedia." Meet Harold Bender.

College and Seminary, Bender's research and writing helped heighten Mennonite interest in Anabaptist history. He began *The Mennonite Quarterly Review* (a journal) and coedited the massive four-volume *Mennonite Encyclopedia* (a fifth volume was added in 1990). Bender's thought was especially significant in the Mennonite Church (MC), but his writings also influenced other Mennonite groups.

In addition to academic commitments, Bender was heavily involved in the everyday work of the church. He volunteered countless hours for many church committees and organizations. For years he served as secretary for Mennonite Central Committee, the relief and service agency. He also promoted the church's global witness through Mennonite World Conference, a group he led for ten years.

Elizabeth Horsch Bender (1895-1988), Harold's wife, collaborated with him on scholarly projects and publications—carrying out research, translation, and editorial work. Elizabeth was also a college professor who taught German, English, Latin, and mathematics.

■ ■ ■

What does it mean for you to be a peacemaker?

Jennifer Lindberg heard a voice. Not a loud demanding one, but a persistent urge at the innermost part of her being: "You must cut out pictures of 100,000 people."

Why? Let Jennifer explain.

"During the Persian Gulf War, there was so much talk about the smart bombs and precision-guided weapons the U.S. was using. A strong belief was circulating that no one was being killed, that the casualties were 'light' or 'insignificant.' When I saw a headline in the newspaper that claimed 100,000 Iraqi soldiers were killed, it seemed so easy, so natural, to brush it off and not worry about it.

"Later we learned there weren't that many soldiers killed," she explained. "But the number was still significant because it represented all persons killed in the war—Iraqis, Kuwaitis, North Americans, and people from other countries."

Even so, Jennifer ignored the voice that was urging her to cut out the pictures. Cutting out pictures of 100,000 people seemed like an incredible amount of work. She was busy enough with her Voluntary Service position in San Antonio, Texas, coordinating a family literacy program for a community center. Then she met a family from El Salvador.

"The girls and their mother had been fleeing their village during the Salvadoran war," Jennifer recalled. "They hit a land mine. The mother was killed, and the two girls' legs were blown off. The girls and their father were in San Antonio to get medical treatment.

"Since I speak Spanish, I was asked to help translate for them. Although I'd been aware of Central American conflicts for a while, I'd never met Salvadorans who had suffered such dire physical consequences.

"For me, that encounter was a time of connections. I now

had a few faces in my mind instead of just statistics. And I understood that for every one of the 100,000 persons killed in the Gulf War, there was a face, a person, a family, a story. The next day I took out my Mennonite Board of Missions calendar and cut it up. I began counting faces."

Soon Jennifer's bedroom floor was a sea of pictures she'd cut from magazines, and she had to jump from the door to her bed. When she finally counted them, the pictures totaled only 2,000. At that rate, she calculated, it would take her sixty years to finish the project.

News of what she was doing began to spread. Soon children and adults across the United States and Canada were snipping and pasting. Within a few months, Mennonite Board of Missions sent Jennifer a full-time helper—Patricia King, a graduate English student from Hickory, North Carolina.

"Peacemaking isn't a lone-ranger kind of activity, and though I had support before Patty came, she brought partnership, community," Jennifer said. "Patty also wrote some articles that were published in a variety of church magazines that helped spread the word."

As the pictures accumulated, Jennifer and Patty began hearing a call to take the display on tour. Unlike the first voice, this came in audible form, from people across North America who wanted to see the 100,000 Faces.

"From the very first day we opened the display, people were always telling us how emotionally overwhelming the Faces were," Patty said, picking up the story. "But I traveled with the display for a full four months before I ever walked through the whole maze myself. I think I was afraid of it, of the power of seeing all 100,000 faces at once. . . .

"When I finally did look at the whole thing, I felt sick, literally sick to my stomach, by the time I was halfway through. About two-thirds of the way through, I had pretty much made up my mind to go to Central America the next year, rather than pursue a graduate degree right away."

Wherever the exhibit of 100,000 Faces traveled, it evoked strong feelings. A few viewers reacted with hostility or rage. A larger number of people strongly disagreed with Patty and Jennifer's stance against the Gulf War, yet sat down to talk with them about it.

"Some of the people who disagreed with us came back to the display a second or third time, to look at the Faces again or to continue our discussion," Patty reported. "I found these instances deeply encouraging. Such one-on-one, mutually respectful exchanges are, I believe, the root of nonviolence in action."

The display was shown in 56 places. The majority of people who saw it were stunned or deeply moved. Some responded with tears, others with action.

"I visited your 100,000 Faces exhibit in Atlanta," a man named Paul wrote. "I am a combat veteran who served on the front lines with the U.S. Army during the Persian Gulf War. . . . After seeing your exhibit, I requested and was granted a discharge, and am no longer in the service. After meeting you and your companion, I now spend many hours speaking with friends and former service buddies about the need to end male-initiated violence.

"If you ever wondered if you were doing the right thing, or if your efforts had an impact, or if anyone cared, you may rest assured, for you are. Please don't stop."

Jennifer heard a voice to bring 100,000 Faces to life. She and Patty heard a call to share the message of those Faces with many other people. The Faces spoke to Paul and changed his life. Now Paul is a peacemaker, calling others away from violence.

What about you? Do you believe that the way of Christ is one of nonviolence and love for all? Do the voices of oppressed people ever haunt you? Are people you know being wounded by verbal or physical violence? How might God be calling you to respond?

The
Russian
Mennonite
story

10

Mennonites move to Prussia and Russia, 1750-1850

"Drunken farmer or sober Mennonite"

In 1676, the low delta regions around Danzig (modern-day Gdansk, Poland) suffered heavy losses from floods and broken dams. Many people blamed the Mennonites for this natural disaster.

In the senate at Marienburg, Poland, a number of deputies argued that God was punishing Danzig, "the nest of the Mennonites," for tolerating these heretics within its jurisdiction. They insisted that the government should expel Mennonites from the country.

The deputy from Marienburg defended the Mennonites because they were, in his view, economically useful to the country. "One can easily tell," he said, "where a lazy, drunken farmer or where an industrious, sober Mennonite lives." One should not drive them out, he continued, but invite even more of them to come into the country.

These comments caused an uproar in the senate. As a result, the Polish-Catholic deputy received a threat of excommunication. He withdrew his remarks, but the senate did not get a majority vote against the Mennonites.[1]

To escape sixteenth-century persecution in the Netherlands, Mennonites fled to the Vistula delta in northern Poland. Polish kings and nobles welcomed the Mennonites because they were good farmers and experts in draining marshland. Neighbors often envied and hated the Mennonites because of their skills and successful farming.

The Mennonite question came up often in the Polish senate. The public pressured the government to limit the Mennonite population and even to expel Mennonites from Polish territory. Mennonites lived under Polish rulers for about two hundred fifty years. In all that time, while discriminated against and harassed periodically by their neighbors, Mennonites generally enjoyed the protection and privileges granted them by their Polish hosts.

A people or a faith?

When the Dutch Mennonites came to Danzig in the 1530s and then were joined by some Anabaptist-Mennonites from South Germany and Austria, they were a religious group adhering to the Anabaptist-Christian faith. However, by the time they left Prussia for Russia at the end of the eighteenth century, they had developed national or ethnic characteristics because of their isolation and life in separate communities. As a group they had experienced hardships and persecutions and had developed a common faith and tradition.

They had also acquired the Low German (Plautdietsch) language, spoken in the dialects of North Germany. Wherever Dutch-Prussian Mennonites live today, many still speak this language: in Russia, Germany, Canada, the United States, Central America, and South America.[2]

Most Poles and Prussians regarded Mennonites, living in "Dutch villages," as an ethnic group. Because the Mennonite religious faith was neither Catholic nor Protestant, other churches called them heretics.

At first the Mennonites in Poland-Prussia spoke and worshiped in the Dutch language. Around 1750 they switched to High German in their church services and schools, but among themselves they spoke their own Plautdietsch dia-

Former Mennonite farm in the Vistula Delta, Poland.

lect. They used the Polish language and later spoke Russian for business transactions and communicating with their non-Mennonite neighbors and servants.

In Russia the government distinguished between Mennonites and other German settlers. Mennonites in Canada, Mexico, and Paraguay are still regarded as an ethnic group, not just a faith.

Today, through missionary work, Mennonites have established congregations in many parts of the world, including Asia, Africa, and South America. While the Germanic ethnic element is still strong among Mennonites in Europe, North America, and some South American countries, Mennonite World Conference emphasizes not ethnicity, but the Anabaptist-Christian faith, which all Mennonites have in common.

Mennonites bump into a soldier-king

Like most Mennonites, the East Prussian Mennonites were law-abiding citizens and dutiful subjects of the Prussian kings. However, when Frederick William I, known as Prussia's soldier-king, came to the throne in 1713, they got into trouble. At first the new king liked the hardworking Mennonites. He promised them religious freedom, allowed them to build their own places of worship, and released them from military conscription.

But the soldier-king had a peculiar obsession. Wherever he found young men six feet or taller, he compelled them to join his "giants guard," which was his pride and joy. Most men felt honored to belong to this elite guard. But for nonresistant Mennonites, belonging to such a military guard was out of the question.

On the night of September 14, 1723, the king's recruiting agents spotted a number of six-footers among Mennonite young men and dragged them off to Königsberg, East Prussia. The agents tried to force the Mennonites into military service by starving them.

When the congregations complained to the king about this injustice and threatened to leave the country, the recruiting agents were punished and most recruits were set free. The

Who would have guessed that being a tall Mennonite man could be such a big problem?

king, however, kept six stately young men and put them under severe discipline. When the king could not force the Mennonite men into service, he grudgingly dismissed them.

The king was furious. He quickly ordered that all Mennonites be expelled from his country. Some actually left for Polish Prussia. However, the king's advisers managed to persuade the soldier-king not to act so hastily against his obedient and industrious subjects, for the country benefited economically from the Mennonite presence.

Frederick William canceled his expulsion order on condition that the Mennonites establish weaving mills and double their economic contribution to his country. There is some reason to believe that Mennonite know-how in weaving and cloth-making later contributed to the establishment of the silk industry among Russian Mennonites.

How to butter up a king

Frederick II "the Great" succeeded the soldier-king and ruled Prussia from 1740 to 1786. During his reign Prussia, Russia, and Austria began to divide Poland among themselves. The city of Danzig, West Prussia, and parts of Poland were granted to Prussia. This is how most Polish Mennonites came to belong to Prussia.

King Frederick II was an enlightened and much-loved ruler. He called himself "first servant of the state" and was a benevolent father to his subjects. He tolerated all religions in his realm and said all people should be "saved in their own ways." King Frederick II invited expelled Mennonites to come back, granted the Mennonites of Königsberg full rights of citizenship, and ordered his recruiting agents to respect the religious convictions of Mennonites.

When Frederick came to Marienburg for a royal celebration, the Mennonite churches nearby met the king and expressed their gratitude to him personally. They presented him with gifts from their farms, including "two well-fed oxen ready for the king's table, four hundred pounds of butter, and twenty cakes of cheese, together with a large assortment of chickens and ducks."

The Mennonites had more in mind than appreciation when they presented the gifts. The king was handed a petition in which the Mennonite churches asked for the liberties they had enjoyed under the Polish rulers, including exemption from military service.[3]

Tolerance was one thing, but to exempt a group from performing their duties such as defending the country was quite another. Moreover, how could the king justify special treatment for one group?

In the end King Frederick II struck what he considered a fair compromise. He issued a *Gnadenprivilegium* (gracious privilege), guaranteeing Mennonites religious freedom "forever," including exemption from serving in the army and protection in practicing their trades according to the laws of the country. In exchange Mennonites had to pay an annual sum of five thousand thaler toward the upkeep of a military academy. Although grateful to the king, the Mennonites were painfully aware that this arrangement compromised their position of nonresistance.

Increasing threats to Mennonite nonresistance

Around 1800 many Europeans feared and hated Napoleon, the French emperor, the way people in World War II feared Adolf Hitler. When Napoleon began to wage war against European states and invaded many countries, rulers did all they could to defeat him. However, Napoleon seemed invincible. One country after another fell to French might.

Like other governments, the Prussian king and government tried to unite their subjects into a force capable of defeating the powerful French. Militancy, patriotism, and intense nationalism swept the country. This fervor caught up the Prussian Mennonites also, and some disregarded their pacifist tradition. Against the will of their elders and congregations, they joined the Prussian military.

A Mennonite leader sides with the military

In 1848 it became painfully evident that times for Prussian Mennonites were changing. German deputies met in Frankfurt, on the Main River, to work out a constitution in which even the king would be subject to the laws of the country. One deputy was a prominent Mennonite, Hermann von Beckerath (1801-1870).

Among other things, the Frankfurt Parliament decided that one's religious conviction could not stand in the way of performing one's civic duty, including military service. A non-Mennonite deputy argued that the government should give special consideration to Mennonites because of their religious beliefs. But von Beckerath argued that Mennonites

David joins the army

David von Riesen of the Elbing Mennonite congregation joined the military voluntarily. After the Russians and Prussians drove Napoleon back, he faced the allied forces at Waterloo, Belgium, in 1815. David von Riesen fought with other Prussians to defeat the French.

After Napoleon's defeat, the young Mennonite soldier returned to his home community, expecting to be accepted and honored by his people. Instead, the elders excommunicated him for violating an important principle of the Mennonite faith. Disappointed and angry, David took the elders to court.

The elders assured the court that their nonresistance was in no way an expression of disloyalty to the state. Their confession of faith was simply an attempt to remain true to their understanding of the gospel of peace.

The royal court in Berlin agreed. In 1818 it ruled that the Prussian Mennonites were sincere Christians and loyal citizens and that von Riesen had no case.

The Mennonite leaders won their case. Yet they must have realized that the struggle to maintain the nonresistant principles of the church was only beginning.

■ ■ ■

should not receive special treatment in the new constitution.

Hermann von Beckerath stated that under absolute rulers, there was no universal compulsory military service, and kings had the power to make special arrangements with minority groups like the Mennonites. Under a new democratic constitution, however, citizens would be equal before the law; privileges and responsibilities would apply to all subjects. To exempt Mennonites from military obligation would be exceptional and unfair to other citizens.

"I declare," von Beckerath concluded, "that it is contrary to the welfare of the Fatherland to provide for any exception in the fulfillment of citizenship duties, no matter on what ground."

This was a hard blow to Prussian Mennonites who were still nonresistant. They submitted a petition to the Frankfurt Parliament, objecting to the views expressed by the Mennonite deputy. Their protest was unsuccessful, and the final draft of the new constitution did not exempt Mennonites. Fortunately, the constitution was not implemented then; for about twenty more years, Mennonites remained exempt from military service.

In 1867 the government removed the special Mennonite privilege. A year later Mennonites were granted permission to serve their country as noncombatants. By this time, however, many Mennonites had left for the steppes of Russia, and some soon left for America.

In time the German Mennonites surrendered their historic principle of nonresistance to the pressures of their state and society. In the Franco-Prussian War, 1870-1871, Mennonites served in the military. In World Wars I and II, German Mennonites enlisted; many were wounded and killed.

God calls in Russian

By the end of the eighteenth century, Prussian Mennonites were looking for a new homeland again. They were worried about the threat to their faith principles and were also experiencing economic hardships and many restrictions. Mennonites could no longer buy land for their young people. Only those who had money could settle in Prussia, and persons of military age had to pay a special tax to a general hospital fund.

Moreover, children of a Mennonite married to a non-Mennonite were regarded as members of the state churches. Both

Catherine II (the Great), Russian Czar (Tsar) from 1762-1796, offered generous terms for Mennonites and other Europeans to come and live in her country.

the state and church had determined to limit Mennonite growth and prosperity. The poor and those without land were hit the hardest.

As if in answer to the plight of Prussian Mennonites, a call came from Russia. Shortly after she came to power in 1762, Catherine II (the Great), empress of all Russians, invited Europeans to settle in Russia. In 1786 George Trappe, Russia's colonization agent, came to Prussia and invited Mennonites to Russia. Trappe could not solicit immigrants publicly, so he handed out promotional pamphlets as Danzig Mennonites left their worship services.

The pamphlets had good news, especially for the less well-to-do. Newcomers to Russia would receive 165 acres of farm land, religious freedom, and freedom from military service "forever." Social, cultural, and educational life could take place in closed settlements. The Russian government offered financial assistance; taxation would begin after the settlers were economically established.

Mennonites are a people of faith, but they are also cautious and practical. Their history taught them to be on guard when dealing with rulers and governments. Before the Prussian Mennonites accepted Russia's invitation, they sent Jakob Höppner and Johann Bartsch to check the new land and to negotiate settlement terms.

Höppner and Bartsch left in 1786, traveling down the Dnieper River in what is today the country of Ukraine. They negotiated settlement terms with Prince Potemkin, the powerful favorite and lover of Catherine the Great. The prince invited them to accompany the empress on her way to the Crimea to inspect her newly acquired territories from the Turks.

North of the Crimea, in the Bereslav region, the two deputies selected an area for settlement. Bartsch and Höppner returned home through Petersburg where the settlement terms were confirmed by the Crown Prince Paul. They received an enthusiastic greeting at home, and a number of families declared their readiness to begin the long journey to South Russia.

No minister for weddings

In 1788, the long trek to South Russia began for 228 families, mostly poor and landless. They had to camp at Dubrovna, north of Kiev, for the winter. They did not have an ordained minister or elder in the group. Mennonites depended much on their church life for spiritual strength and social and cultural activities. For this they needed ministers.

Mennonites in Prussia generally chose ministers from among the more well-to-do farmers. The government did not issue exit visas to propertied citizens, however, so the migrants left without an ordained minister. Laymen could, of course, preach the Word of God and lead the congregation in devotions. Only ordained elders could administer baptism and communion or officiate at weddings. The need for a minister was obvious when ten couples requested marriage at Dubrovna.

The home congregations suggested that the group select three men who could function as ministers. Among the three men chosen was Bernhard Penner; later he was ordained as the first elder among the Russian Mennonites.

An even more serious crisis was the bad news the group received concerning the place of settlement. In the spring of 1789 when the immigrants were ready to continue south along the Dnieper River, they learned that they could not settle in Bereslav, the choice of the deputies. They would have to settle farther north along the Chortitza, a small tributary of the Dnieper.

Prince Potemkin said plans were changed because the war between Russia and Turkey was going on farther south. The real reason may have been the prince's wish to settle the Mennonites in an area that belonged to him.

The group was disappointed when they arrived in what became the Chortitza settlement. The area along the Dnieper river was a barren, rocky, and hilly steppe, so unlike the flat and fertile fields of their Vistula delta homeland. Some of the pioneers wanted to return to Prussia immediately or wait until they could move farther south.

They soon realized, however, that they could not go back or move on. They had to make the best of the situation. They blamed Bartsch and Höppner for all their troubles, even charging that they had betrayed and deceived them. Later the Mennonites excommunicated the two men, and the Russian authorities imprisoned Höppner for alleged dishonesty, which was never proved. A hundred years later, in 1889, the descendants of the first settlers erected two monuments in honor of Bartsch and Höppner.

Before long the Chortitza area was subdivided, and the pioneers built their first primitive dwellings and worked the land. When the settlers planned their first communion, they faced another problem: Bernhard Penner had no proper boots for the occasion, only footwear worn by poor peasants.[4] The more prosperous members of the group found a pair of boots so the elder could administer communion in proper style.

The first communion service was a moving occasion. People wept, remembering the happy homes they had left in Prussia. But the pioneers were determined to start their new settlement with God's help and to make the best of the situation.

Four mother settlements

As Prussian Mennonites continued to arrive in Russia, they established four mother colonies or settlements. Mennonites later called *Chortitza,* established in 1789, the "old colony." The *Molotschna* settlement, established in 1804 along the Molochnaya River flowing into the Sea of Azov, became the largest colony in South Russia (today Ukraine).

Mennonites established the *Am Trakt* and *Alexanderthal* settlements along the Volga River in 1853 and 1859. Other settlements were formed as branch or daughter colonies. One of the largest was *Bergthal* east of Molotschna, an offshoot of Chortitza.

The Chortitza settlers were the first Mennonite pioneers in Russia. Their experiences blazed a trail for others to follow. When the Molotschna settlers arrived, the Chortitza settlers taught them how to begin and what to avoid in settling their area. The Volga settlers moved directly to their destination in 1853, but they too benefited from the settlement experiences of Mennonites in the south.

The Molotschna settlers got a much better start than the Chortitza settlers did. The first group had no ordained leaders; the Molotschna settlers brought their ministers and teachers with them. The first Chortitza people had been poor and landless in Prussia, with little experience in farming. The Molotschna settlers were more well-to-do farmers and experienced in agriculture. The soil and climate in the Molotschna settlement were more conducive to farming than in Chortitza. The Molotschna colony was closer to cities and towns along the Sea of Azov, where they could sell their agricultural and industrial products. Hence, Molotscha became more prosperous than Chortitza.

Riders of the steppe and other neighbors

The first Mennonite settlers may have thought they would live on an empty steppe, far away from other people. In fact, many other peoples and tribes were living in what today is Ukraine. By 1773, fifteen years before the first Mennonites arrived, the region had one hundred sixty thousand inhabitants. By 1812 there were one and a half million people living there.

In Chortitza, where a giant "thousand-year-old" oak tree stood, *Cossacks* had lived for many years before the Men-

Centre for Mennonite Brethren Studies, Winnipeg

Famous oak tree in Chortitza, South Russia, considered sacred by the Cossacks. The tree provided shelter for the earliest Mennonite settlers from Prussia.

nonites came. The Russian government had moved the Cossacks to the southeast, but the first Mennonite settlers still came across some of these steppe horsemen and fierce warriors. There were also *Nogai-Tartars*, who were ranging between the Russians to the north and the Turks to the south, often changing sides in wars between Russia and Turkey. At first the Nogais saw the Mennonites as a threat to their nomadic life. They murdered four Mennonites and sometimes stole livestock from Mennonite farmers. In time, however, Mennonites traded with the Nogais and learned from them how to live on the steppe.

Other steppe inhabitants included the Russian *Old Believers*, persecuted by the tsars and the Orthodox Church. The *Dukhobors* (spirit wrestlers) emphasized the Holy Spirit and were pacifists like the Mennonites. Leo Tolstoy, the great Russian novelist, helped the Dukhobors settle in Canada. The Mennonites had extensive dealings with the *Molokans* (milk drinkers). *Gypsies* traveled through the Mennonite settlements, and *Jewish* merchants sold their wares among Mennonites.

As Russia consolidated the territories won from the Turks, *Russian peasants* moved further south in Ukraine. Mennonites hired many of these people as workers on farms, in industry, and as domestics.

On the west side of the Molochnaya River were *Lutherans* and German *Catholics*. Their colonies were similar to those of the Mennonites. The relationship between them and the Mennonites was cordial but not close. They were kept apart by their differences in faith, culture, and language, and the fact that the Russian government differentiated between the German "colonists" and the Mennonites.

Mennonite firsts in Russia

Mennonites lived in Russia for some 150 years before their established life there came to an end. In this time they encountered several firsts. Before coming to Russia, Mennonites were a persecuted people because of their faith and way of life. In Russia, however, the government welcomed and respected them. They also met new realities and problems they had not known before.

1. Russian Mennonites were isolated on the steppes and free to develop independent living patterns, including local government. They set up their own church-state, a state within the Russian state. Lines became blurred between government affairs and the church. This created problems, as we shall see in the next chapter.

2. Through thrift and hard work, Mennonites in Russia became quite prosperous. P. M. Friesen, a Russian-Mennonite historian, has noted that a godly life, diligence, and industry contribute to prosperity. In turn, prosperity contributes to materialism and worldliness. This happened to many Mennonites in Russia.

3. For centuries rulers had persecuted Mennonites. In Russia, Mennonites developed a genuine love for their government and the tsars. They strongly supported their country, contributing to the government's war effort financially and providing other noncombatant support. In their literature, Mennonites sang the praises of the tsars and war heroes.

4. Perhaps for the first time in their history, Mennonites in Russia developed feelings of superiority over their non-Mennonite neighbors. They certainly felt superior to their Russian workers and sometimes treated peasants with contempt. In the first half of the nineteenth century, it was rare for Mennonites to marry non-Mennonites. They considered Catholic and Lutheran Germans a notch lower than themselves socially, culturally, and certainly religiously.

5. In Russia, Mennonite faith and ethnicity became almost identical. It was nearly impossible to separate culture, social life, and religious faith. To get married or hold office in a Mennonite colony, one had to receive baptism and belong to the church. A Russian Mennonite was a member of an ethnic group. Thus Mennonite peoplehood, begun in Prussia, was confirmed and further developed in Russia. The Russian government considered Mennonites an ethnic group, distinct from all other German settlers. Sometimes being Mennonite had little to do with faith and a Christian life.

6. In Russia, for the first time, Mennonites experienced religious reform on a large scale. The low spirituality and shallow moral life in the nineteenth century led to divisions, ruptures, and the formation of new groups. Two examples of new churches established in Russia are the *Kleine Gemeinde* (from 1814; since 1952 the Evangelical Mennonite Church in Canada) and the Mennonite Brethren Church (from 1860).

Pressures of the world

In Prussia and Poland, Mennonites were caught between two opposing forces. Pressures for adaptation and assimilation pushed them to integrate into their host societies. Yet the power of tradition and faith pulled Mennonites back to their spiritual heritage. Under sixteenth- and seventeenth-century Polish rule, Mennonites maintained their identity and faith. Their differences with the Catholic Poles helped them keep their unique faith identity.

Under eighteenth- and nineteenth-century Prussian-German rule, however, the push to integrate into society was much stronger. Mennonites spoke German and were culturally similar to their German neighbors. Some Mennonite leaders compromised their faith principles in the interest of greater social and political acceptance. German governments were less willing than earlier Polish rulers to honor the beliefs and practices of Mennonites.

Mennonites not willing to give in to the forces of assimilation decided to leave their Prussian homeland, hoping to maintain their traditional ways and to establish a new home for their children. While the Swiss Mennonites looked for a new homeland in America, many Prussian Mennonites believed that God was leading them to Russia.

On the long trek to South Russia, Mennonites thought of themselves as the children of Israel on their way to the Promised Land, a land which God had prepared for them. They found, however, that they could not leave their human nature and habits behind. Human weaknesses, combined with new circumstances in Russia, brought new threats to their faith and identity as a people.

In this chapter, we have considered the factors and circumstances that led Mennonites to Russia. In the next chapter we'll focus on how Mennonites established institutions in their Russian "commonwealth."

11

The Mennonite commonwealth in Russia, 1850-1917

Robbers attack a leader

Late on a dark evening, Jakob Höppner, one of the leaders of the Chortitza Mennonites, returned home from a business trip. Two companions were with him.

As they drove into the yard, they found it strange that none of Höppner's family came out to greet them. Rain began to fall, and by a flash of lightning, Höppner and his friends saw two strangers standing before them. One raised a large knife, and the other pointed a rifle at Höppner. The knife came down and cut a button off Höppner's clothes. The other man pulled the trigger of his rifle.

Höppner would have been a dead man, but the rifle's wet powder failed to explode. Meanwhile, one of Höppner's friends had rushed off to get help. The two intruders vanished in the darkness.

When the men were caught and brought to justice, Höppner learned what had happened. The robbers were merchants from a nearby town who came to Höppner's home on the day he left. They broke into the house and tied up the occupants. Then they waited for Höppner to return, knowing he was a rich man and would be carrying money.

They got that information from some jealous Mennonite settlers who told the robbers that Höppner received money

from the Russian government for official services he had
performed. Begrudging Höppner his position and wealth,
these discontented settlers wanted to have the Mennonite
leader killed.

How Mennonites lived in Russia

Mennonites in South Russia lived in their own towns.
Safety was a major reason for establishing compact villages,
rather than living on scattered farms.

Towns had a simple plan: a street with twenty to forty
homesteads on each side. Farmland and pasture surrounded
the village. Each property had three buildings: a house facing the street, with an attached barn, and a shed connected
to the barn—all under one roof.

The church and the school were near the center of the village. At the end of the town were small lots and houses for
Mennonites who had no land.

Some people have described the Mennonite colonies as
self-governing "states within the state" or "common-
wealths." Russian Mennonites organized their lives demo-
cratically. Each village elected a mayor and assistants, who
were responsible for roads, education, and assisting the
poor. A settlement or colony had a number of villages.
Chortitza colony eventually consisted of eighteen villages;
Molotschna had fifty-eight. A chief mayor and his assistants,
elected by all farmers in the villages, governed the colony.

The colony government was responsible for law and
order, fire and insurance regulations, and inheritance laws.
Elders and ministers were responsible for spiritual life. But
since government and church matters were closely related,
lines between them often blurred. This led to serious problems.

The Mennonite democracy existed in an empire ruled by
the Russian tsar and his government in dictatorial fashion.
To attract good settlers like the Mennonites, however, the

government granted them considerable freedom. In exchange, the government expected Mennonites to be examples to the society around them. At times, Mennonite filled this role well, as the story of Johann Cornies demonstrates.

An enlightened dictator

Centre for Mennonite Brethren Studies, Winnipeg

Johann Cornies (1789-1848) was a well-to-do Mennonite farmer, educator, and agricultural leader in South Russia.

Johann Cornies (1789-1848) was born near Danzig, West Prussia. His father had been a sailor, which no doubt awakened his son's interest in the wider world. When the Cornies family migrated to Russia, they established a homestead of 175 acres in the Molotschna colony. Johann's father acted as the community's doctor, using healing herbs that grew in the steppes. A self-taught young man, Johann Cornies worked at various jobs, impressing his employers with his diligence, intelligence, and sense of responsibility. After his marriage to Agnes Klassen in 1811, he acquired his own farm. His star began to rise dramatically.

In 1830 Cornies established an experimental station along

the Yushanlee River where he bred pure strains of horses, cattle, and sheep. He imported the best breeding animals from all over Europe, including merino sheep from Spain.

By 1847 he owned 500 horses, 8,000 sheep, and 200 head of cattle. Cornies also cultivated about 25,000 acres of land, planted tree saplings that he sold to the settlers, and introduced the potato to Russia.

Within his lifetime, five million trees, including many fruit trees, were planted in forty-seven villages. Forests began to take shape on the treeless South Russian steppes. With the introduction of irrigation and crop rotation, the Mennonite farms flourished.

When Cornies was twenty-eight, the Russian government took note of his accomplishments. He was appointed life-long chair of the Agricultural Society, a committee that regulated the farming life of the settlements. Since Cornies had been appointed by the government, not the colonists, he had almost unlimited powers. P. M. Friesen calls Cornies an "enlightened despot," a dictator who ruled for the benefit of his subjects.[1]

Not all Mennonites appreciated Cornies. Some spiritual leaders resented his influence, believing that he secularized many aspects of Mennonite life. When those conservative leaders opposed him, Cornies dealt with them harshly, even exiling them from the colonies.

From babysitting to high schools

Before Cornies took over, education among Russian Mennonites was inadequate. Classes met in homes, and teachers were generally unqualified. Basic reading, writing, and arithmetic were taught by rote from an ABC booklet or primer, the catechism, and the Bible. Students who could not memorize lines or numbers received physical punishment.

Using the Agricultural Society, Cornies reformed the

Not all Mennonites liked Johann Cornies, so one village thought it'd be cool to play "trick or tree" with him.

Trees planted upside-down

Not everyone liked Johann Cornies. From one village came persistent reports that trees planted according to the instructions of the Agricultural Society had all died. This was surprising, for the soil was good, the saplings of the best quality, and the instructions for planting and watering detailed.

The Agricultural Society sent inspectors to investigate. When the mayor led them into the garden, the inspectors saw that the mayor and his villagers had played a joke on Cornies and the Society. They had planted the trees with their branches in the ground and their roots in the air!

Incredulous and angry, the inspectors rushed back to report what they had found. Cornies did not laugh. The saplings cost money, and the mayor had opposed the orders of the Society and its leader. In opposing the Society's orders, the mayor had also opposed the Russian government and the tsar himself, under whose control the Society worked.

The mayor had to appear before the congregation and answer for his misdeed. The church excommunicated him and imposed the ban. He was a shunned man; his community would have nothing to do with him, and his family couldn't even eat with him. Members of the mayor's congregation even beat him physically, a practice not uncommon among Mennonites at that time.

People pleaded with their mayor to repent, confess his fault, and return to his church. But the mayor remained unrepentant to the end of his life. When his wife died, the mayor was not allowed to eat the funeral meal with the mourners. Historian P. M. Friesen, critical of the congregation's actions, concludes his account of this case by adding, "May God judge him graciously!"

■ ■ ■

colonies' educational system. He studied the latest European educational theories and published rules on how to teach. Cornies introduced required textbooks and programs of study, and appointed trained and licensed teachers. He established the first high school and teacher training institute in Ohrloff. It became the basis for the high schools and teacher training institutes in the Mennonite colonies.

The new Mennonite educational system became a model for Russia. Attractive buildings and skilled teachers attracted promising students who valued education. Earlier the farmer-preachers controlled education and carried the most influence in settlement life. Then trained teachers began to replace the old leadership in the pulpits and community.

Women enjoyed greater freedom. Mennonites established special girls' schools, modeled on the Russian system, where female and male teachers taught inquisitive young women. By the end of the nineteenth century, Mennonite young people began to attend Russian and European universities, preparing themselves for nonfarming occupations.

For the old guard among Mennonites, these were radical developments. Some leaders thought Cornies was a dangerous influence.

Cornies' educational goals reached beyond the schools. He taught people of various ethnic backgrounds how to farm and administer their villages. He transformed Mennonite

Centre for Mennonite Brethren Studies, Winnipeg

Girls' School in Chortitza, South Russia, as it appears today. The building is still used by a school.

towns into models for other groups. Houses were solidly and beautifully constructed. Farms were in good order, with painted, well-built fences. Streets and yards were clean.

Cornies placed Mennonite farmers in non-Mennonite villages as teachers. He encouraged Hutterites to abandon communal life, which they did for a short time. In 1839 he and his wife, Agnes, took Russian young people into their house to train them to become leaders among their own people.

I wish to remain a simple farmer

Critics saw Cornies as proud, stubborn, and intent on destroying traditional ways of life. At heart, however, he remained humble and deeply committed to the Mennonite-Christian faith. When the government offered him high positions, he declined, saying he wished to be "nothing but a Mennonite farmer who, at the time of his baptism, promised not to govern or carry arms in accordance with his Christian duty."[2]

Nevertheless, Cornies did accept a gold medal of merit. In addition, Tsar Alexander I honored him highly by visiting the Cornies home in 1825. Two years later Tsar Nicholas I received him as a special guest.

When Johann Cornies died in 1848, the church in Ohrloff could not contain all the people who came to pay their last respects. A long procession of Mennonite, Jewish, Russian, Molokan, and Nogai mourners followed the coffin to the cemetery. Later a marble shaft with the top broken off, symbolizing Cornies' unfinished work, was placed in his honor.

Cornies had summed up his life this way: "I feel constrained . . . to work while there is yet time, for surely the night will come when no one can work. I depend on no man nor do I pay any attention to the slander of those who disagree with me, for I place my trust in God my Savior."[3]

His admirers placed him side by side with Menno Simons.

Historian P. M. Friesen writes, "And we call upon our . . . brothers and sisters in Russia and America: Let us remember our two teachers, Menno and Cornies!"[4]

Farmers without land

Though many sixteenth-century Anabaptists lived in towns and cities, Mennonites later took to the soil. They followed the advice of Menno Simons, who encouraged his followers to work the land, milk cows, and avoid urban life.

For Mennonites in Russia, farming and godliness went hand in hand. People who had no land had problems with landholding Mennonites, the colonial authorities, and the church.

By 1870 at least two-thirds of all families in Chortitza and Molotschna were landless. The problem required immediate attention if the Mennonite commonwealth was to survive.

Johann Cornies knew that with large families and the lack of additional land, it was only a matter of time before there would be a land crisis. He established industries to provide employment for landless young people, but these industries did not develop fast enough to absorb the rising number of Mennonites.

Russian laws forbidding the division of individual farms and the landholders' resistance to giving up their profitable rented crown lands and pastures compounded the problem. The rich farmers and estate owners could buy or rent land for their children from Russian nobles. Poorer Mennonites with large families had no such option.

The situation created two classes: the landholding minority who could vote, and the landless majority who couldn't. Landless Mennonites appealed to their spiritual and colonial leaders for help. But the leaders belonged to the landholding class and showed little desire to aid their landless brothers and sisters.

When pleas for assistance were ignored in the Mennonite

community, the landless took their grievances to the Russian government. Sympathetic teachers and pastors helped them prepare documents to present to the authorities. One helpful minister, Franz Isaac, later wrote a book on the difficulties of the landless. It is our best source of information about this sad chapter in Russian Mennonite history.[5]

The problems of the landless were eventually solved when the Russian government granted permission to divide farms for the children. Crown lands and pastures were subdivided and sold or rented to the landless. The colonies bought land from Russian nobles and helped establish daughter colonies for those who wished to farm.

Meanwhile, the manufacture of farming implements and other industries provided additional employment, and many young people acquired education and entered non-farming jobs.

In the 1870s, eighteen thousand Mennonites left Russia for North America. This solved the problems of overpopulation and landlessness. However, the stresses and strains had put the Mennonite faith and sense of community to severe tests and pointed to the need for revival.

Early signs of revival

When the church is in need, God often sends reformers to call people back to discipleship. In 1814 Klaas Reimer (1770-1837) was the founder of the *Kleine Gemeinde* (German for "small congregation"), the first group to remind Mennonites in Russia that they had become neglectful in their faith, materialistically minded, and worldly.

Reimer came from Danzig to settle in Molotschna with the intention of calling his people to repentance. His convictions came from reading the Bible, Anabaptist literature, and *Martyrs Mirror*. As a result of his study, the shallow spirituality of the Russian Mennonites burdened him. Finding little support from other ministers, Reimer and eighteen to twenty like-minded persons withdrew from the large Mennonite church to form the Kleine Gemeinde.[6]

Reimer and his church believed the principle of nonresistance was no longer taken seriously. Though Mennonites did not enlist in the Russian army, they supported the government financially to fight Napoleon, the French emperor. Moreover, church members compromised their peace position by using physical punishment on lawbreakers.

Second, the Kleine Gemeinde objected to the moral tolerance among Mennonites, including alcohol abuse at weddings and other celebrations. One document says: "You know yourselves how the poor blind people act at these wedding feasts, the one proud, the other still prouder, the pipe in one hand and the songbook in the other as if the living God, and the dying Lord Jesus could be honored thereby."

Third, to foster humility, the Kleine Gemeinde did not approve of praising the dead at funerals. They especially believed it was hypocritical to speak well of the departed who had not led a godly life.

The Kleine Gemeinde remained a small, often despised church. Eventually, its members moved to Canada and the United States. Yet Reimer and his group had planted the seed of much-needed reform. Other individuals and groups eventually emerged to continue the reform which the Kleine Gemeinde had begun.

Origins of the Mennonite Brethren

The 1860s were a time of much religious turmoil among the Russian Mennonites. The Peters Brethren, or Breadbreakers, followed Hermann Peters (1841-1928) to the Crimea and later to Siberia. They broke bread as Jesus did at the first communion, and they rejected many "worldly" activities such as reading newspapers, discussing politics, and taking photographs. Their outlook resembled the Old Order

Amish. Some of them later settled in Oklahoma.

The Friends of Jerusalem or Templers emphasized the Lord's second coming, good education, and building the temple in Palestine. Some settled in Palestine. Today there are still some Mennonite Templers in Australia, where they moved when they experienced hardships in Palestine.

Bernhard Harder (1832-1884), minister, evangelist, teacher, and poet, was one of the most severe critics of the shallow faith and life among his people. He preached like an Old Testament prophet against materialism, drunkenness, and general worldliness among Mennonites. In revival sermons, he called people to repentance and commitment to Christ.

Through his poetry he often criticized Mennonite immoral living. In a poem "To the People Whom I Dearly Love," Harder reminds Mennonites of their early Anabaptist martyrs and their faith. Then he criticizes the fathers for neglecting their children and depriving them of the necessities of life because of their heavy drinking.[7]

People who were drawn to Christ through Harder's sermons and poetry could not understand how he could criticize his church so severely without leaving it. But Harder believed he should work for reform from within his church, even though he sympathized with those who eventually left and organized the Mennonite Brethren Church.

A minister in the German-Lutheran colonies south of Molotschna greatly influenced the group that later established the Mennonite Brethren Church, the most successful Russian Mennonite reform group. Eduard Wüst (1818-1859) preached with great emotion, emphasizing the grace of God, repentance, and the new birth. Some Mennonites went to hear him, and some churches invited him to preach on special occasions and to hold Bible studies in homes.

The followers of Wüst were called "brethren." While Wüst stressed evangelical faith and God's free grace, he failed to emphasize discipleship or following Jesus in life. Some of his followers disregarded Christian discipleship and stressed unwholesome emotions and a false freedom.

Wüst died in 1859, one year before the establishment of the Mennonite Brethren Church. Some Mennonite Brethren historians believe that "it was perhaps providential that the man to whom so many Brethren were emotionally attached" died when he did. According to them, Wüst was a Moses who led people "out of the bondage of a lifeless tradition . . . to a joyous assurance of a personal faith." But he was not equipped to be a Joshua to lead the "redeemed people into the promised land of a believers church."[8]

After Wüst's death, the brethren who had followed him needed to reorient their understanding of the church. For their view of the church, they looked to their Anabaptist tradition and the New Testament.

Mennonite Brethren withdraw

The break with the old church came suddenly. Toward the end of 1859, the brethren asked Elder August Lenzmann (1823-1877) of the Gnadenfeld Mennonite congregation to administer the Lord's Supper to them separately because they did not want to take communion with unconverted church members. Lenzmann, while sympathetic to the request, felt that private communion would foster spiritual pride and cause disunity in the church.

In late November the brethren celebrated communion among themselves. At a stormy church meeting, someone suggested that Johann Claassen (1820-1876) and his followers step out of the church so that communion could be discussed more freely. Claassen and his people left the church meeting. Had there been more patience and less harshness on both sides, the break might have been prevented. As it was, reason took a back seat to high emotion.

On January 6, 1860, eighteen heads of families signed a founding document. They addressed their declaration "to

Centre for Mennonite Brethren Studies, Winnipeg

Peter Martin Friesen (1849-1914) and his wife, Susanna. Friesen was a Mennonite Brethren minister, teacher, and historian in South Russia.

the total body of church elders of the Molotschna Mennonite Church." In it the dissidents state that by the grace of God, they have recognized the "decadent condition of the Mennonite Brotherhood and can . . . no longer continue therein."

They separated themselves from the "satanic lives" of

many church members and accused the spiritual leaders of not dealing with the deplorable conditions within the Mennonite brotherhood. They would continue, however, to pray for the salvation of the spiritually blind. They also state repeatedly that in their principles of faith they are "in full agreement with Menno Simons."[9]

The religious and colonial leaders did all they could to shut out and discredit the new group. Mennonite Brethren teachers lost their positions, and businesses were boycotted. Some Brethren were imprisoned and beaten, the group was blackmailed before the Russian authorities, and they were threatened with exile. Eventually, through the hard work of Johann Claassen, the government recognized the Mennonite Brethren as a legitimate Mennonite body. In time they were given settlement land in the Caucasus regions.

The Mennonite Brethren Church saw itself as an agent of renewal among Russian Mennonites. The young church emphasized individual conversion and baptism upon a genuine confession of faith. A memorized confession, based on the catechism, was not sufficient. They believed baptism by immersion—not pouring or sprinkling—best symbolized the death and resurrection of the individual in Christ.

As zealous evangelists, they tried to draw Mennonite and non-Mennonite people to Christ and to their fellowship. The Brethren believed that ethnic Mennonitism was not identical with true Christian faith. Mennonites needed to experience the grace of God and become committed followers of their Lord.

The Mennonite Brethren contributed significantly to the reformation of the old church. Leaders such as Bernhard Harder were encouraged in their work for renewal by contacts with the Mennonite Brethren. As time passed, the old congregations accepted many ideas and practices from the Mennonite Brethren which they considered to be right and scriptural.

In the words of historian Cornelius Krahn, the Mennonite Brethren gave the Russian Mennonites "a rebirth of personal piety, a living piety in which the individual believer receives assurance of the forgiveness of his sins, and orders his life definitely according to the teachings of Christ, particularly the Sermon on the Mount."[10]

Claas Epp founds the Bride Community

On June 25, 1880, a group of thirty-five Mennonite families gathered to celebrate a special communion service in the Volga colony of Am Trakt. Their minister, Claas Epp, whose father had founded the colony in 1853, preached an inspiring sermon. He spoke of the end-time in glowing words and told the people that they must prepare for the Lord's second coming.

To meet Christ, he said, believers would have to make a seventeen-hundred-mile trek to South-Central Asia, well beyond the Caspian Sea. That was where the Bride Community, as he called his faithful, would find a haven of refuge from the antichrist, who would soon appear. There the faithful would experience the rapture.

Epp made his proclamations when major changes were taking place in imperial Russia. Mennonite privileges, including exemption from military service, were ending. As noted earlier, eighteen thousand Mennonites had left for North America. But Claas Epp and his followers believed Mennonites should serve their Lord and await his coming in remote central Asia, not on the other side of the Atlantic.

Epp arrived at his view by studying prophetic books of the Bible, especially Revelation, and reading an eighteenth-century German novel. Like the fictional hero, Epp believed he would lead his people to their promised land.

Epp was a well-to-do farmer, a husband and father, and an energetic and popular preacher. Claiming to have the gift of prophecy, Epp declared Christ would return in 1889. When he urged his followers to leave their homes and loved ones in 1880, they gladly obeyed him. Even the fifteen weeks of travel through heat, cold, rivers, and deserts was not too much for them.

Waiting for the second coming

A group of about six hundred people left for Asia under Epp's leadership. Fourteen children died on the way and were buried in the sand. But the people were full of hope.

Arriving at their destination, they lived among people of different cultures, including Tartars, Turkmens, Kirghizes, and Uzbeks. The natives often harassed and robbed the non-resistant Mennonite settlers. We have already described at the beginning of this book how local bandits murdered Heinrich Abrahms when he refused to sell them his wife.

The Mennonites' crops often failed, and there were economic hardships. But Claas Epp and other preachers tried to keep their people's faith and hopes alive by pointing them to the speedy return of Christ.

March 8, 1889, was to be the day. Epp, surrounded by his flock, seated himself on a table on a hill. They waited for the Lord to descend. When Christ failed to appear as predicted, Epp explained that because his clock had leaned to one side, he had mistaken the date. So he set the clock straight, and the dial pointed to 1891. But that date also came and passed without the Lord's return.

Some of Epp's followers began to doubt the preacher. But Epp continued in his madness, eventually declaring that he was the son of Jesus and thus the fourth person in the Trinity. He even changed the baptismal formula: "In the name of the Father, the Sons, and the Holy Spirit."

Many of Epp's followers left, and those who remained excommunicated him. Epp died a lonely man in 1913.[11]

Some historians have called this episode one of the strangest in the Mennonite story. Yet similar things have happened before and since. You will recall the Münster Anabaptists of 1534-1535. In recent times tragedies in other religious groups have shocked the world. When people blindly follow charismatic leaders instead of the God of the Bible, the results are often bizarre and tragic.

The commonwealth comes to an end

Russian Mennonites enjoyed a good life. They had religious freedom and were fairly independent in their local government. They had good schools, where they studied German and Russian classical writers. They enjoyed music and art, and read foreign and local newspapers.

Mennonites took pride in their prosperous farms and well-kept estates. They also developed various industries, including factories that produced farm implements and mills run by wind or other power.

Hardworking Russian Mennonite farmers and industrialists hired non-Mennonite servants, both male and female. Most Mennonites treated their workers well, but some held their hired help in contempt and exploited them. Later this came back to haunt them.

By the second half of the nineteenth century, imperial Russia was changing. Russia's wars in the Crimea and against the Turks convinced the government that the army needed reform and modernization. Industrial developments in Europe affected Russia as well. Russian factories, coal mining, railway building, and the increasing importance of city workers threatened the peaceful existence of Mennonites and made them vulnerable to outside influences.

Toward the end of the century, Russian nationalists thought of German-speaking settlers as foreigners who benefited from life in Russia but remained loyal to Germany.

All was not well within the Mennonite communities. Material prosperity, ethnic pride, and worldliness blinded many Mennonites to spiritual values and their faith tradition. Greed and selfishness led to the struggle over land. All this was evidence of the spiritual illness of Russian Mennonites. Efforts at church reform could not heal the internal problems. External events soon took over and directed the course and outcome for the Mennonite commonwealth.

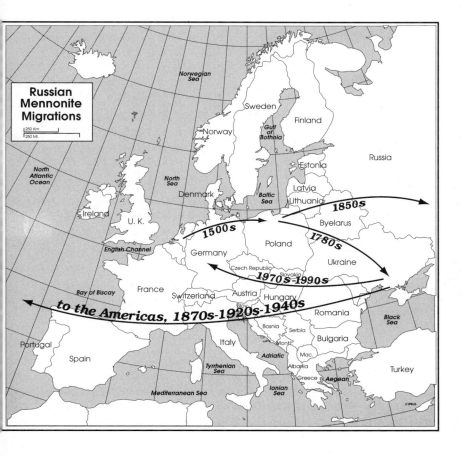

12

Migration and loss, 1874-1945

Troubling news

Early in 1871 distressing news reached the Mennonite colonies in South Russia. One of their most cherished principles, nonresistance, was under attack. The government in St. Petersburg was about to end this and other special privileges that earlier tsars had granted to Mennonites "for all time."

Religious and civic leaders in Chortitza and Molotschna met and decided to send six delegates to the capital to discuss their concerns with the tsar. Only two of the delegates had a good command of the Russian language. In St. Petersburg they could not see the tsar, but other government officials received them, and they talked.

Russians: It's too bad that after seventy-five years in Russia, Mennonites still don't speak Russian. This is a sin!

Mennonites: We are beginning to do all we can to make up for this neglect.

Russians: It's too late.

Mennonites: We object to serving in the military, which is against our faith.

Russians: Your confession of faith will not be affected. We expect you to render medical services, but not right now. Perhaps some twenty-five years down the road, you'll be asked to take up arms.

Mennonites: We can't even serve in the medical corps if it is
  connected with the military.
Russians: Then you'll have to look for another country
  where no obligation toward the state exists.
Mennonites: As Mennonites we acknowledge the authority
  of the state. We obey it and pray for its rulers.
Russians: What would you do in case of war?
Mennonites: We would meet the enemies, be reconciled to
  them, even embrace them in love. But we would not
  kill.
Russians: No state could exist if all people thought as you
  do.
Mennonites: If all people were nonresistant, there would be
  no wars.

The Russians laughed and dismissed the delegates, telling
them that they should think further about serving as medical orderlies.

Mennonites sent several more delegations to St. Petersburg, but the meetings weren't encouraging. Once the delegates were told that it was hypocritical of them to talk about
peace, love, and nonresistance. "We have rooms of files concerning quarrels and fights within your settlements," the
Russians said. They were referring to the difficulties Mennonites had about land ownership and religious issues in
the 1860s.

Because of the government's demand for military service
many Mennonites began to consider emigrating to America.

Leaving for America

When the Canadian and U.S. governments learned that
Russian Mennonites were planning emigration, they did all
they could to attract as many Mennonite farmers as possible
to their countries. Canada offered incentives:

- Complete exemption from military service.
- Free land—160 acres in Manitoba for each family.
- Complete freedom of religion.
- The right to instruct their children in German.
- Complete control over their schools.

The U.S. offer was similar, although the Americans could not guarantee military exemption. They assured the Mennonites, however, that the government would respect their faith principles.

In the summer of 1873, twelve Mennonite delegates traveled to North America to inspect conditions for settlement in Manitoba, the Dakotas, Minnesota, Nebraska, and Kansas. When they returned to Russia with positive reports, a number of Mennonites were ready to move. They believed that in North America they could follow their faith principles and provide a safe future for their children.

The possibility of losing thousands of industrious farmers alarmed the Russian government. To persuade Mennonites to remain in Russia, the government sent General von Totleben, a German Lutheran and war hero, to the colonies. He described life in North America: Mennonites would have to drain swampy areas and cut trees to prepare farmland. There would be no native people to work for them. And there were no guarantees of military exemption in United States.

In Russia, von Totleben said, Mennonites could perform alternative service: plant trees and do other forestry work, serve in hospitals or as firefighters in the cities, or work in factories and in southern ports. Above all, the general told the Mennonites, the tsar would be most pleased if they stayed in Russia.

Mennonites agreed that the Russian offers were fair and just. They chose to work in forestry units where they could supervise their young men and support them spiritually. A minority of Mennonites, however, were fearful of the future and did not trust government promises. They moved to Canada or the United States.

The more conservative Mennonites decided to leave—the Kleine Gemeinde, the Bergthal colony, the Hutterites, and some from Chortitza and Molotschna. Beginning in 1874 and continuing into the 1880s, eighteen thousand Russian Mennonites made the difficult land and sea voyage to the plains of Canada and the United States. Some Mennonites from Poland and Prussia joined the immigrants.

Of those who came to North America, eight thousand settled in Manitoba, Canada. They included members of the Kleine Gemeinde, the Bergthal colony, and some of the other more conservative Mennonites. The Canadian government guaranteed them military exemption and settlements on compact reserves.

About ten thousand Mennonites, including the Hutterites, settled in the American Midwest because of its more advantageous climate and soil conditions, as well as its closeness to markets. They also believed that the United States would honor their religious principles. Thus religious and economic reasons contributed to the first emigration of Russian Mennonites to North America.

Mennonites of Swiss background had earlier come to America and Canada. Now they generously assisted the Russian Mennonites arrivals. Pennsylvania and Ontario Mennonites gave advice and material help, opened their homes to the immigrants, and helped them to settle in their new homeland.

The Native people on the prairies were also helpful, teaching Mennonites how to adapt to the harsh climate and establishing friendly relations with them. Thanks to their industry, assistance from others, and the governments' goodwill, Russian Mennonites soon developed thriving communities in North America.

Breadbasket of the world

One important economic contribution of Mennonites to America was the introduction of winter wheat. In 1874 the Mennonites from Russia sowed the first winter wheat seed in America which they had brought with them. They experimented with different varieties and then found that the hard red Turkey winter wheat was best suited to the soil and conditions of Kansas. This wheat gradually spread to the neighboring non-Mennonite counties of Kansas and other parts of the midwestern states. Today Kansas is known as the "breadbasket of the world."

The Mennonite most responsible for helping Kansas develop economically was Bernhard Warkentin (1847-1908). Born in Russia, Warkentin settled in Halstead, Kansas, in 1873. He married Wilhelmina Eisenmaier, and in 1886 moved to Newton, where he established the Newton Milling and Elevator Company. A year earlier he made arrangements in South Russia for a large shipment of hard winter wheat to Kansas for distribution among the farmers. Warkentin organized banks, including the Kansas State Bank of Newton, of which he was the director and president. He was also active in the founding of Bethel College.

Warkentin died in 1908 in Beirut, Syria, where he and his wife were traveling. A pistol accidentally discharged in the adjoining compartment, killing Warkentin. He was buried in the Greenwood cemetery in Kansas.

■ ■ ■

The Revolution of 1917

Mennonites who remained in Russia experienced great prosperity, educational progress, and increasing involvement in their society and state. However, certain signs pointed to troubles in the future. While the tsarist government continued to value and protect the Mennonites, passionate Russian nationalists, called Slavophiles, began to view all German-speaking settlers with suspicion and hatred. They said the Germans became rich at the expense of Russian peasants and neglected their duty to the state. While Mennonites benefited from living in Russia, the Slavophiles charged, their hearts were really in Germany.

Mennonites defended themselves by saying they were loyal Russian subjects, they had supported war efforts by transporting goods and healing wounded soldiers, and they had contributed substantially to the economy. The attacks in the press continued.

Here and there peasants began to rob Mennonite estates and even murder well-to-do farmers. Bandits brutally murdered Hermann A. Bergmann (1850-1919), a wealthy estate owner and prominent member of the legislative assembly. Things did not look good for the defenseless Mennonites.

The Revolution of 1917 was the beginning of the end of the Mennonite commonwealth in Russia. At first some Mennonites, especially the intellectuals, sympathized with the poor in their drive for fair land distribution and greater justice. But when Vladimir Lenin and the Bolsheviks violently overthrew the tsarist government and murdered Tsar Nicholas II and his family, Mennonites knew they would have serious problems. The Soviet government continued its reforms, forcing farmers into collectives, closing Mennonite schools and churches, and exiling leaders to Siberia.

Anarchy and civil war

Before Mennonites experienced the full force of antireligious and atheistic propaganda and lost their material possessions and cultural life, they faced a terrible challenge. In March of 1918, the Soviet government made peace with Germany and Austria and withdrew from the First World War (1914-1918). Germany took possession of the Ukraine.

Jubilant Mennonites believed that all lawlessness would end and they would be able to resume their former existence. According to some reports, "pretty blonde Mennonite girls carried bunches of flowers and their mothers offered zwieback [buns] and thick slices of ham to the astonished but delighted young liberators."

Their joy did not last long. When Germany was defeated a few months later, German troops withdrew from the Ukraine. German soldiers warned Mennonites that Russian peasants would take terrible revenge against German settlers, and they should prepare to defend themselves.

The Mennonites' experiences were worse than the Germans predicted. The White Army, seeking to reinstate the tsar, fought the Red Army of the Communists; anarchist and lawless bands of peasants were caught between the two forces. In the civil war and chaos, Mennonite colonies suffered all the horrors of war, famine, and disease.

Terror comes to the settlements

Nestor Makhno (1889-1934) was the terrorist Mennonites feared most. Born in a large Russian village north of Molotschna, Makhno may have worked as a young man for a Mennonite farmer. In 1908 he was arrested for revolutionary activities and sentenced to life imprisonment. Released after the Revolution of 1917, he went back to his home village to become the leader of a peasant army of about a hundred thousand men, according to some estimates.

The Makhnovites' rallying cry was "Liberty or death!" On their black flag was the inscription "Anarchy is the mother of all order." Makhno had a superb military mind. He was

Suffering and horror

Statistics cannot describe what individual families experienced. Dietrich Neufeld in *A Russian Dance of Death*
tells us what happened. In the house of the . . . physician in Tiege, the bandits made an exhaustive search for
valuables they believed to be there. The doctor's only
valuable possessions were his two beautiful daughters.
The man who called himself the leader gave the doctor
a choice between giving up his life or surrendering his
daughters to him for his sexual pleasure. One daughter
saved her father from his dilemma by offering herself
voluntarily.[1]

The young woman was raped, but she saved her
father's life. There are reports of family members sometimes being forced to witness the terror and brutaliza-
tion of their loved ones.

Another example of terror is the story of William Martens and his family. Martens knew he was a target of the
bandits. When the Makhnovites attacked his village, Martens' wife persuaded him to hide in the garden behind
the house, which he reluctantly agreed to do. But he
couldn't stay hidden for long, as Neufeld reports.

"The burning of the homes, the shrieks, and raving
madness allowed him no rest. Slowly he stole closer to
the house, and when he was sure the bandits had left it,
he hurried to the door. Just before he reached it, he
stumbled over a corpse. It was his wife. His heart cried
out. In his agony he called out to heaven. . . .

"Then he remembered his children. Horror of horrors!
The mutilated remains of all five lay scattered about the
rooms, the oldest of eleven years alongside the young-
est. Their hands looked as if they had protectively tried
to ward off the saber strokes."[2] Martens survived this
particular horror, but he died in the disease epidemic
that followed.

■ ■ ■

cunning and ruthless in dealing with his victims. His men moved on swift light-spring wagons, manned by the driver and a couple of machine-gun operators. Cavalrymen armed with revolvers, rifles, and sabers were part of Makhno's army.

Effective fighters, the Makhnovites would suddenly appear out of nowhere and do their grisly work of robbing, raping, and killing, usually in the dead of night. Then they would abruptly disappear into the darkness.[3]

Many Mennonite villages suffered Makhno's terror. The Chortitza settlements suffered more than Molotschna. The Chortitza groups had a population of 15,000 before World War I. Many Chortitza villages were destroyed, with no residents left. Makhno's men killed nearly 400, including children, raped 92 women, and burned 16 villages to the ground. Then a typhus epidemic struck the colony, affecting 8,000 persons; 1,200 died. Bandits took 113 horses, 1,717 cows, 1,073 hogs, 40,000 bushels of wheat, and 10,000 bushels of barley. The dead were buried in mass graves.[4]

Mennonites defend themselves

Mennonite men were torn between defending their women, children, and possessions, and remaining faithful to their principle of nonresistance. Church leaders and members agonized about what to do. They decided that the matter of self-defense should be left up to the conscience of each individual. Mennonites reasoned that if there were a government in control, they would obey it, no matter how oppressive it was. But there was chaos and anarchy all around, and the bandits were not a legitimate government force. Hence, Mennonites needed to do whatever they could to provide protection for themselves and their possessions.

Young men organized Self-Defense (*Selbstschutz*) units to guard their villages and ward off the attacks of the anarchists. Before the German army left in fall of 1918, it had trained Mennonites in the skills of warfare and provided them with arms and ammunition. Mennonites were taught to shoot and plan defensive strategy. When the Mennonites and other German settlers eventually confronted the anarchists, they achieved some notable military successes, particularly in the Molotschna area.

According to some estimates, the Makhnovites lost over nine hundred men in the encounters, while the Self-Defense units lost only a handful of men. However, it is doubtful that resistance did much good. The anarchists took terrible revenge, particularly on those villages that had taken up arms against them.[5]

Some Self-Defense units fought the Red Army by mistake and were severely punished. A Red Army general told the Mennonites angrily that when it came to fighting for their country, Mennonites claimed to be nonresistant; but when it came to defending their own possessions they were quite ready to take up arms.

In violently resisting their oppressors, Mennonites acted contrary to their historic peace position. Dietrich Neufeld declared, "A Mennonite who surrenders the fundamental idea of peace and affirms war has judged himself. He is henceforth no longer a Mennonite."[6]

This is harsh criticism, but there is some truth to it. However, Russian Mennonites were severely pressed. Later they repeatedly acknowledged their failure to follow the biblical way of peace.

Help comes from abroad

War and anarchy ended, the Soviet government established law and order, and Mennonites tried to rebuild their lives. The war had shattered their communal life. Their cattle and farm horses were gone, and the crops suffered from drought. Soon famine and diseases ravaged the villages. Children and old people died prematurely, and families hoped and prayed for help.

Centre for Mennonite Brethren Studies, Winnipeg

Children line up for food distributed by MCC in the 1920s in Europe.

Help came from Dutch and German Mennonites who collected funds and materials for Soviet Mennonites. American and Canadian Mennonites donated money and sent packages. In 1920 Mennonite Central Committee (MCC) was created to coordinate the Mennonite famine relief program in Russia. Without the effort of MCC and the many other relief agencies, thousands of Russian Mennonites would not have survived.

Foreign assistance helped to establish hundreds of feeding kitchens in Mennonite villages. Relief workers issued forty thousand daily food rations at the peak of the operation.

In addition, relief efforts helped farmers reestablish their agricultural life. Mennonites from abroad sent fifty tractors to replace the many stolen draft horses. American Mennonites gave sacrificially. They collected about $1,200,000—a large amount at that time. Russian Mennonites have often expressed their gratitude to their brothers and sisters abroad for saving them from total destruction.

Desperate people

Life in the Soviet Union showed signs of improvement, but Mennonites were uncertain about their future under Communism. The Soviet program of restructuring the economy included nationalization of all landholdings, redistribution of large landholdings, and seizure of church property.

The government took complete control of education, promoting "atheistic propaganda designed to root out all consciousness of God and religion from the minds and hearts of the youth of the land."[7] In addition, the new government sent religious leaders, teachers, and preachers into Siberian exile.

Then Mennonites began to look for another country. Canada was more open than other places. From 1923 to 1929, twenty-two thousand Russian Mennonites emigrated to Canada.

Centre for Mennonite Brethren Studies, Winnipeg

"Red Gate" through which Mennonites passed on their way to Germany in 1929.

Centre for Mennonite Brethren Studies, Winnipeg

Group of Mennonites leaving Lichtenau, South Russia, in 1924 for Canada.

Centre for Mennonite Brethren Studies, Winnipeg

Group of Mennonites leaving Prenzlau, Germany, in 1930 for South America.

Canadian officials knew that the newcomers would, like the Mennonites who had immigrated earlier, contribute substantially to the economy, especially as farmers in the western provinces. The Canadian Mennonite Board of Colonization, under the presidency of David Toews (1870-1947), and the Canadian Pacific Railway were in charge of settling the immigrants on the prairies. The CPR still had vast stretches of sparsely settled land in western Canada.

The Soviet authorities were reluctant to let their good farmers go. Nevertheless, men like Benjamin H. Unruh (1881-1959) and B. B. Janz (1877-1964), through their contacts with political leaders, managed to acquire exit visas for their desperate people. When Mennonites on their way to Germany passed through the Red Gate in Riga, Latvia, they thanked God with tears of joy for deliverance from an oppressive regime.

By 1929, however, it became practically impossible for Mennonites to leave the Soviet Union. Due to Canadian internal politics and the beginning of the economic depression, Canada closed its doors to immigrants. The Soviet Union no longer issued exit visas to prospective emigrants.

Alarmed, thousands of Mennonites sold or left their homes and possessions and traveled to Moscow, hoping to leave the Soviet Union for a country that would accept them. Government authorities sent many back to their homes in the Ukraine or exiled them to regions beyond the Ural Mountains. Some courageous and desperate Mennonite women and their children demonstrated in Moscow's Red Square, appealing to the authorities to consider their plight and allow them to leave.

Concerned about the negative publicity in the Western press, the Soviets allowed four thousand Mennonites to leave. Germany established temporary homes for the refugees. American and European Mennonite leaders looked for countries to receive their people. About a thousand Mennonites went to Brazil. Two thousand settled in the Paraguayan Chaco, where Canadian Mennonites had established a colony in 1926. About one thousand joined their relatives in Canada.

Fleeing across a frozen river

To escape the famine and political conditions in the European part of the Soviet Union, some Mennonites started new settlements in the vicinity of Blagoveshchensk, Russia. This is in the Far East part of the country, along the Amur River between Russia and China. They believed that by living far away from the centers of Soviet power and close to China, it would be easier for them to escape across the Pacific Ocean to America.

Mennonites in these villages administered their own economic and social life when the Russian government started collective farming. This made it possible to plan for escape across the river. The story of how 217 Mennonites from the village of Shumanovka escaped across the Amur River into China shows the risks Mennonites were willing to take to be free.

The collective farmers of Shumanovka had a good harvest in 1930. Jacob Siemens, the leader, and his fellow-administrators were intelligent and well-loved leaders. They devised a daring plan to lead the entire village to China and eventually to America. The success depended on diligence, hard work, secrecy, even deception. Failure would mean imprisonment, exile, perhaps death.

After the harvest was in, Siemens and his men suggested to the Soviet authorities that their collective might profitably work in the far-away forests during the slack winter months. To prepare they needed sleds, more horses, and other equipment. The Mennonites' eagerness to work in the cold winter months surprised the Soviets, but they agreed to the plan.

As they prepared to "work in the forest," the villagers were informed about the real intentions of the administrators. The plan had to be kept secret. Alexander, a Chinese guide who had frequently crossed the Amur River, agreed to guide the Mennonites to the Chinese side. For payment he demanded several good horses.

On December 16, 1930, in the dead of night, the villagers heard the signal—"Prepare to leave!" The temperature was forty below zero. Fast and mysterious activities began in all of the households. Cattle were set free. Clocks were wound and lamps were lit to leave the impression that all was normal. Women and children got into sleds and were covered with heavy blankets. In a short time, sixty sleds began moving in a long line through the village street, with Alexander riding ahead of them.

The twenty-kilometer distance through snow-covered fields and past other villages took several hours. When the caravan reached the river, dawn was breaking. They could see faint outlines of mountains, the Lesser Khingan Range to the southwest. These "blue mountains of China," as Mennonites called them, reminded the oppressed people of the hope for freedom in the Americas.

Getting the horses and heavy-laden vehicles safely onto the frozen river and across it was not easy. The steep river bank was three meters deep, forcing the men to hold horses and sleds with all their might so as not to damage them. They abandoned sleds that broke.

Once on the ice, the caravan moved swiftly, with the occupants casting fearful glances backward, hoping and praying that no border guards would see them. In the past, some fugitives had been captured and killed. This time, miraculously, all went well.

On the other side of the river, generous Chinese people took the Mennonites into their houses and looked after their needs. Later the refugees boarded buses and trains that took them south to the Chinese city of Harbin. There American and German authorities provided food and shelter for the group. From this city the refugees eventually left for the Americas, establishing new homes and beginning new lives beyond the blue mountains of China.[8]

"He'll never come back!"

The Mennonites who remained in the Soviet Union faced most difficult times. They lost their spiritual leaders and church life. Soviet authorities harassed, blackmailed, and abused them. Labeled kulaks, wealthy and oppressive farmers, Mennonites had their human and political rights taken away. During Stalin's purges in the 1930s, the police arrested, imprisoned, exiled, and shot many "undesirable elements."

Most men in the Mennonite villages faced arrest and exile. Women and children struggled for a meager existence on the newly established collective farms. The following story of Anna, Nicholas, and their three children, in one of the Mennonite villages in Ukraine, illustrates what happened to many others.

It was in the fall of 1937. The family had gone to bed, hoping that they would be spared what had happened to many of their relatives and friends in the last few weeks. Nicholas, a veterinarian, was a useful and productive citizen, but that did not guarantee him any security. Trumped-up charges against his father, an expert horticulturist, had led to his recent arrest and imprisonment.

After midnight the family heard a loud knock on the window and a voice demanding that the door be opened. Anna turned to her husband and murmured, "Now they've come to get you." She dressed and began to sob quietly.

Nicholas got up, lit a lamp, dressed, and opened the house door. Two secret policemen entered and ordered Nicholas to get ready to go with them. They searched drawers for documents and valuables, including possible mail from relatives in North America. It was a crime to have connections with a foreign country. When they finished, they took Nicholas by his arms and led him to the door.

Nicholas turned to say good-bye to Anna and their children. At the bed of his six-year-old son, he whispered, "My dear boy, perhaps I'll never see you again—be good to Mother."

Anna was weeping uncontrollably. One of the policemen said, "Don't cry; your husband will soon be back."

Angry at the mockery, Anna snapped, "Don't give me that! I know how he'll return. He'll never come back!"

Soon after the outside door closed, Anna and her children heard a car drive away. The children never saw their father again. During the first few weeks, Anna visited her husband in the local prison, taking him food and clothing.

One day Nicholas returned his shoes, telling Anna that he did not need them anymore. When Anna examined them at home, she found the insides soaked with blood. Guards had apparently tortured Nicholas until he signed the trumped-up charge against him—that he had poisoned a number of cattle in the collective!

Nicholas and many others were exiled to one of the many camps beyond the Ural Mountains, and Anna never saw her husband again. Later in Canada, after World War II, Anna received word from the International Red Cross in Moscow that her husband had died in the 1940s.

In *The Gulag Archipelago,* Russian author Aleksandr Solzhenitsyn graphically describes the suffering of many people under the Soviet secret police. According to some estimates, between forty and sixty million people died in Stalin's labor camps.

A war that changed the Mennonite world

When Germany invaded the Soviet Union in 1941, Mennonites believed their life would change for the better. Indeed, during the German occupation of the Ukraine and other parts of Soviet Russia, Mennonites began to revive their religious life and values. They resurrected their educational system and reorganized their communities according to their traditional principles.

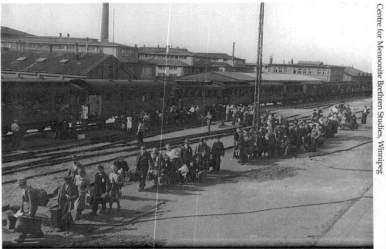

Mennonites leaving Bremerhaven, Germany, in 1948 for their new homes in Canada. Pictures taken by Peter J. Dyck of MCC, May 16, 1948.

Their hopes were dashed because the German "liberators" supported strange beliefs that included superiority of the Germanic race, anti-Semitism, and the Hitler *Führer*-cult. They rounded up Jews and killed them. The Nazis viewed and treated Slavic people with contempt. One Mennonite grandmother told her ten-year-old grandson, "We are grateful to the Germans for liberating us from Soviet Communism. But what the Germans are doing to the Jewish people is most terrible. This will come back to haunt them." She spoke for other disappointed Mennonites.[9]

In 1943 the tide of war turned. Russian armies defeated the seemingly invincible German armies at Stalingrad and near Moscow, forcing them to retreat westward. Some Mennonite villagers had been evacuated eastward before the German armies came. The rest now began a long and difficult trek westward. Some thirty-five thousand Mennonites reached German-occupied Poland and Prussia, their homelands 150 years earlier.

But in January 1945, shortly before the end of the war, the Red Army caught up with them. They sent about twenty-three thousand Mennonites back to the Soviet Union. Only twelve thousand reached the western part of Germany, occupied by the victorious Western Allies. Through the efforts of Mennonite Central Committee and other groups in North America, six thousand Mennonites found new homes in Canada, and another six thousand in South America, most of them in Paraguay.

"Green Hell" becomes a new homeland

A trek of oxcarts moved slowly into the Gran Chaco of Paraguay. The Mennonite men, women, and children with their few belongings had come from Soviet Russia to a new homeland. But what a strange land this was! There were no white inhabitants for hundreds of miles, only a few bands of roving Indians. Poisonous snakes, annoying insects such as

C. F. Klassen

Cornelius F. Klassen (1894-1954) was a tireless worker on behalf of Mennonite refugees. Born in Russia, Klassen joined the Mennonite Brethren Church in his youth. Friends were constantly impressed by his deep faith and dedicated life. During the troubled times of the Russian Revolution and the early Soviet state, Klassen was one of several delegates who went to Moscow to negotiate with the government on his people's behalf. He assisted many families in leaving the Soviet Union before he himself immigrated to Canada in 1928.

After World War II, he returned to Europe under the Mennonite Central Committee to head the massive task of negotiating release for ten thousand Mennonites seeking to emigrate to South America and Canada. Klassen was also concerned about the church remaining in Europe. He worked to revive and strengthen the spiritual life of German Mennonites traumatized by war. When confronted by seemingly insurmountable challenges, he was fond of encouraging others with a positive "God can!" He died in Germany, still assisting refugees.

■ ■ ■

grasshoppers and mosquitoes, and anthills ten feet in diameter and up to four feet high—it all seemed so foreign and threatening.

The soil, so important to Mennonite farmers, was salty and dry. The tall bitter grass was not even fit for cattle. The trees had bottle-like trunks—trunks that would soon serve as coffins for the dead. During the first year, eighty-eight children and old people died. In the Menno colony, established two years before, 147 died of a typhoid epidemic and the difficult climate.

Strangest of all were the skies above. In Russia and Canada, the settlers had known the Big Dipper. In Paraguay, they gazed in amazement at the Southern Cross, something they had never seen before. At noon the burning sun beat down from a northern sky, and the scorching winds also blew from the north.

"Dear God, is this to be our new homeland?" many newcomers asked.

"What does 'Chaco' mean?" someone asked.

"Green Hell," another replied with a sneer.

A young man said, "I won't stay here!" He was one of the first to leave.

Most newcomers stayed, however. They built simple huts, cleared the land, and dug wells. Wells often caved in during digging because of the sandy soil. Most of the wells dug had salty and bitter water. A "sweet" or fresh-water well was cause for celebration. It became the life-giving center of the village.

Growing European or North American wheat crops was out of the question. New crops had to be developed, including Kaffir corn, peanuts, beans, and cotton. Soon even the juicy watermelon Mennonites loved could be grown. Eventually oranges and other citrus fruit were also grown.

Migration to Paraguay

There were two migration movements from Russia to Paraguay. Refugees from Moscow who were unable to go to Canada established the *Fernheim* colony in 1930. By 1932 more than two thousand Mennonites migrated to the Paraguayan Chaco. This included a few from Poland and 367 persons who came by way of Harbin, China.

Financially assisted by Mennonite Central Committee, these people soon established their church and educational institutions, including elementary and high schools. As early as 1935, they set up a mission, "Light to the Indians." Today there are many Indian converts to the Mennonite-Christian faith who live near the Mennonite settlements and who conduct their own congregations and schools.

In 1947-1948, a group of 4,500 Mennonites founded the colonies of Neuland in the Chaco and Volendam, on the east side of the Paraguay River and near the Friesland colony, begun in 1937. They had escaped deportation to the Soviet Union after the war and had no place to go but to Paraguay. Most of them were women and children who had lost their husbands and fathers in Europe. They were happy to find peace and freedom. Their early years in Paraguay were difficult and often discouraging. Mennonite Central Committee greatly assisted this group as well.

Like their forebears in imperial Russia, the Paraguayan Mennonites enjoyed the goodwill and protection of their government. They conducted their own religious, social, economic, and political affairs in freedom.

In 1980 the Fernheim colony celebrated the fiftieth an-

The *Volendam* took many Russian Mennonite refugees to South America.

Mennonite villages in the Paraguayan Chaco. The settlers named villages after their lost homes in Prussia and Russia.

niversary of its existence. A film produced for the occasion, *Home for the Homeless*, portrays the difficult beginnings, progress and community building, and eventual prosperity. The theme song of the film is hauntingly beautiful and expresses longing for a permanent homeland: "We are a people in the stream of time, drifted to this world's shores. We remain restless and full of pain until our Savior calls us home."

More sinned against than sinning

In the depth of his despair, Shakespeare's King Lear cries out, "I am a man more sinned against than sinning!" Of the Russian Mennonites, it also can be said that the sins committed against them were greater than the sins they themselves committed.

In Russia, Mennonites became rich and proud. They often forgot the needy around them and treated the poor in their midst with contempt.

Yet Mennonites did contribute positively to Russian society, particularly in the areas of farming, education, industry, and culture. But when the times of trouble came, their enemies forgot this.

Mennonites became targets of greed, banditry, and state terror. They suffered all the cruelties that fate and human beings could inflict: dispossession, exile, torture, and death. Their beautiful homes and prosperous communities were destroyed beyond recognition. Historian C. Henry Smith observes, "Never since the days of the [sixteenth-century] martyrs have the Mennonites suffered as much as during the twentieth century in Russia."[10]

The suffering of the Russian Mennonites also brought out the best in them and Mennonites elsewhere. Many of the victims of terror suffered patiently, expressing deep faith and commitment to God. Some leaders who suffered exile or death during Stalin's purges became true martyrs in the tradition of their Anabaptist forebears.

European and American Mennonites who rescued their brothers and sisters manifested true Christian love. They performed their good deeds sacrificially and in the name of Christ. When Russian Mennonites left the Soviet Union in the twentieth century, and later when Soviet Communism ceased to exist, Mennonites throughout the world viewed these developments as answers to their hopes and prayers.

Where does your citizenship lie?

Fred's questions came to a climax at the end of his freshman year of college. It happened during an award ceremony for cadets in the U.S. Army Reserve Officers Training Corps.

Fred served in the color guard. Just before the program began, his lieutenant demanded that Fred remove his silver necklace and ring, both of which had clearly-engraved Celtic crosses on them.

Fred felt this demand was a direct challenge to his faith. He always wore the crosses as symbols of his loyalty to God. On the university campus, they had provided opportunity for conversation about his beliefs. Fred told the lieutenant he would rather remove his uniform than take off his ring, and he started to do just that.

Fred's sergeant saw what was happening and quickly intervened. He told Fred he could wear the ring and tuck the necklace under his shirt for the ceremony.

During the program, Fred's lieutenant gave a speech entitled "The Army Way." The speech forced Fred to evaluate his faith and future in the ROTC program. He heard the lieutenant define success in the army as obeying orders.

"Your job is not to think or question the order," the officer said. "Your orders come before your family, your loved ones, your faith, your beliefs, and even your own thoughts."

As he listened to the lieutenant, Fred thought about what had happened with the uniform. If the lieutenant would substitute "God" and "church" for "officers" and the "army," the speech would make sense, Fred thought.

In one of the chapel windows, he noticed a stained glass engraving of Christ with the words "You are the light of the world." It seemed to Fred that Christ's face was sad and depressed. Was Christ disappointed with him?

The next day, a week before the end of the semester, Fred dropped his uniform on the sergeant's desk. "Because of my religious convictions, I can't be in the army," he said. On the way out of the building, his lieutenant confronted him. "You can't hide behind your religion," he said. "You can go home to your draft-dodger friends, but the army will catch up with you."

Fred's decision created tension with his parents. Raised in a Christian home, he was majoring in theology and planned to become an army chaplain. He would have become a fourth-generation career military man.

Fred is still trying to sort out the issues. But for now, he feels that he cannot wear the uniform because of the conflict he senses between the military and his Christian faith.

Many Mennonites in the past have had to decide whether to put on their country's military uniform. Most have refused, but others have done so when required by their government. Though more than 10 percent of all countries now grant conscientious objector status, Mennonites in many nations find their faith severely challenged when they are drafted into the military.

What do you think? How should conscientious objectors respond in lands where exemption from the military is unavailable? Did Fred make the right decision by turning in his uniform? Does a government's requirement to wear a uniform come down to a question of citizenship (Phil. 3:20; John 18:36)?

Do you feel any conflict between allegiance to Christ's kingdom and your government? Where does your citizenship lie?

Anabaptism grows around the world

13

Mission, migration, and mutual aid, 1890-1940

"Give us friends!"

In the summer of 1910, three American Mennonites arrived in Edinburgh, Scotland. Jonas S. Hartzler (1857-1953), Joseph S. Shoemaker (1854-1936), and Alfred Wiebe (1888-1973) had traveled to Great Britain to attend the World Missionary Conference. Hartzler and Shoemaker were directors of a Mennonite mission board, and Wiebe would soon begin church work among Native Americans.

The Edinburgh Conference was a huge gathering of European and North American missionaries. The meeting lasted for ten days, and the thousands who attended heard reports, listened to sermons, and swapped stories.

The conference marked a new era in modern mission activity. Never before had so many people gathered to talk about the church's witness. More importantly, the meeting challenged churches and missionaries to relate to believers in other parts of the world as fellow sisters and brothers.

A Christian from India who addressed the conference begged Western churches to expand their vision of mission. "You have given your goods to feed the poor," he said. "You have given your bodies to be burned." Yet, he pleaded, the younger churches hoped for more: "We also ask for love. Give us friends!"[1]

Like the others at the World Missionary Conference, Mennonites in the early twentieth century faced two challenges—sharing their faith with others and accepting them as friends. During this time new Mennonite fellowships emerged around the world through mission efforts and migration.

Within a few years of the Edinburgh meeting, European and North America Mennonite missionaries were working in more than a dozen locations. Meanwhile, significant groups of Mennonites from Canada and Russia moved to Latin America and established new communities there. By 1940 Mennonites were living on five continents and speaking many languages.

Beyond Europe and North America

Mennonites had accepted the challenge of world missions before the Edinburgh conference. In 1851 Dutch Mennonite Pieter Jansz (1820-1904) sailed for the Indonesian island of Java, where he engaged in an active ministry of preaching and writing. Jansz studied the island's culture, translated the Bible into Javanese, and produced a local dialect dictionary. Through patient work and encouragement, he helped plant the Indonesian Mennonite Church.

In addition Jansz became an advocate for the Javanese people. He feared that Dutch colonialism hurt the native economy and robbed the East Indies of raw materials. Jansz published pamphlets attacking the colonial system and spoke against the opium drug trade, which Western nations encouraged at the expense of native Asians.

Russian Mennonites followed Jansz into overseas mission work. Among them were Abraham (1859-1919) and Mary Martens (d. 1917) Friesen, who went to southern India and assisted Baptists in evangelization efforts.

India was also the first country to which North American Mennonite overseas missionaries went. Mennonite layman

George Lambert (1853-1928) visited India in the mid-1890s and wrote a book about his travels. When severe famine struck India, Lambert asked North American Mennonites to donate food and money for the hungry. In 1897 he returned to India to distribute the donated grain.

Lambert's publicity sparked an interest in India and its people. By 1900 several North American Mennonite groups were sponsoring church workers in that country. Eventually a number of Indian Mennonite congregations grew out of these efforts. In addition to missionary preachers and teachers, the church supported Indian Christians as traveling evangelists. As the years went by, native believers became increasingly active in carrying the church's message.

Mennonite Library and Archives, Bethel College, North Newton, Kan.

Caroline Banwar was the first physician to staff the Champa, India, Mennonite mission dispensary. She worked at the clinic for about a decade after her 1924 graduation from medical school.

By the 1920s, one Indian Mennonite group near Hyderabad organized its own church body, the Andhra Church Conference. This group—without Western missionary administration—assumed responsibility for sending its own preachers to surrounding towns and villages.

North American Mennonites had first come to India to distribute food to the hungry. They continued to respond to the physical as well as the spiritual needs they saw around them. One of the

Mennonite Historical Library, Harleysville, Pa.

Missionary Annie Funk with Girls' School in India, 1908.

"I have no fear"

Annie C. Funk (1874-1912) was a Mennonite teacher from Bally, Pennsylvania. She devoted most of her life to mission work, serving schools in rural Tennessee and urban New Jersey.

In 1906 she sailed for India to work with Mennonite missionaries in Janjgir. When friends warned her of the dangers of such a long trip, she assured them, "Our heavenly Father is as near to us on sea as on land. My trust is in him. I have no fear." In India, Annie continued teaching and founded a school for Indian girls.

In 1912 when her mother became ill, Annie made hasty plans to return home. Arriving in England, she arranged last-minute passage on the *Titanic*, a new ocean liner making its first Atlantic voyage. Tragical-

ly, the ship never completed that journey. On April
15, 1912, the *Titanic*—which many claimed was un-
sinkable—went down in icy waters.

Annie was not one of the survivors. Friends later
heard an unconfirmed report that she had given
someone else her place on a lifeboat.

■ ■ ■

Mennonites' first tasks was caring for orphans whose parents had died during the famine. The missions also established schools and medical clinics.

Women physicians such as Florence Cooprider Friesen
(1887-1985) and Ella Garber Bauman (1895-1989) played especially important roles in the clinics since local custom
frowned on male doctors treating female patients. Indians
also helped staff the clinics. Caroline Banwar (1901-1952), a
medical doctor and member of the Champa Mennonite
Church, helped begin the Mennonite hospital near her
home.

Responding to Russian needs

By 1919 North American Mennonites received word of
severe suffering in another part of the world. Russia had
plunged into a disastrous revolution and civil war. Amid the
violence and banditry, poor harvests and bad weather produced a famine. Mennonites living in the Russian Ukraine
appealed to their brothers and sisters for help. In January
1920 they sent a four-member delegation to Europe and
North America, describing their plight and asking for assistance.

Speaking to American and Canadian Mennonites, the delegates expressed appreciation for the many relief committees which collected donations and offered aid. But, the Russians warned, conditions in the Ukraine were so chaotic that
only an organized and coordinated relief effort could suc-

ceed. The delegates begged North American Mennonites to cooperate with one another and form a single, united relief agency.

After some discussion and initial hesitation, seven Mennonite relief and service groups met in the summer of 1920 and formed Mennonite Central Committee (MCC). Peter C. Hiebert (1870-1963), a Mennonite Brethren educator from Hillsboro, Kansas, headed the new organization.

By the time MCC officially organized, its first workers were already at sea and heading for their base in Constantinople (now Istanbul), Turkey. After arriving there, volunteers Orie O. Miller (1892-1977) and Clayton Kratz (1896-1920?) crossed the Black Sea and landed in the Ukraine. They toured Mennonite villages, met with church leaders, and made plans to bring relief aid. Miller returned to Turkey to arrange supply shipments, while Kratz stayed behind. Suddenly the battle lines changed, and Kratz found himself in an area controlled by Soviet forces. He was arrested by military officials and was never heard from again.

The turbulence in Russia prevented MCC workers from distributing any food until December 1921. By that time the

Archives of the Mennonite Church, Goshen, Ind.

Fordson tractors donated by Mennonites through MCC, near Alexandrowsk, Ukraine, 1922.

civil war was winding down, but food shortages and famine conditions were even more severe. The American Relief Administration, a government agency coordinating foreign aid efforts, assigned MCC to work in the Mennonite-populated part of the Ukraine. For three years MCC operated an extensive food distribution system there, feeding seventy-five thousand people (about 80 percent were Mennonites). The program probably saved as many as nine thousand individuals from starvation.

Until 1927 Mennonite Central Committee also coordinated relief supplies to Mennonites living in Siberia. As time passed, Soviet farms once again began producing healthy crops, and the emergency feeding programs closed. With the Russian relief work completed, some people thought MCC should disband, and it almost did. But in 1929 Russian Mennonites issued another appeal. This time many were trying to leave the Soviet Union and wanted help in emigrating. Once again, MCC mobilized money and volunteers to help the refugees, many of whom settled in South America.

Moving to Latin America

Meanwhile, some Canadian Mennonites had also been moving to Latin America in search of greater religious freedom. Since 1890 conservative Mennonites in Manitoba and Saskatchewan had repeated conflicts with provincial school officials. Before Canada adopted its policy of multiculturalism, the government used public schools to establish cultural uniformity throughout the country.[2] Public instruction sought to produce loyal citizens and good British subjects.

However, some Mennonite parents did not want that kind of education for their children. They hoped that their students would grow up appreciating the German language. They also objected when public schools made children sing patriotic songs like "God Save the King." In protest, some Mennonite villages refused to cooperate with the public

**Old Colony
Mennonites
in Mexico.**

Mennonite relief sales

Each year Mennonite relief sales raise money for Mennonite Central Committee (MCC) relief and service ministries. Sale organizers auction donated goods, such as quilts, furniture, and livestock. MCC uses sale proceeds to distribute food, clothing, and other material aid to refugees and victims of war and natural disaster around the world.

Mennonites held their first two relief sales the same year MCC organized. Both events raised money to assist Russians suffering from famine and civil war. In the late spring of 1920, Mennonites near Reedley, California, held an auction to assist fellow church members in Siberia. And in December, Mennonites at Herbert, Saskatchewan, raised $1,100 for MCC with their own sale.

The first regularly scheduled relief sale began in the mid-1940s. The first well-publicized auction took place in 1957 near Morgantown, Pennsylvania. Today, more than three dozen relief sales annually raise over $3.5 million for MCC relief ministries.

■ ■ ■

school program and curriculum.

By the early 1920s, the governments were determined to force Mennonite parents to comply with public school laws. Provincial Courts handed down thousands of fines and judgments, upheld by the Canadian Supreme Court and the Privy Council in England. Tired of fighting, conservative Mennonites started thinking about leaving Canada. During 1919 and 1920, they sent several delegations to look for land and educational freedom in Mexico and Paraguay.

The president of Mexico invited the Mennonites to his country with promises of military exemption, full religious freedom, and the right to manage their own schools. During the mid-1920s, nearly seventy thousand Mennonites accepted the Mexican offer. Most settled in the northern states of Chihuahua and Durango.

At first the settlers had great difficulty farming in a new, dry climate. Disappointed, some returned to Canada. But those who remained eventually established somewhat successful farming colonies. By 1940 the growing group needed more land. Some families established new Mexican settlements, while others moved to Belize, Bolivia, and more recently, Argentina.

Others from Manitoba and Saskatchewan moved directly to Paraguay and founded the Menno Colony in 1928, the first Mennonite settlement in the country. They were soon joined in the Chaco by the Mennonite refugees fleeing the Soviet Union.

Mennonite World Conference

In 1925 amid all their mission work, migrations, and relief campaigns, Mennonites paused to remember the four-hun-

Delegates to the first Mennonite World Conference, 1925, assembled at Basel, Switzerland.

dredth anniversary of the birth of the Anabaptist movement. That year Christian Neff (1863-1946), a pastor and historian from Weierhof, Germany, invited Mennonites to gather in celebrating the past and thinking about the future. Neff's meeting drew perhaps one hundred people, mostly Europeans. The group held meetings in Basel and Zurich (Switzerland), heard historical lectures, and discussed the plight of the Russian Mennonites.

Because of the unstable political situation in the Soviet Union, the Swiss government would not allow the Russian delegates into the country. Instead, Russians met members of Neff's party at the border and suggested a plan for forming a global Mennonite conference devoted to fellowship and mutual aid. Although the assembly did not act on the details of the Russian plan, they did agree to continue meeting every few years. Their assembly marked the beginning of Mennonite World Conference as a regular international fellowship.

Neff continued to coordinate the group's gatherings for the rest of his life. World Conference meetings in the 1930s focused on Anabaptist history and the church's work with refugees. At first Europeans and North Americans dominated World Conference gatherings. But in time, as the church's mission efforts continued, Mennonite World Conference grew to include younger churches from around the world.

Freeing a cage full of birds

Although Mennonite missionaries remained active in the early twentieth century, they did not begin every new Mennonite fellowship. One new Mennonite church emerged through the witness of an Indonesian couple, apart from Western missionaries.

Tee Siem Tat (1872-1940) was an Indonesian printer and business person. Around 1917 he became ill, but neither traditional healers nor modern medicine was able to cure him.

His wife, Sie Djoen Nio (1875-1962), was a Christian and urged Tee to read the Bible and pray for healing. Tee found the Bible so exciting that he soon began preaching to his neighbors and friends.

One day in the midst of his teaching, he realized that he was no longer sick. Tee was so happy, according to one story, that when he met a boy going to market with a cage full of birds to sell, he paid the lad for all of them. Tee opened the cage and let the birds go, saying that since he had found freedom in Christ, he could not help but free the trapped birds to symbolize his joy.

Through his study of the Bible, Tee came to believe that baptism was meaningful only for those who could confess their faith. He was disappointed to learn that most of the missionaries in Indonesia baptized infants. So when Tee met the Mennonites and learned that they baptized believers, he asked them to baptize him along with twenty-five other new Christians who regularly met at his home.

For the rest of their lives, Tee and Sie worked as traveling evangelists, driving from village to village and preaching the good news. They organized the Muria Christian Conference, a Mennonite group planted through native witness.

Christian cooperation

For the most part, however, newer Mennonite fellowships in Asia, Africa, and Latin America grew from the work of organized missions. Mennonite Church planting efforts were only a small part of the larger Christian mission movement of the time. As the Mennonite delegates to the 1910 Edinburgh Missionary Conference had discovered, many denominations were engaged in active witness throughout the world. Frequently, Christian groups cooperated with one another to present the gospel.

In 1911 when Mennonite missionaries went to the Belgian Congo (now Zaire), they discussed their plans with other church mission boards. They did not want to duplicate or interfere with already-established work. Mission groups also helped one another find willing volunteers. For a time Alma Doering (1878-1959), a Lutheran missionary, recruited staff and money for the Mennonites' Congo Inland Mission.

Mennonites in East Africa were also careful to work with other Christian groups in their region. In 1934 when the first Mennonite missionaries arrived in Tanganyika (now Tanzania), they met with the Tanganyika Missionary Council and asked where they should locate. Council members directed them to a place near Lake Victoria, where there was no local Christian witness.

Many church groups worked together in China. In 1865 an English missionary, J. Hudson Taylor, had founded the China Inland Mission, which brought together volunteers from many denominations. His work was successful, and hundreds of mission workers followed his example. By the first quarter of the twentieth century, there were nearly ten thousand Protestant missionaries in China.

Among these were workers representing a variety of Mennonite mission boards, as well as independent Mennonite missionaries. In China they also coordinated their work with other denominations, independent faith missions, and local congregations.

Henry J. (1879-1959) and Maria Miller Brown (1883-1975) were among the first Mennonite missionaries to China. Arriving in 1909, the Browns soon settled near the city of Kaizhou (now Puyang). Henry operated a small medical dispensary and began preaching and teaching. Maria engaged in village evangelism. In 1913 eight people asked Henry to baptize them and organize a church. The next year Mennonites in North America decided to support the Browns' work, and soon more missionaries arrived.

A decade later ten congregations were related to the Browns' mission, in addition to Mennonite congregations in other parts of China. Eventually, with the assistance of more volunteers, the mission opened elementary schools, a high school, a Bible school, and a hospital. By 1940 the Chinese Mennonite Church had more than 2,000 members.

"Not the Jesus of Christendom"

To be successful, mission churches needed more than numbers. Native leadership and local ownership were crucial. It was often difficult for missionaries to turn control over to Chinese Christians. At times Westerners tried to hold onto their authority, but most tried to give native churches their independence, knowing that was a part of their mission.

In China, local leaders emerged in a number of Mennonite congregations. For example, missionaries noted the many contributions of lay leader Li Ching Fen. Moderator of her congregation, she regularly engaged in aggressive, independent witness in her community. All who knew her respected her work.

Two other important Chinese Mennonite leaders were James Liu (1904-1991) and Stephen Wang (b.1905). Liu's parents had become Christians through Henry Brown's preaching. Liu later studied at the Mennonite high school where he met Stephen Wang. The boys became good friends. Wang's father was a Confucian teacher who had become a Christian evangelist and worked as a traveling preacher for the Mennonites.

After finishing high school, Liu and Wang continued their studies at a Beijing university. They also arranged to spend two years in the United States at Bluffton (Ohio) College and Bethel College (North Newton, Kansas). In 1932 they returned to China, eager to assume responsibility in the Chinese church. Liu served as the principal of the Kaizhou Mennonite High School, and Wang became a teacher there. Wang also took charge of church youth activities. In 1940 the

James Liu (left) and Stephen Wang (right), Chinese Mennonite leaders.

Chinese Mennonite Conference elected Liu as its first chair.

The 1930s were difficult years for the Chinese church as it faced new opposition and stinging criticism. Many Chinese were growing suspicious of Christianity, charging that Chinese Christians simply accepted Western culture and corrupted China with foreign ideas. Unfortunately, the accusation was partly correct. Some mission workers had been too closely tied to Western politics and had preached their culture instead of Christ.

Nevertheless, native leaders like Wang and Liu struggled to make their faith authentically Christian and Chinese.

Wang believed that the church must reject the temptations of imperialism and nationalism. Christians have integrity only as they follow Jesus, he reasoned. In 1936 he wrote that he had no faith in "the Jesus of Christendom with its economic and military might." Rather, he looked to "the Jesus of the Galilean ministry and the redemptive work in Jerusalem." This Jesus, Wang said, "is being discovered by and is discovering the young men and women of China today."[3]

The church faced other difficulties as well. War with Japan and civil strife that ended in revolution turned Chinese society upside down after 1940, and all foreign missionaries had to leave. Fortunately, because the church had adopted the stand Stephen Wang had suggested, it was able to survive the unrest and difficult circumstances.

Not all Mennonite groups around the world were as strong as the Chinese believers. In many cases mission churches lacked native leaders. In other places local Christians were waiting to be accepted and treated as friends. Hardship and migration had marked the lives of others, already wounded by war and famine. Nevertheless, the Mennonite family was larger than it had been at the turn of the century. Many Mennonites had learned to share and cooperate in new ways, and dozens had volunteered their lives for lifelong missionary service. Looking ahead, many Mennonites were hopeful about the future of their family of faith.

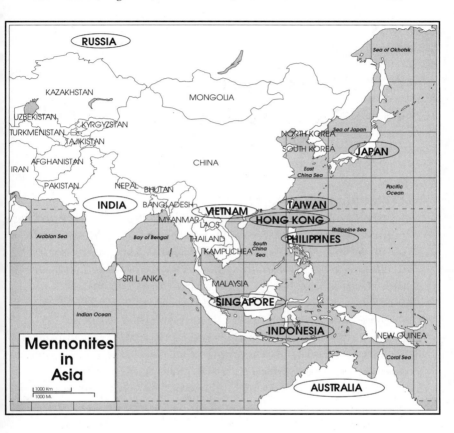

Mennonites in Asia

14

Learning to serve together, 1940-1970

"This thing is in our blood"

As nations around the globe mobilized forces during the Second World War (1939-1945), North American Mennonite young men needed to take a stand. Once again they had to decide whether or not they would go to war. In Canada, most Mennonites hoped to perform alternative civilian service instead of joining the armed forces.

Some military officials, on the other hand, wanted Mennonites to serve in the army medical corps. When church leaders rejected that idea, one officer decided to test the Mennonites' commitment.

"What will you do if we shoot you?" he asked the church leaders.

Jacob H. Janzen (1878-1950), an elder from Waterloo, Ontario, who had experienced the horrors of the Russian revolution before coming to Canada, responded quickly. "Listen, Major General, I want to tell you something. You can't scare us like that. I've looked down too many rifle barrels in my time to be scared in that way. This thing is in our blood for four hundred years, and you can't take it away from us like you'd crack a piece of kindling over your knee. I was before a firing squad twice. We believe in this."[1]

In the end, church and state reached an agreement on Alternative Service Work. Mennonites could spend time in a variety of work camps, fighting forest fires, reclaiming timber, or clearing land for the Trans-Canada Highway. Later the government reassigned most conscientious objectors (COs) to farm and factory work, but they remained civilians.

In the United States, a similar program known as Civilian Public Service (CPS) allowed Mennonites to work in forestry service, state psychiatric hospitals, and regional health projects. Fifty-four percent of drafted American Mennonites and 38 percent of conscripted Canadian Mennonites joined combatant or noncombatant wings of the military. A majority, however, selected alternative service as a way of making a constructive contribution in an increasingly destructive world. Though not faced with conscription, some women also took part in these service assignments.

In all, some seventy-five hundred Mennonites, Amish, Hutterites, and Brethren in Christ participated in Canadian Alternative Service. In the U.S. nearly forty-seven hundred served in CPS. Only a few COs ended up in jail because of their stand.

Most North American Mennonites fared relatively well during World War II. But many of their brothers and sisters in other parts of the world suffered considerably. The war destroyed Mennonite communities in eastern Germany and the Soviet Union. Mennonites in western Germany, France, and the Netherlands endured the conflict's intense bombing campaigns.

In China, Japanese forces imprisoned several Mennonite missionaries and disrupted church life. In Indonesia, Dutch colonial officials jailed two German Mennonite church workers. In both of these Asian countries, sporadic persecution broke out against Christians. Suspicious officials on both sides charged the church with supporting the enemy. Some fiercely anti-Christian groups used the chaos of wartime as an opportunity to attack believers.

An officer and a peacemaker

It was Christmas Eve 1941, and Siegfried Bartel was in the trenches on the Russian front. As a German army officer, he felt he had a duty to be with his men during the holiday when they were separated from family.

"Listen to this," one of the soldiers said, and motioned for Siegfried to join him in the no-man's land between enemy lines. In the minus-43-degree weather, the ground acted as a conducting wire, and the soldier had attached a listening device to the earth.

Siegfried put on the headphones. He was startled by what he heard: the enemy troops were singing Christmas carols!

Siegfried suddenly realized that he "was hearing Russian soldiers singing about the birth of Christ. Were those enemy fighters also remembering warm family times as they sang?" he wondered. "Were they also wondering what 'peace on earth' meant during times of war?"

Although Siegfried was a Mennonite, he had had no problem with joining the army four years before. His church had supported his decision to enlist. As the war continued, however, he occasionally had some moments of doubt. He was deeply disturbed when he had to order a military execution, but he tried to quickly extinguish his misgivings by reminding himself of his patriotic duty.

After the German surrender, he was able to reunite with his wife, Erna, and their sons in western Germany. In 1951 they emigrated to British Columbia and began farming.

Siegfried never forgot his wartime memories or his lingering questions. Through years of Bible study and conversation with other Christians, he gradually came to what he called his "second conversion"—his acceptance of Christ's way of peace. He also experienced God's forgiveness and freedom from the guilt he had carried since the war.

In Canada, Siegfried spent many years working as an executive with Mennonite Central Committee. Later he often traveled to share his story in churches across North America. Wherever he went, he wanted to tell people of the importance of God's call to peacemaking, and the forgiveness and joy that God offers to all.

Looking back, Siegfried still remembers that Christmas Eve on the front: "My pacifism, which I cherish so much today, may have been born on that moment."[2]

■ ■ ■

Reshaping the church

The effects of the war were long lasting and profound. In North America the generation who spent years in alternative service were eager to find new opportunities for witnessing and sharing. These young people used their vision and energy to initiate scores of creative ministries for neighbors near and far, such as community evangelism and church planting, church-sponsored mental health care, Mennonite Disaster Service, and the SELFHELP Crafts program.

At the same time, Mennonite mission activity around the world expanded as never before. During this time, North American and European church workers took the gospel to more than fifty new locations. Although Mennonite missions had been active before 1940, the Mennonite church truly became a worldwide family during the postwar decades.

Equally significant were the political changes which followed the war. Asian and African peoples who had watched Europeans fight totalitarian oppression started seeking their own freedom from colonial rule. Mission churches increasingly felt the tension between native independence and Western interference. During the 1960s many Mennonite mission churches became self-sustaining. Native leaders also emerged and assumed responsibility for church life and work.

All of these events, growing out of the ashes of war, profoundly reshaped the emerging Mennonite family.

Reaching out in North America

During the 1940s, and 1950s, North American Mennonites launched major evangelism and church-planting efforts. Some undertakings, like the outdoor tent revival meetings which thrived after 1951, called members of older Mennonite communities to new faith and deeper commitment. Other mission efforts, however, took Mennonites into dozens of new communities. Mission advocate Joseph D. Graber (1900-1978) urged every congregation to have a mission outpost. Dozens of families left established homes and moved to new communities, where they helped nurture young churches.

These church planting efforts took Mennonites into urban centers such as Winnipeg, New York City, and Denver, as well as rural regions such as Alberta's Peace River Valley and Michigan's Upper Penisula. The scores of new congregations which formed during these years began to shift Mennonite populations away from their historic communities and enlarged the church's fellowship to include people of many backgrounds. Within several decades, cities such as Vancouver, Los Angeles, and Toronto became home to hundreds of Mennonites who were Chinese, Cambodian, Indonesian, Lao, and Vietnamese.

Meanwhile, Mennonite young people also urged their church to take a role in reforming mental health services. Conditions in American mental hospitals shocked the fifteen hundred CPS volunteers assigned to psychiatric work during World War II. Overcrowded and underfunded, state mental facilities seemed more like prisons than places where people received help and care. Some patients even suffered violent treatment at the hands of frustrated, overworked hospital employees.

Alarmed by what they saw, CPSers asked their church to establish mental health centers where patients could receive proper care in a Christian environment. In 1947 Mennonites began Brook Lane Psychiatric Center near Hagerstown, Maryland. Soon other church-related hospitals opened in California, Indiana, Kansas, Manitoba, Ontario, and Pennsylvania.[3]

Mennonite Disaster Service (MDS) was another grassroots service effort which emerged after the Second World War. In 1950 a group of former CPS workers from Hesston, Kansas, organized a group to help with cleanup and repair after natural disasters. The next year heavy rains sent the Little Arkansas River over its banks, flooding Wichita. The Mennonites went into action, filling sandbags and building dikes.

Soon MDS units organized in other states and provinces. Since then thousands of volunteers have scooped mud from flooded homes, cleared tornado and hurricane wreckage, and rebuilt ruined structures.

Through the years MDS teams also assisted survivors of other tragedies. In the 1960s, for example, MDS volunteers helped rebuild five African-American and two Choctaw Indian church buildings which had been fire-bombed by racial terrorists.

A third postwar endeavor offered Mennonites the opportunity to help economically disadvantaged women in other parts of the world. In 1946 Edna Ruth Miller Byler (1904-

Edna Ruth Byler selling some of her early SELFHELP needle-point products from the Middle East, 1965.

1976) of Akron, Pennsylvania, traveled to Puerto Rico with her husband to visit CPS volunteers working on the island. There Byler met Olga Reimer Martens (1913-1989) and Mary Hottenstein Lauver (1916-1990), who were organizing a women's sewing project.

Martens and Lauver encouraged Puerto Rican women to embroider traditional designs on napkins and tablecloths with the hopes of later selling the finished pieces to American tourists. When Byler saw the beautifully crafted linens, she decided to buy the embroidery herself and market it directly in North America.

Sales were so successful that Byler continued purchasing native needlework, selling it from her home and in churches across North America. By returning her profits to the producers, Byler helped skilled women support themselves and their families. "I'm just a woman trying to help other women," she often told people who asked about her vision and commitment.[4]

Gradually she added crafts from many other countries, included products made by men, and developed the Mennonite Central Committee SELFHELP Crafts program. Today SELFHELP continues to market the crafts of artisans from around the world who would otherwise be unemployed or underemployed.

Growth around the world

As the development of the SELFHELP Crafts program shows, the Mennonite world was becoming increasingly global and interconnected. Mission and service tied churches together across continents.

During the late 1940s and 1950s, Mennonite young people served in the PAX (Latin for *peace*) program, rebuilding ruined towns in Germany and Austria. Others constructed homes for refugees in Algeria or assisted with relief work following the Korean War (1950-1953). After 1962 North American Mennonite schoolteachers began volunteering for service in Africa through the Teachers Abroad Program.

In places like Taiwan (Republic of China), Mennonite efforts to care for physical and spiritual needs gave birth to new Mennonite churches. In 1948 MCC medical volunteers arrived in Taiwan to assist Canadian Presbyterian missionaries. Mennonites established mobile medical units to serve people living in the Taiwanese mountains and opened several eye clinics in coastal towns. Six years later, an MCC volunteer couple partnered with local Taiwanese Christians and began a weekly Sunday school in their community. Each Sunday, a local accordion player roamed the town announcing it was time for the school to begin.

When the autumn weather cooled, MCC constructed a small building for the Sunday school. Soon regular worship services and evening Bible studies began, and American

Children gathered on Sunday afternoon in a "street Sunday school" behind a Buddhist temple, with Paul Lin, youthful pastor in the church in Taiwan, telling the story of the lost sheep.

mission workers arrived to help shepherd the emerging congregation. The group organized as a Mennonite church in 1955 with a Taiwanese minister, Samuel Hsieh, as its first pastor. Within months the group opened a neighborhood kindergarten.

About the same time, MCC founded the Mennonite Christian Hospital in the city of Hualien. Today it remains an important medical facility in Taiwan. Gradually, the Taiwanese assumed responsibility for the hospital and other mission projects on the island. By 1964 seven congregations formed the Fellowship of Mennonite Churches in Taiwan. Foreign mission workers are only advisers and assistants.

An explosion of mission

The decades following 1945 saw an explosion of worldwide Mennonite mission activity. Between 1946 and 1966, Mennonites opened mission work in fifty-two new places, expanding the Mennonite global fellowship.

Witmarsum Mennonite Church in the state of Santa Catarina, Brazil.

Mennonite bookstore, Cuauhtémoc, Mexico.

The spear of the Moros

Through their mission, Light to the Indians, Russian Mennonite settlers in Paraguay tried to reach out to neighboring Native peoples. In 1958 the Mennonites decided to befriend members of the Moro tribe.

The Moros were a private people who had little contact with outsiders. Moreover, at the time many Moros were angry with all white settlers since a foreign oil company was pushing them off their land, and some of the firm's workers had brought new diseases into the area.

In August 1958 Mennonite missionaries David Hein and Kornelius K. Isaak (1928-1958), accompanied by a Lengua Indian guide, made the 223-kilometer trek to the Moros' territory. In September, the missionaries finally met a group of about fifty Moro men.

The Moros reacted angrily, and one man threw a sharp spear which hit Isaak. Back at the Mennonite hospital, Isaak died, praying for the Moro people.

Years later, through contacts with other missionaries, some of the Moros became Christians. In 1988 they visited the Mennonite colony of Filadelfia and met Isaak's family. The Mennonites and the Moros expressed sorrow and forgiveness for what had happened thirty years before.

Symbolizing their reconciliation, Mary Born Isaak and her grown children posed for a picture with Jonoine, the man who had killed their husband and father. Despite what had happened, they stood together as brothers and sisters in Christ.

■ ■ ■

In 1950 French Mennonites began mission work in the Chad. Two years later, the French joined Dutch, German, and Swiss Mennonites in forming the European Mennonite Evangelization Committee. The group began sponsoring church work in Asia and Africa, as well as in Europe.

Meanwhile, North American Mennonites began planting churches in Colombia, the Dominican Republic, Mexico, and nearly a dozen other Latin American countries. In 1951 MCC volunteers John R. and Clara A. Regier Schmidt of Mountain Lake, Minnesota, worked with Paraguayan Mennonites to pioneer a new mobile treatment program for Hansen's disease (leprosy).

The Schmidts' clinic, commonly called Kilometer 81 because of its location along a national highway, cares for patients in their villages. The program allows those with leprosy to continue physical therapy and exercise at home instead of spending days confined in a hospital. The clinic's work has been quite successful.

"Scales fell from my eyes"

In Japan, Mennonite missionaries faced unique cultural obstacles. Many Japanese associated Christianity with the American forces which occupied their islands following World War II. Hence, some were suspicious of the church's message. Yorifumi Yaguchi (b. 1933), who later became a leader in the Japanese Mennonite church, doubted all organized religion because of its role in justifying violence. He was skeptical of Christians who preached about the Prince of Peace and then dropped atomic bombs.

However, Yaguchi embraced the church after he learned that not all Christians approved of killing. As he described it, "When I first met some pacifist Christians, it was a big shock." The Mennonite missionaries explained that "they had not fought but had obeyed God. They had been critical of their own government and had been praying for the

Mennonites Down Under

After World War II, many people left the ruins of Europe and started new lives "down under" in Australia and New Zealand. Among these settlers were Dutch Mennonites Foppe and Aaltje Hazenberg Brouwer.

In 1964-1965 while on a family vacation in the Netherlands, the Brouwers attended Foppe's home church. They received baptism and returned to Australia eager to establish contact with Australian Mennonites.

The Brouwers placed an advertisement in a Dutch-language Australian newspaper and asked other immigrant Mennonites to write to them. Eventually, they built a mailing list of several hundred and began producing a Mennonite newsletter.

In 1978 the Brouwer's home congregation in the Netherlands ordained them for ministry. The next year the first Australian congregation organized under their leadership in Fennel Bay, New South Wales.

More recently their congregation began the Care and Share ministry, which provides low-cost fresh fruits and vegetables to Fennel Bay residents who otherwise could not easily buy them.

Other Australians, such as Ian (b. 1940) and Ann Duckham, also caught the Anabaptist vision and began church work on the continent's west coast. These leaders, along with several North American mission workers, are nurturing the Mennonite witness down under.

■ ■ ■

Japanese people during the war. It was a revelation for me. Scales fell from my eyes, and I could finally see the work of Christ."[5]

For several years, MCC sponsored a peace ambassador in Tokyo. One person who joined the church through this witness was economics professor Gan Sakakibara (1898-1994). Committed to spreading the gospel of reconciliation, Sakakibara wrote a number of books on Anabaptism, including *The Anabaptist Heritage of Conscientious Objection* (in Japanese).

In addition to planting new Mennonite fellowships, missionaries also partnered with other denominations and assisted existing churches. In 1954 Mennonites helped organize the interchurch United Mission to Nepal. Five years later Mennonite Bible teachers responded to the invitation of an African Independent Church (AIC) in Nigeria. The AIC has native Christian groups developed without direct connections to Western missionary work. Although AICs are self-supporting, several asked Mennonite teachers to join them in ministry. By the late twentieth century, Mennonites had worked with AICs in more than six countries.

Independence

While Mennonite church planting and mission activity was increasing, another significant change took place among the world's younger churches. Across Africa and Asia, national independence movements gained strength and forced Western colonial powers to grant them freedom.

After World War II, India (in 1947) and Indonesia (1949) were among the first nations to achieve independence. Then the West African nation of Ghana (1956) became the first of dozens of new states to emerge on that continent. In 1960 and 1961 alone, nineteen new African countries were born. By 1970 few colonies remained.

This new wave of nationalism and political independence had important implications for younger churches. First, the

Africa Inter-Mennonite Mission

Mennonite missionaries Stan Nussbaum and Jim Egli work with African Independent Church leaders in Lesotho in the early 1980s.

governments of many new nations wanted Western missionaries to go home. The Indian government, among others, decided to gradually reduce the number of foreign church workers in the country. As the missionaries left, native Christians took control of their church's witness, finances, and administration.

In other cases, governments did not force missionaries to leave, but the independence movements made local Christians eager to assume more responsibility. Most missionaries also understood that locally administered churches would have more integrity in the new independent states. Nevertheless, the transition from mission control to local control was not always easy. In many cases the process took years and sometimes involved misunderstandings and confusion.

Many native leaders emerged in the newly independent Mennonite churches. Although missionaries had long ordained native evangelists and ministers, leaders with broader authority now rose to guide their people. Among this new generation of leaders were Pyarelal J. Malagar (b. 1920) and

Zedekia Marwa Kisare (b. 1912). In 1955 Malagar became the first Indian leader of the Mennonite Church in India. Twelve years later Kisare was ordained as the first native head of the Tanzanian Mennonite Church.

Digging his own grave

Sometimes freedom from the rule of oppressive foreigners led to divisive ethnic strife and civil war. In some places Mennonites were caught in the battlefields of revolution.

In 1960 the Belgian Congo (now Zaire) became an independent state. Unprepared for freedom by its former colonial rulers, the new nation plunged into ethnic violence. Some Zairian rebel groups, associating Christianity with the old colonial government, attacked the churches.

One night soldiers captured Mennonite pastor Kasai Kapata. "We shall not hear your preaching any longer; that we will end," they said.[6]

The rebels ordered Kasai to dig his own grave with a hoe. After forcing him into the pit, the soldiers covered him with dirt up to his neck. Unable to agree on how to kill Kasai, the soldiers left, arguing with one another. Three days later, one of the rebels returned. Quietly he dug the pastor out. As a boy he had been one of Kasai's Sunday school students, and he did not want to see Kasai executed.

Other Mennonite leaders were not so fortunate. Rebel leaders murdered one of Kasai's co-pastors, Kakesa Pierre. In some cases ethnic tensions surfaced among the Mennonites. Even so, some leaders tried to work as peacemakers during the civil strife.

When rival ethnic groups threatened to attack one another near the village of Zairian Mennonite Pastor Kuamba, he called the factions to reconcile. Armed only with his Bible, Kuamba walked between the shouting bands of warriors and cried out, "My friends, . . . my kinsmen. Why are you rushing into the direction of fighting rapidly like this? Take

Africa Inter-Mennonite Mission

Ngongo David, longtime pastor and second president of the Mennonite Church in Zaire, 1961-1971. He served during the transition to national church control.

your thinking out of the path of war. Don't you fear the warnings of our ancestors about shedding human blood? Fighting will destroy everything. It will divide us perpetually. We are Christians. There is another way to resolve our differences." Moved by his appeal, local leaders agreed to negotiate their differences.[7]

"Always looking and praying"

By the late 1960s, the Mennonite family had spread to many countries. More importantly, many new fellowships were independent and self-supporting. Although the transition had often been difficult, administration was passing to local, native Christians.

More significant was the witness that continued. Tanzania's bishop Kisare likely spoke for many new leaders: "My greatest fulfillment as bishop hasn't been in adminis-

Africa Inter-Mennonite Mission

Africa Inter-Mennonite Mission

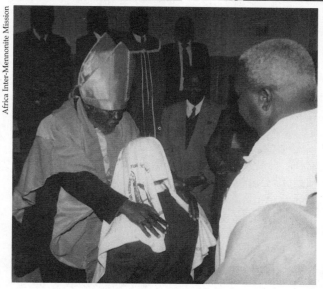

Africa Inter-Mennonite Mission

These photos illustrate a significant event in 1994. Since 1981, Mennonites Jonathan and Mary Kay Larson had served the church in Botswana. African Independent Churches in Gaborne, Botswana, ordained Bible teacher Jonathan Larson. He had been licensed as a Mennonite pastor in North America but was never ordained before going to Africa. The AICs in Botswana requested permission from the General Conference Mennonite Church to ordain him; permission was happily granted. Keynote speaker was seventy-one-year-old bishop Jackson Mbakile of Christ the Word of God Church, who had studied under Larson for ten years. The ordination itself was led by Archbishop Israel Motswasele of the Spiritual Healing Church.

tration. My greatest joy has always been in seeing men and women come into a right relationship with God. I am always looking and praying for God's breaking into our congregations through the Holy Spirit, bringing men and women into a right relationship with each other and with God."[8] Around the world many Mennonites shared Kisare's joy and joined him in prayer.

Mennonite high schools

An important part of North American Mennonites' mission in recent years has been the ministry of church-sponsored secondary education. Each year Mennonite schools provide thousands of young people with an education that combines knowledge, faith, and service.

Before 1900 several Mennonite communities sponsored secondary schools, but most of these institutions later evolved into liberal arts colleges. In Canada, the arrival of thousands of Russian Mennonites in the 1920s and 1930s, revived interest in church schooling. During the 1940s, these immigrants helped launch secondary institutions across the provinces. Their schools often drew on the long Russian Mennonite tradition of church-sponsored education.

In the United States, Mennonite high schools emerged for the most part after World War II. Some parents and church leaders grew concerned with the nationalism promoted in public schools, while others objected to the secular atmosphere they saw in public classrooms and athletics.

Over time, Mennonite secondary education has changed significantly. Earlier, church high schools often tried to shield students from certain academic subjects, or to promote knowledge of German culture and language. Today, however, Mennonite secondary schools are committed to integrating faith and learning. Schools are no longer places to withdraw from the world, but rather places where young people can engage the world with informed minds and Christian perspectives.

Changing student bodies represent another important shift. At one time these institutions served primarily young people from ethnic-German Mennonite families. But by the late twentieth century, growing numbers of students from a variety of racial, ethnic, and religious backgrounds enrolled each year.

The Canadian Association of Mennonite Schools (CAMS) and the Mennonite Secondary Education Council (MSEC) coordinate the work of twenty-three secondary schools spread across ten states, five provinces, and Puerto Rico. Several smaller Mennonite groups also sponsor independent church-related high schools.

■ ■ ■

Caribbean Sea

North
Atlantic
Ocean

VENEZUELA

GUYANA

COLOMBIA

SURINAME

ECUADOR

PERU

BRAZIL

South
Pacific
Ocean

BOLIVIA

CHILE

PARAGUAY

URUGUAY

ARGENTINA

South
Atlantic
Ocean

**Mennonites
in
South America**

500 Km

500 Mi.

FALKLAND

SOUTH
GEORGIA

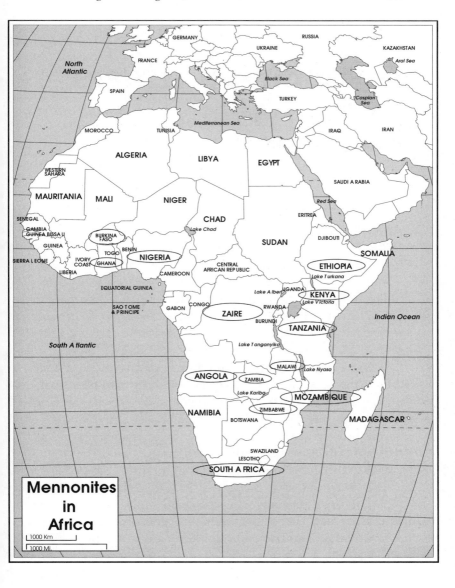

Mennonites
in
Africa

15

Becoming partners in a global community

African Anabaptism

Raymond Affouka Eba grew up in the West African country of Côte d'Ivoire. The only son of an important village leader, he quickly became a successful businessman. Spiritually, however, he found himself searching. For a number of years, he experimented with occult powers. Later he became heavily involved in secret societies, trying to find meaning in the ritualistic and mystical practices of these groups.

Then in 1984 at age thirty-three, Eba discovered in Christianity the peace and purpose for which he had been looking. He became an active evangelist and church planter, and he used his business profits to support young churches. As a pastor he won the respect of many believers and soon had oversight of 268 congregational cell groups.

Many Christians looked to Eba for guidance, and he began instructing local church leaders. In addition to presenting Bible studies, Eba began teaching the new pastors about church history. During his own study, Eba came across the Anabaptist movement. Although the sixteenth-century Radicals had lived centuries earlier in a culture quite different from his own, they grabbed his attention. Three Anabaptist characteristics in particular attracted Eba: their understanding of the Bible and their approach to it, "the spirit of peace" prevalent among Anabaptist groups, and the Anabaptists' understanding of the Lord's Supper in which Jesus was believed to be present in the gathered community rather than in the bread and wine. Pastor Eba was excited about his new discovery. "The more I study the Anabaptists," he said, "the more I realize that being converted means being born anew, so one's whole life is changed. The quality of life in Christ is the proof of conversion."

After praying and fasting, Eba decided to create a West African version of the churches formed by the early Anabaptists. "I felt God called me to start this Anabaptist church," he recalls. In 1994 he launched the Protestant Anabaptist Church of Côte d'Ivoire. The initial group of sixteen members quickly grew. Two years later, the fellowship had about two hundred members.

In 1995 Eba met James Krabill, a Mennonite mission worker teaching in Côte d'Ivoire. Although Eba expressed interest in learning about North American Mennonites, Krabill knew that Eba's group was "going to be an Anabaptist church no matter what we [North Americans] either said or did." The new fellowship was an indigenous expression of faith. Pastor Eba "came to Anabaptism and actually started a denomination and nine churches without ever meeting a Western missionary," Krabill realized.

Still, Eba anticipates building connections with Anabaptist churches in other parts of the world. Krabill provided Eba with French-language editions of Anabaptist works, and both of them hope that Pastor Eba may be able to link with other Anabaptist communities, possibly through Mennonite World Conference.[1]

Cooperative witness

Raymond Eba's experience illustrates some of the emerging patterns of mission and ministry around the world. Indigenous Christian movements increasingly take the lead in

Cooperating with other Christians

In addition to cooperating with one another, Mennonites have also begun working with other Christian groups.

Six Canadian denominations participate with MCC Canada in the work of the Canadian Foodgrains Bank. Developed in 1975 by MCC staff person John R. Dyck (1913-1988) of Winnipeg, Manitoba, the Foodgrains Bank gives farmers an opportunity to share their resources with others in need. The Bank manages grain supplies which church aid agencies use for famine relief.

During the 1970s and 1980s, MCC and the Baptist World Alliance cooperated in the huge task of translating and publishing Russian-language Bible commentaries for Christians in the Soviet Union. Soviet Baptist leaders chose the commentaries and proofread the Russian translation. British Baptists prepared the printing plates, and American Mennonites printed and bound the books.

MCC coordinator Peter J. Dyck (b. 1914) called the project "a leap of faith" since Baptists and Mennonites produced the commentaries before they had official permission to send them to Russia. Just as the volumes were finished, the Soviet government allowed churches to import 150,000 volumes.

Mennonites have also joined other historic peace churches in bringing the message of reconciliation. In 1987 Mennonites and the Church of the Brethren began sponsoring Christian Peacemaker Teams (CPTs). CPT members place themselves in violent situations around the world. Using prayer, negotiation, and direct action, team members become a presence of peace and seek to reduce hostility and tension.

■ ■ ■

sharing God's good news with their neighbors. Meanwhile, North American Mennonites are learning how best to help these young churches, while working to increase connections between Anabaptist believers around the world. By the later twentieth century, growing cooperation and partnership in the global community were becoming an important part of the church's witness.

No longer do missionaries come only from Europe and North America. Mennonite fellowships in Africa, Asia, and Latin America have begun sending their own church workers to neighboring peoples. In the mid-1960s, the Indonesian Mennonite Muria Christian Church organized its own mission agency. Soon they planted congregations in their country's populous capital city, Jakarta. Later they sent missionaries to other Indonesian islands. At times they invited European and North American Mennonites to join them as partners in their new Asian mission projects.

There have been other cooperative ventures as well. In 1971 Argentine and North American Mennonites began a joint mission in Bolivia. In the mid-1970s another mission and service partnership developed in Colombia. There Colombian Mennonites have been cooperating with MCC and North American businesspeople through Mennonite Economic Development Associates (MEDA). The three-way partnership combines agricultural development, health care, and other social services.

Full circle

In some cases mission has moved full circle. Mennonite fellowships begun with the help of North American church workers now send missionaries to the United States. One example is the Amor Viviente (Living Love) Church in Honduras.

In 1973 American church planters opened a youth coffeehouse near a Tegucigalpa high school. The center offered

Eastern Mennonite Missions, by Dale D. Gehman

The Amor Viviente congregation in Tegucigalpa, Honduras, in celebrative worship.

teens a place to socialize, share their problems, and talk with trained counselors. Coffeehouse Bible studies eventually gave birth to the Amor Viviente Church. The new congregation committed itself to ministering to the whole person. This included establishing a drug and alcohol rehabilitation and treatment center. The church's practical involvement in the community and Spirit-filled worship services drew others to the congregation. Members met in small house fellowships around the city, inviting neighbors and friends to join them.

Amor Viviente's witness soon moved beyond Honduras. In the 1980s the church sent missionaries to Spain and the United States. A decade later the group had planted congregations in Costa Rica, Louisiana, New York, and Florida.

Increasingly, Mennonite global witness is carried by younger churches apart from Western mission efforts. During the 1970s, for example, Zairian Mennonites ministered to Angolan refugees fleeing their country's civil war. Through the Zairian witness, several Mennonite fellowships developed among the Angolans. In the 1980s when the refugees returned home, they took their new faith with them and established the Evangelical Mennonite Brethren Church of Angola.

Twentieth-century persecution

Although friendly cooperation and pleasant church growth are important themes in recent Mennonite life, they are not the whole story. Suffering and persecution have also been a major part of many peoples' lives. Although some North American Mennonites assume that the age of the martyrs ended with the *Martyrs Mirror*, it did not. In fact, the twentieth century has produced more Christian martyrs than any other.

Mennonite Christians, like Colombian church leader José Chuquin, have been among those killed for their faith. Chuquin was committed to working nonviolently to help the poor and oppressed, but in 1991 guerrilla soldiers killed him while he traveled with an evangelical aid worker in Peru.

During the 1980s, political violence was an almost daily fact of life for some Latin American Mennonites. International tensions between the United States and the Soviet Union ignited regional conflicts in Central America. Honduran Mennonites living near their country's border with Nicaragua responded to the fighting by sheltering Nicaraguan refugees.

In retaliation, on Palm Sunday 1986, U.S.-supported Nicaraguan Contra rebels crossed the border and took over the Honduran Moriah Mennonite Church building. Turning the meetinghouse into a military base, the soldiers attacked local Christian families and captured Nicaraguan refugees they hoped to force into their militia. Nevertheless, the Honduran Mennonites continued to shelter refugees as they were able.

This experience made many Honduran Mennonites more conscious of their Christian responsibility to witness for peace and care for others. One church leader described his acceptance of Christian nonviolence as his second conversion. "I've been converted twice. Maybe my conversion to

Call him "missionary": Mennonites and the Vietnam War

Like other Asian and African colonies, Vietnam declared its independence after World War II. After years of struggling against its former French rulers, the country plunged into a long and bitter civil war. When the United States took sides in the conflict, hundreds of thousands of American troops became involved in the fighting.

Beginning in 1954, North American Mennonites were active in Vietnam. By the mid-1960s, a small Vietnamese Mennonite Church formed.

As the war grew more intense, American Mennonites in Vietnam found themselves in a difficult situation. They were citizens of a nation at war, yet trying to represent the kingdom of God.

Some Vietnamese understood the Mennonites' dilemma. When children in Saigon called Mennonite volunteer Luke S. Martin (b. 1933) an *American*, a Vietnamese adult corrected them: "Call him *missionary*," the man instructed the children. "The missionary does not kill Vietnamese."[2]

Others were less willing to accept the church's presence. Guerrilla forces captured Mennonite hospital volunteer Daniel Gerber (1940-1962?) of Kidron, Ohio. Gerber was never heard from again.

Vietnamese church members also felt the conflict's pressures. During the war the Saigon government forced several Vietnamese Mennonites into the army. At least one, Phan van Khai, deserted the military rather than kill others. Sheltered by his congregation for the rest of the war, he avoided arrest.

Back in the United States, other Mennonite young men also faced conscription. Most chose alternative service, but some refused to cooperate with the military system and moved to Canada.

When the struggle ended in 1975, virtually all foreigners fled Vietnam. Four MCC workers were among the handful of Westerners who remained to work with the church. Today Vietnamese Mennonites affiliate with the Evangelical Church of Vietnam. In 1995 Vietnamese Mennonites began meeting publicly again. The next year the government returned the group's church building, confiscated twenty years earlier.

■ ■ ■

the love of neighbor was really my first conversion. I used to think that salvation was something just for me."[3]

By 1995 Honduran Mennonites had helped lead a successful drive to amend their country's constitution and end obligatory military service during peacetime.

The church goes underground

During the 1980s, perhaps no Mennonites suffered more intensely than those in Ethiopia. Known as the Meserete Kristos Church (the church whose foundation is Christ), the Ethiopian Mennonite fellowship experienced a profound revival in 1974. In the words of church leader Dagne Assefa, "There was a new life and openness in the worship services" and "a new hunger for the word of God."

At the same time, a revolutionary movement drove the Ethiopian emperor from power. Although the new government did not immediately oppose the church, it became nervous as the revival-inspired Meserete Kristos Church grew. Officials pressured church members to join pro-government political groups. Several Mennonite school students spent time in prison for refusing to chant patriotic slogans.

Despite the pressure, the church continued to grow. "Because of its willingness to suffer for Christ," Assefa explained, the church "became a power that the government

Eastern Mennonite Missions, by D. Michael Hostetler

Community halls once used by the Marxist government for communist gatherings are now used by the Meserete Kristos Church for worship. Ethiopia, 1992.

had to reckon with. The more the government infringed upon the freedom of the church, . . . the more the work of God was done. When the government restricted the church from going out into the world in any manner, the world came to the church to see what God was doing."[4]

Finally in 1982, the state moved to crush the Meserete Kristos Church. The government took over all church property, programs, and money. Officials converted church buildings into political indoctrination centers. They also jailed six church leaders. For the next ten years, the Meserete Kristos Church went underground. Unable to meet publicly, members gathered in small groups in one another's homes. Although evangelism was illegal, they continued to invite neighbors and co-workers to join them.

Because the underground church was so secretive, not even church leaders knew the extent of its growth. Then in the early 1990s, when a new and more tolerant government

eased restrictions on the church, everyone had a big surprise.

The Meserete Kristos Church had five thousand members
before going underground. A decade later it emerged from
hiding with fifty thousand members and thousands more
waiting to be baptized. By the mid-1990s Ethiopian Mennonites counted some eighty-three thousand members. Eventually the new government returned church property and
allowed members to buy land for new buildings. Ten years
of persecution and opposition had not crushed the church—
it had multiplied it.

Singing old songs in a new land

Mennonites living in the Soviet Union also experienced up-
heaval mixed with joy during the 1980s and 1990s. Since the
end of World War II, Russian Mennonites had lived under
harsh Soviet rule. Because of their German ethnic background and their Christian convictions, the fifty-five thousand Russian Mennonites lost opportunities for education,
travel, and contact with their extended families. Eager for religious fellowship, many Mennonites affiliated with Baptist
churches.

In the mid-1980s, however, conditions in the Soviet Union
began to change rapidly. Soviet authorities allowed hundreds—and then thousands—of Mennonites to leave for
Germany. Germany offered religious and educational freedom, as well as better economic opportunities. Fearful that
the door of immigration might close at any time, Russian
Mennonite families hurried to pack their bags. By the mid-
1990s, after the collapse of the Soviet Union, fewer than four
thousand Mennonites remained in the new Commonwealth
of Independent States.

In Germany these ethnic German immigrants were known
as *Aussiedler* and accepted as returning citizens. For the Aussiedler, life in their new homeland was not always easy.

Festival Quarterly, by Kenneth Pellman

Russian Mennonite Aussiedlers (German resettlers) worship at a Mennonite Thanksgiving festival in Germany in 1979.

Although the Mennonites were still German in many ways, they were unfamiliar with various aspects of modern German culture. Germany was a foreign land to them.

Many Aussiedler organized independent congregations and continued traditional church practices from the Soviet Union. For example, most avoid costly clothing, jewelry, television, and films. Unpaid ministers serve congregations which sing old hymns with conviction and enthusiasm.

Even Germans who find Aussiedler practices quaint or unusual admit that these people are sincere and committed. While some of them identify themselves as Mennonites,

Eastern Mennonite Missions, by Dorothy Beidler

Luke Beidler and Pak Yakub, members of the missionary team in West Kalimantan, Indonesia, starting out for the weekend of teaching in the village of Jelemuk. Over one hundred persons attended the Bible classes and worship services.

many more consider themselves to be Baptists.

For those Mennonites still in the Soviet Union, new questions weigh heavily. Some wonder if they, too, should leave and join their brothers and sisters in Germany; others ask whether they should remain in Russia and join the Baptists. Many believe that the two-hundred-year-old Russian Mennonite story may be drawing to a close.

New experiences in worship and renewal

In addition to growing cooperation in mission and the persistence of suffering, late twentieth-century Mennonite life has also included a wide range of renewal movements and worship styles. Since 1970 many Mennonites have experienced the work of the Holy Spirit through the charismatic renewal movement. Especially important among some Latin American Mennonite groups, the movement has also touched Mennonites in Africa and North America.

Seeking deeper Christian fellowship and commitment, other Mennonites established intentional communities

Leonor de Méndez: a Guatemalan pastor's life

When María Leonor Argueta de Méndez remembers her childhood, she does not have warm, happy feelings. Raised in Guatemala City, Guatemala, Leonor was taken from her mother at an early age. For five years she and her sister lived with their father and stepmother, who beat them.

When a doctor reported the abuse, Leonor and her sister returned to their mother. But even then life was difficult.

"I was a very troubled person, very lonely," Leonor remembers. "I had few friends."[5]

As a teenager Leonor began attending a Pentecostal school where she found a new, more-stable life. Later she married Mario, a young Pentecostal minister. After a critical illness forced Mario to change jobs, the de Méndez family returned to Guatemala City and opened a printing business.

Maria Leonor de Méndez, from Guatemala, at the 1993 General Council meeting of the Mennonite World Conference in Bulawayo, Zimbabwe.

Festival Quarterly, by Merle Good

There Leonor started witnessing to neighbors and customers. She and Mario began a house church which eventually grew to include ninety people. Later this fellowship joined a nearby Mennonite congregation.

Leonor and Mario serve on the church's pastoral team. Leonor also preaches and teaches in several other Mennonite congregations in the city.

Leonor graduated from SEMILLA, the Central American Mennonite seminary based in Guatemala City. She has also represented Latin American Mennonites on the executive committee of Mennonite World Conference. Although she still mourns her lost childhood, Leonor has found a joy-filled Christian ministry as an adult.

"I have felt gradual growth and a sense of call," she said.

■ ■ ■

Festival Quarterly, by Merle Good

Worship time at the 1993 General Council meeting of the Mennonite World Conference in Bulawayo, Zimbabwe.

where members live together, share resources, and join in regular worship and service. Mennonite pastor José Gallardo helped establish one such intentional community in Burgos, Spain. By combining evangelism and practical service, the group developed an extensive ministry among the sick, homeless, and social outcasts of their community.

Bible study and leadership training have been another source of church renewal, especially among Mennonites in Africa, Asia, and Latin America. During the 1950s, Indonesian Mennonites opened their own seminary. Mennonites in Latin America established Bible schools and seminaries in several countries, as have Indians and Zaireans. African Mennonites and Brethren in Christ pioneered programs in Theological Education by Extension (TEE). TEE participants remain in their home communities instead of moving to central campuses, allowing pastors to continue working while they study.

Mennonites from many countries have also found strength through regional assemblies for worship and fellowship. African church members were among the first to gather in this way. In 1962 they formed the African Mennonite and Brethren in Christ Fellowship. Nine years later the first Asian Mennonite Conference assembled. The Mennonite European Regional Conference and the Central American Mennonite Conference soon followed.

These groups cooperate in a variety of projects. For example, the Central American Conference produced a Spanish-language Mennonite hymnal, *Alabanzas de libertad* (Praises of liberation). In 1973 during a severe Bangladeshi famine, the Asian Conference organized a worldwide Mennonite relief effort.

Growing in world fellowship

At the turn of the twenty-first century, no group represents the richness and diversity of the Mennonite family of faith better than Mennonite World Conference (MWC). Since its beginnings in 1925, MWC has continued to grow and expand in size and scope. In the 1990s, MWC related to 194 different Mennonite, Brethren in Christ, Amish, and Hutterite groups in 61 countries.

One of MWC's major tasks is sponsoring a worldwide assembly every six years or so. MWC has tried to expand participation beyond Europe and North America. In 1967 World Conference established a special travel fund to help members with fewer resources who wish to attend.

In 1972 MWC gathered for the first time outside Europe or North America, in Curitiba, Brazil. Delegates from thirty-three nations discussed the implications of the conference theme, "Jesus Christ Reconciles." That year MWC also elected its first non-Western president, Ethiopian pastor Million Belete.

By 1994 Argentine pastor and MWC president Raúl O. García (b. 1930) could announce that for the first time more Mennonites and Brethren in Christ lived in Africa, Asia, and

Latin America than in Europe and North America. As the end of the century approached, Mennonites were preparing for the 1997 world conference assembly in Calcutta, India.

More than fifty years earlier, Mennonite leader Martin C. Lehman (1883-1963) looked forward to a time when his church could experience a truly international communion service in which all "nations, races, and cultures" would participate. "We would all partake of the sacred emblems," Lehman wrote, "united in Christ Jesus; no race prejudice, humbly washing each other's feet—brown, black, and white."[6]

Today more members of the Mennonite family are beginning to catch Lehman's vision. Increasingly they realize that international partnership strengthens the faith community and it also enables the church to offer its most powerful witness to the larger world. Whenever Christians join across national, racial, and cultural barriers, they testify to God, who reigns over human divisions and unites disciples in love—a God who is always faithful.

Do you see many members forming one body in Christ?

Luis A. Lumibao (b. 1957) turned to run from the charging police. In the stampede of demonstrators, he fell and broke his left arm. But with a corrupt dictator ruling his homeland of the Philippines, Luis was afraid to go to the hospital for treatment. If he did, the police might arrest him.

Fear and anger were nothing new to Luis. The military had drafted him during his university days, issuing him an M-16 carbine and a Bible. Though he considered the pair a contradiction, the Filipino government refused to recognize conscientious objectors. Luis could not avoid the required military training, but he took part in protests against the dictatorship. Over the years, he used several aliases to avoid capture.

Nonviolent demonstrations eventually forced the dictator out, though the military has been slow to give up its power. Meanwhile, the former protestor has become a Mennonite church leader, teacher, and traveling pastor.

Luis grew up in the region of Pantabangan, five hours north of Manila. He first learned to know Mennonites when his community was facing a crisis. Neighbors and friends of Luis has been forced out of their valley homes, due to a controversial hydroelectric project. Mennonites, including James Metzler, offered assistance to people who had been displaced. Metzler led Luis to a renewed commitment to Jesus and to the Christian ideals Luis had partly absorbed as a child.

Today Luis travels to many parts of the Philippines, planting churches and teaching. Picture a modern-day apostle Paul riding an overcrowded bus up and down rugged mountain roads from one village to another. Before long, he's off to the next town.

The work is exhausting. And sometimes Luis gets frustrated

with older church members, many of whom aren't sure a
person who looks so young has enough experience to be a
pastor. Yet Luis has taught most of the Mennonite pastors and
church planters in the rural and urban areas of his country.
He feels energized by the growth of the Filipino Mennonite
Church.

In addition to serving Mennonites in his home country,
Luis is involved in the worldwide Mennonite fellowship. In

**Never one to seek a cushy lifestyle, Luis Lumibao rides rickety
buses on rough roads in the Philippines as he plants churches
and teaches new converts.**

the summer of 1990, a devastating earthquake struck the Philippines. Luis helped clear debris and carry bodies out of the rubble—including those of his own niece and cousin. Then he walked 100 kilometers to the airport and caught a flight to the Mennonite World Conference assembly, where he represented his local community to brothers and sisters from around the world.

At one time, Luis could not have imagined himself as a traveling evangelist. But God calls many different members—from various backgrounds and walks of life—to form one body in Christ.

Another leader is Naka Gininda (b. 1910), who has served for many decades as a Brethren in Christ pastor in the African nation of Zimbabwe. In the 1950s her household was among many families the colonial government forcibly relocated. Sad and lonely, the resettlers were without their familiar churches and pastors.

One person suggested they meet for worship anyway and perhaps form a house church. Naka Gininda recalls the surprise she received soon after that: "One Sunday I was late [for worship]; I sent my children on ahead. When I got to the service, I found that they had chosen me to be pastor."

Naka Gininda, busy mother of nine children, a pastor? "I was afraid! Oh, I prayed about it," she said. "God [promised to] give me the message, that I was just the instrument. Then I was no longer afraid."[1]

Indeed, villagers and other Brethren in Christ leaders quickly saw that Naka Gininda was a powerful woman of prayer. They also appreciated her sermons filled with Scripture quotations. She led village women in making bricks to construct a church building. When rebel soldiers sought to keep the group from worshiping there, the believers met around Naka Gininda's kitchen fire. Even after soldiers beat her severely and kidnapped one of her sons, she continued to deliver the messages God gave her.

Advancing age didn't stop her. Naka Gininda continued to serve her congregation well into her seventies. She also worked as an evangelist, spreading the gospel to people of surrounding villages. Having felt God's power in her own life, she wants others to experience it too. As Naka Gininda has learned, God does extraordinary things with ordinary people who are willing to listen and share.

Today Mennonite and Brethren in Christ churches from many countries, including the Philippines and Zimbabwe, support hundreds of full-time mission workers, engaged in all types of witness and service. They include former student activists like Luis Lumibao and busy grandmothers like Naka Gininda. God's ever-expanding work is not reserved for a few people who all look and act the same. By God's grace many different members are being built into one body around the world.

In the Mennonite fellowship spanning more than sixty nations and six continents, Europeans and North Americans are no longer in the majority. The Mennonite family speaks many languages, worships in a wide variety of ways, and looks quite different from one place to another.

If someone asks you, "What is a Mennonite?" what would you say? How do you feel about the family of faith including so many races and cultures? How do you see many members forming one body in Christ (Romans 12:5)?

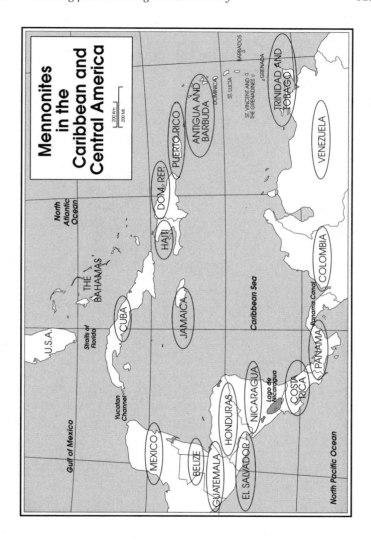

Epilogue

Continuing the Anabaptist story: A twenty-first-century faith

Being a part of the story

When Luis Correa (b. 1938), a pastor in Colombia, explains why he is a Mennonite, he thinks of stories. Some are experiences of church members working for peace and justice in Latin America. Others involve friendships with Mennonites from other parts of the world.

Not all of his stories are pleasant. In one case, Correa left a congregation in deep disappointment. Yet he recalls all these stories of faith and failure as he sorts out who he is.

"For me history is very important," Correa says. "A people without history is a people without a future."

The biblical people of Israel also told stories when they talked about their relationship with God. Moses began with the wanderings of Abraham and Sarah when he explained who he was (Deuteronomy 26:5-10). Later Joshua told the same story—and added to it (Joshua 24:2-13). The writer of Psalm 136 and the priest Ezra did the same (Nehemiah 9:6-37). Early Christians such as Stephen (Acts 7) and Paul (Acts 13:16-41) continued to proclaim the ongoing drama.

All of these people grounded their faith in the history of God's faithfulness. As they came to know God—like Luis Correa—they joined the story and made it their own.

Faith and failure

Our overview of Mennonite history has covered centuries and crossed continents. Preachers and peasants, martyrs and missionaries, reformers and rascals have all played a part. Often their experiences were inspiring and heroic. Amazing accounts of courage and strength call us to greater faith. Stories of personal sacrifice and loving service encourage our deeper commitment. Everyday tales of God's work in ordinary lives give us hope. Their history is a source of strength, wisdom, and power.

But some aspects of the Anabaptist and Mennonite story are embarrassing and make us uneasy. Mennonites suffered failure and pain. Some were unfaithful, even hypocritical. At times they lost sight of God's activity and God's story.

When we encounter unfaithfulness or hypocrisy in our history, it is tempting to become disgusted and throw out our story. We may want to hide our past, embarrassed that it includes mistakes and failures. We may even get angry and reject our story as too narrow and confining. Often we're eager to forget our history and want to start all over again. After all, we reason, we'd be better off simply being faithful in the present rather than bothering with the past.

"Having roots has a lot of value"

Although we may be tempted to ignore our stories—or even think of them as getting in the way of more important things—Luis Correa challenges us to remember and join in the telling. He reminds us that we are part of a larger family of faith, a family we know through its story. "Having roots," Correa observes, "has a lot of value."[1]

Roots provide nourishment and stability. They give us a place to begin and source from which to grow. In the heat of our lives, our roots keep us from withering. As one church leader observed, a neatly arranged bouquet may appear more attractive than an average flower bed. But, beautiful as they are, cut flowers cannot survive for long. Nor can they produce new seeds.

Like the people of Israel and the early Christians, today's church must know its story well enough to invite others to join in its telling and make it their own. Only when the family of faith knows its own roots will it be able to support new growth.

Christian faith

The Anabaptist and Mennonite story is not an isolated tale, growing by itself. It is part of a larger story, rooted in the Christian tradition. Menno Simons' favorite verse, 1 Corinthians 3:11, pointed to the basis of Mennonite faith: "For no one can lay any foundation other than the one that has been laid; that foundation is Jesus Christ." For Menno and other Anabaptists, salvation came through Jesus. Christians "are in Christ and Christ is in them," Menno said.[2]

Mennonites root their story deeply in the biblical drama. Uneducated Anabaptists were so closely connected to the story of Scripture they could debate leading theologians. Anabaptist writers filled their books and tracts with references to the biblical narrative. Twentieth-century Mennonites, such as Indonesian pastor Tee Siem Tat, have continued to search the Bible to keep their story firmly rooted in that story of God's redeeming action.

As Mennonites share their story, they must continue to rely on God's grace, Jesus' work, and the Holy Spirit's witness. Only as their experience grows out of a deep relationship with God will it continue to have meaning.

Reconciling ministry

Those who carry the Mennonite story have been especially concerned with continuing Christ's ministry of reconciliation. Salvation, as they proclaimed it, involves more than peace between God and individuals. It also brings love into all human relationships. "Christ never hated anyone," Felix Manz said, "neither did his true servants, but they continued to follow Christ in the true way."[3]

Offering the good news of salvation and reconciliation demands the rejection of violence. Discovering new paths of peacemaking has been central to this story. Mennonites like Confederate soldier Christian Good do not see anyone as an enemy. They seek instead to heal the injustice, abuse, and poverty which accompany broken relationships.

As Mennonites continue their story into the twenty-first century, the ministry of reconciliation will remain essential. In a world marked by violence and brokenness, peace and wholeness are desperately needed. But bringing the good news of healing to a hostile world takes enormous energy and solid commitment. Only deep roots can sustain that kind of peacemaking.

Covenant people

The church as a gathered body of believers played an especially important role in the Anabaptist and Mennonite story. The early Hutterite leader Peter Riedeman described the church as a "lantern of righteousness, in which the light of grace is borne and held before the whole world" so that everyone "may also learn to see and know the way of life."[4]

The church's life together has been essential in telling the story. Leaders like Mennonite Brethren minister Johann Claassen spent their lives trying to build the church into a community with a clear and consistent witness. Such a witness attracted future church leader Rowena Lark, and thousands of others around the world.

As Mennonites take their story into the future, they will need to carry it as a church. In a fragmented world torn by factions and rivalries, the church witnesses to a sovereign God. As brothers and sisters practice mutual aid and care for one another, they point to the reign of God. Their story of life together offers encouragement and hope to new generations.

Daily discipleship

Finally, those who carried the Anabaptist and Mennonite story have emphasized the importance of daily discipleship. *Nachfolge Christi* (following after Christ) was a regular theme in Anabaptist teaching and hymns. A song written by Michael Sattler and included in the Anabaptist's *Ausbund* hymnal begins with these lines: "When Christ with His teaching true, Had gathered a little flock, He said that each with patience, Must daily follow Him bearing his cross."[5]

For disciples like Michael Sattler, Mennonites who lived through the Russian revolution, or members of the Ethiopian Meserete Kristos Church, following Christ involved persecution and death. For others, such as Edna Ruth Miller Byler, listening to God's call meant marketing third-world crafts as "a woman trying to help other women." For countless others, everyday lives of kindness and morality offered a striking witness in a world of lies and compromise.

A twenty-first-century faith will be carried by believers who commit themselves to daily lives of honesty and integrity. At times, such faith commitments will also bring suffering and persecution. Only those rooted in daily discipleship can endure that kind of opposition.

These roots will nourish the Mennonite story as it continues into the future. As neighbors hear and claim the story for themselves, new lives will enrich the telling. And by God's grace, the drama will continue.

Notes

Introduction: Ghosts and echoes

1. For a longer version of this story, see John Allen Moore, *Anabaptist Portraits* (Scottdale, Pa.: Herald Press, 1984), 74-75.

2. For this tragic story, see Thieleman J. van Braght, *Martyrs Mirror of the Defenseless Christians* (Scottdale, Pa.: Herald Press, 1938), 481-482; and *Mennonite Encyclopedia* (Scottdale, Pa.: Herald Press, 1955-1959, 1990) 2:185.

3. This and other stories can be found in Fred Richard Belk, *The Great Trek of the Russian Mennonites to Central Asia, 1880-1884* (Scottdale, Pa.: Herald Press, 1976).

4. Gerlof D. Homan, *American Mennonites and the Great War, 1914-1918.* (Scottdale, Pa.: Herald Press, 1994), 104.

5. *The Weekly Budget*, Sugarcreek, Ohio, March 20, 1918, 2.

Chapter 1: The apostles build the church

1. See C. John Cadoux, *The Early Christian Attitude to War* (New York: The Seabury Press, 1982), 149-151.

2. Cadoux, 105; John Driver, *How Christians Made Peace with War* (Scottdale, Pa.: Herald Press, 1989). For Scripture samples on Jesus' peaceful teaching and life, see Matthew 5:44; 26:52; John 18:36.

Chapter 2: The church gains power and wealth

1. This chapter has benefited much from Kenneth Scott Latourette, *A History of Christianity* (New York: Harper and Brothers, 1953).

Chapter 3: Reformers shake the church

1. Roland H. Bainton, *Here I Stand: A Life of Martin Luther* (New York: Mentor Books, 1978), 15.

2. For this reply and other dramatic events, see Bainton, 140-145.

3. Bainton, 209-216.

Chapter 4: The Swiss Brethren break with Zwingli

1. See *The Chronicle of the Hutterian Brethren*, vol. 1, trans. and ed. by the Hutterian Brethren (Rifton, N.Y.: Plough Publishing House, 1987), 43-47. For this chapter, also see John Allen Moore, *Anabaptists Portraits.*

2. George H. Williams, ed., *Spiritual and Anabaptist Writers* (Philadelphia: The Westminster Press), 73-85.

3. Williams, 83.

4. *The Radicals,* 1989, produced by Sisters and Brothers, is available from Gateway Films/Vision Video or through Provident Bookstores.

5. For the Schleitheim text, see *The Schleitheim Confession,* trans. and ed. by John H. Yoder (Scottdale, Pa.: Herald Press, 1977). Scripture references are identified in the notes.

6. For an account of the trial, see *Martyrs Mirror,* 416-418.

7. Guy F. Hershberger, ed. *The Recovery of the Anabaptist Vision* (Scottdale, Pa.: Herald Press, 1957), 30-31.

8. Hershberger, 42-54; Harold S. Bender, *The Anabaptist Vision* (Scottdale, Pa.: Herald Press, 1944).

Chapter 5: Anabaptism develops in Holland

1. Menno Simons, *The Complete Writings of Menno Simons, c. 1496-1561,* trans. from the Dutch by Leonard Verduin and ed. by John Christian Wenger, with a biography by Harold S. Bender (Scottdale, Pa.: Herald Press, 1956), 670.

2. Quoted in Magdalene Redekop, "Escape from the Bloody Theatre: The Making of Mennonite Stories," *Journal of Mennonite Studies* 11 (1993): 10.

3. See the story of Swaen Rutgers in Harry Loewen, *No Permanent City: Stories from Mennonite History and Life* (Scottdale: Herald Press, 1993), 24-26.

Chapter 6: Radical reform comes in South Germany and Moravia

1. *Mennonite Encyclopedia,* 2:846.

2. *Mennonite Encyclopedia,* 2:849.

3. *Mennonite Encyclopedia,* 2:35.

4. *The Chronicle of the Hutterian Brethren,* 1:81.

5. Linda Huebert Hecht, "An Extraordinary Lay Leader: The Life and Work of Helene of Freyberg, Sixteenth Century Noblewoman and Anabaptist from the Tirol," *Mennonite Quarterly Review* 66 (July 1992): 336.

6. *The Chronicle,* 1:83.

7. *The Chronicle,* 1:145.

8. Walter Klaassen, ed., *Anabaptism in Outline: Selected Primary Sources* (Scottdale: Herald Press, 1981), 266.

9. Roland H. Bainton, "The Anabaptist Contribution to History," in *The Recovery,* ed. Hershberger, 317.

Is your life a witness?

1. Moore, *Anabaptist Portraits,* 98.

Chapter 7: Seeking peace and finding division, 1600-1750

1. Paul Klaeui, "Hans Landis of Zurich (d. 1614): The Last Swiss Anabaptist Martyr," *Mennonite Quarterly Review* 22 (Oct. 1948): 209, with quote adapted.

Chapter 8: Mennonites settle in North America, 1683-1860

1. This petition is reprinted in Richard K. MacMaster, et al., *Conscience in Crisis: Mennonites and Other Peace Churches in America 1739-1789, Interpretation*

and Documents, Studies in Anabaptist and Mennonite History, no. 20 (Scottdale, Pa.: Herald Press, 1979), 266-267.

2. Quoted in Titus Peachey and Linda Gehman Peachy, *Seeking Peace* (Intercourse, Pa.: Good Books, 1991), 101.

Chapter 9: War and renewal, 1860-1940

1. Peter S. Hartman, *Reminiscences of the Civil War* (Lancaster, Pa.: Eastern Mennonite Associated Libraries and Archives, 1964), 10-11. Peter Hartman (1846-1934) lived in Virginia's Shenandoah Valley during the Civil War.

2. Hubert L. Brown, "The Larks: Mission Workers," in *Mennonite Yearbook, 1981* (Scottdale, Pa.: Mennonite Publishing House, 1981), 9.

Chapter 10: Mennonites move to Prussia and Russia, 1750-1850

1. C. Henry Smith, *Story of the Mennonites,* Newton, Kan.: Faith & Life Press, 1981) 169. See also P. M. Friesen, *The Mennonite Brotherhood in Russia,* (Fresno, Calif.: Board of Christian Literature, 1978), 48-49.

2. For an informative book on Low German, see Reuben Epp, *The Story of Low German and Plautdietsch* (Hillsboro, Kan.: The Reader's Press, 1993).

3. See Smith, *Story of the Mennonites,* 177.

4. The practice of ministers wearing boots was based on the German translation of Ephesians 6:15 ("gestiefelt"—wearing boots). The King James Version reads, "your feet shod with the preparation of the gospel of peace."

Chapter 11: The Mennonite commonwealth in Russia, 1850-1917

1. P. M. Friesen, *The Mennonite Brotherhood,* 198. On Cornies, see also 190-199. The following articles on Cornies are helpful: Harvey L Dyck, "Russian Servitor and Mennonite Hero: Light and Shadow in Images of Johann Cornies," *Journal of Mennonite Studies* 2 (1984): 9-28; and "Agronomist Gavel's Biography of Johann Cornies (1789-1848)," 29-41. Cf. Harry Loewen, "Reflections on Harvey L Dyck's Images of Johann Cornies," *Journal of Mennonite Studies* 3 (1985): 148-154.

2. Friesen, *The Mennonite Brotherhood,* 192-93.

3. Friesen, 190.

4. Friesen, 199.

5. Franz Isaac, *Die Molotschnaer Mennoniten* (Halbstadt, South Russia, 1908).

6. For a fine article on Klaas Reimer, see Al Reimer, "Klaas Reimer: Rebel Conservative, Radical Traditionalist," *Journal of Mennonite Studies* 3 (1985): 108-117.

7. Friesen, *The Mennonite Brotherhood,* 949-955.

8. John A. Toews, *A History of the Mennonite Brethren Church: Pilgrims and Pioneers* (Fresno: Board of Christian Literature, 1975), 31-32.

9. For the complete text of the Secession Document, see P. M. Friesen, *The Mennonite Brotherhood,* 230-232.

10. Quoted in Toews, *A History,* 84.

11. For a full-length study, see Belk, *The Great Trek.*

Chapter 12: Migration and loss, 1874-1945

1. Al Reimer, ed. and trans., in Dietrich Neufeld, *A Russian Dance of Death: Revolution and Civil War in the Ukraine* (Winnipeg: Hyperion, and Scottdale, Pa.: Herald Press, 1977), 84.

2. Reimer in Neufeld, *A Russian Dance,* 84-85.

3. On Nestor Makhno and the terror the Makhnovites spread, see Dietrich Neufeld, *A Russian Dance of Death;* Gerhard P. Schroeder, *Miracles of Grace and Judgement* (Lodi, Calif., 1974); and Victor Peters, *Nestor Makhno: The Life of an Anarchrist* (Winnipeg: Echo Books, 1970).

4. Smith, *Story of the Mennonites,* 315.

5. Neufeld, 80.

6. Neufeld, 80.

7. Smith, *Story of the Mennonites,* p. 321.

8. For a more complete story, see Harry Loewen, *No Permanent City,* 134-138.

9. Loewen, *No Permanant City,* 216.

10. Smith, *Story of the Mennonites,* 340.

Chapter 13: Mission, migration, and mutual aid, 1890-1940

1. *World Missionary Conference,* 1910: *The History and Records of the Conference: . . .* (New York: Fleming H. Revell [1910]), 9:315.

2. Multiculturalism became official federal policy in Canada in 1973.

3. Stephen Wang, "The Chinese Christians and Their Environment," *The Mennonite* 21 (Apr. 1936): 17.

Chapter 14: Learning to serve together, 1940-1970

1. Robert S. Kreider and Rachel Waltner Goossen, *Hungry, Thirsty, a Stranger: The MCC Experience* (Scottdale, Pa.: Herald Press, 1988), 61.

2. Quotations from Siegfried Bartel, *Living With Conviction: German Army Captain Turns to Cultivating Peace* (Winnipeg: Canadian Mennonite Bible College Publications, 1994).

3. In 1910 Russian Mennonites had opened a mental health institution in the Ukraine. After 1932 Henry and Magda (Maria) Unrau Wiebe, Russian Mennonite immigrants to Canada, opened their home near Stratford, Ontario, to patients needing mental health care. In 1947 the Mennonite Brethren Church took over their work, which became the Bethesda Mental Hospital, at Vineland. Thus, the Ontario hospital had a different background than the other institutions which grew out of the war experience.

4. Steven Nolt interview with William T. Snyder, Akron, Pa., 30 August 1989.

5. Dieter Götz Lichdi, ed., *Mennonite World Handbook, 1990: Mennonites in Global Witness* (Carol Stream, Ill.: Mennonite World Conference, 1990), 38.

6. John B. Toews, *The Mennonite Brethren Church in Zaire* (Fresno, Calif.: Board of Christian Literature, General Conference of Mennonite Brethren Churches, 1978), 145.

7. Levi O. Keidel, *War to Be One* (Grand Rapids, Mich: Zondervan, 1977), 122.

8. Zedekia Marwa Kisare, *Kisare: A Mennonite of Kiseru,* ed. Joseph C. Shenk (Salunga, Pa.: Eastern Mennonite Board of Missions and Charities, 1984), 111.

Chapter 15: Becoming partners in a global community
1. Tom Price, "New Anabaptist Church Emerges in Ivory Coast Independent of Mennonites," *Gospel Herald* 89 (May 7, 1996): 10.
2. Wenger, *A People in Mission*, 79.
3. A. Grace Wenger, *A People in Mission, 1894-1994* (Salunga, Pa.: Eastern Mennonite Missions, 1994), 68.
4. Assefa, Dagne, "Dis-Quest," *Festival Quarterly* 10.4 (Nov. 1983-Jan. 1984): 14.
5. Merle Good, "Pastor with a Lost Childhood," *Festival Quarterly* 20.3 (Fall 1993): 12-13.
6. Martin C. Lehman, *Our Mission Work in India* (Scottdale, Pa.: Mennonite Publishing House, 1939), 100.

Do you see many members forming one body in Christ?
1. Quotation from Mennonite Central Committee *Women's Concerns Report*, no. 81, Nov.-Dec. 1988.

Epilogue: Continuing the Anabaptist story: A twenty-first-century faith
1. Lichdi, *Mennonite World Handbook, 1990,* 49.
2. Menno Simons, *Writings,* 506.
3. *Martyrs Mirror,* 415.
4. Klaassen, *Anabaptism in Outline,* 112.
5. John Howard Yoder, trans. and ed., *The Legacy of Michael Sattler* (Scottdale, Pa.: Herald Press, 1973), 141.

Index

For further reading

To read more about the Anabaptist and Mennonite story, you can consult the notes and a wide variety of sources.

Two general histories survey the Anabaptist and Mennonite experience: Cornelius J. Dyck, *An Introduction to Mennonite History: A Popular History of the Anabaptists and the Mennonites*, 3d ed. (Herald Press, 1993); and C. Henry Smith and Cornelius Krahn, *Smith's Story of the Mennonites*, 5th ed. (Faith & Life Press, 1981). *The Mennonite Encyclopedia*, vols. 1-4 (1955-1959) and vol. 5 (1990, Herald Press), includes history, biography, and theology. It is often a good place to begin a search for more information.

For more on the Anabaptists, see J. Denny Weaver's book *Becoming Anabaptist: The Origin and Significance of Sixteenth-Century Anabaptism* (Herald Press, 1987). An in-depth book on the Anabaptists is George H. Williams, *The Radical Reformation*, 3d ed. (Sixteenth Century Journal Publishers, 1992). Also see C. Arnold Snyder, *Anabaptist History and Theology* (Kitchener, Ont.: Pandora Press, 1995).

For some of the Anabaptists' own writings, see the following: Classics of the Radical Reformation (Herald Press), a series that provides these sources in modern English. Walter Klaassen, ed., *Anabaptism in Outline: Selected Primary Sources* (Herald Press, 1981), organized topically. *The Complete Writings of Menno Simons, c. 1496-1561*, ed. by John C. Wenger (Herald Press, 1956). C. J. Dyck, translator and ed., *Spiritual Life in Anabaptism* (Herald Press, 1995), with classic devotional resources.

For more about Mennonites in North America, check two fine sets of books—The Mennonite Experience in America (Herald Press), and The Mennonites in Canada. The first series chronicles Mennonite life in the United States: Richard K. MacMaster, *Land Piety, Peoplehood: The Establishment of Mennonite Communities in America, 1683-1790* (1985); Theron F. Schlabach, *Peace, Faith, Nation: Mennonites and Amish in Nineteenth-Century America* (1988); James C. Juhnke, *Vision, Doctrine, War: Mennonite Identity and Organization in America, 1890-1930* (1989); and Paul B. Toews, *Mennonites in American Society* (1996).

The other series includes two books by Frank H. Epp, *Mennonites in Canada, 1786-1920: The History of a Separate People* (Macmillan, 1974); and *Mennonites in Canada, 1920-1940: A People's Struggle for Survival* (Macmillan, 1982). The third volume is by Ted D. Regehr, *Mennonites in Canada, 1940-1970: A People Transformed* (University of Toronto Press, 1996). A local Mennonite historical society or historical library can recommend many fine regional, conference, or congregational histories.

For more about the Russian Mennonite story, see John Friesen, ed., *Mennonites in Russia, 1788-1988* (Canadian Mennonite Bible College Publications, 1989); James Urry, *None But Saints: The Transformation of Mennonite Life in Russia, 1789-1889* (Hyperion Press, 1988); and John B. Toews, *Czars, Soviets, and Mennonites* (Faith & Life Press, 1982).

You can read about Mennonites in other parts of the world in Diether Götz Lichdi, ed., *Mennonite World Handbook, 1990: Mennonites in Global Witness* (Mennonite World Conference, 1990); and Paul N. Kraybill, ed., *Mennonite World Handbook: A Survey of Mennonite and Brethren in Christ Churches* (Mennonite World Conference, 1978). You might also consult Mennonite mission histories. *The Courier* is a quarterly newsletter from Mennonite World Conference, with articles about Mennonites from all continents.

The authors

Harry Loewen chaired the Mennonite studies department at the University of Winnipeg in Manitoba, Canada, from 1978 to 1995. He is the author of eight previous books, including *Luther and the Radicals* (1974), and is founding editor of *The Journal of Mennonite Studies.*

A member of the Mennonite Brethren denomination, Harry grew up in the Soviet Ukraine and escaped to the West in the aftermath of World War II. You can read part of his story in chapter 43 of his book *No Permanent City* (Herald Press, 1993). In chapter 12 of this book, he is the six-year-old boy whose father was arrested.

Steven Nolt has a deep interest in the Mennonite church's past and future. He holds degrees in history and church history from the University of Notre Dame, South Bend, Indiana; Associated Mennonite Biblical Seminary, Elkhart, Indiana; and Goshen (Ind.) College. Steve is the author of *A History of the Amish* (1992) and co-author of *Amish Enterprise: From Plows to Profits* (1995).

Carol Duerksen is a freelance writer from Goessel, Kansas. She is co-author of *Runaway Buggy* (1995), co-editor of *With*, a magazine for Anabaptist teenagers, and writer of Sunday school curriculum for youth.

Elwood Yoder teaches Bible and history at Eastern Mennonite High School in Harrisonburg, Virginia. He holds a master's degree from Temple University in Philadelphia.